A square, cream-colored envelope lay on Megan's pillow, holiday greetings from the hotel, no doubt. Iris picked it up. "A special card for someone?"

"It's probably from the maids. Open it, if you want. They're probably inviting us to enjoy the tree in the lobby or something."

Iris used one blade of her scissors to open the thick envelope. The paper inside was white, with a torn top edge, and Iris turned almost as pale as the paper. In fact, she looked as if she might fall down.

"Iris, what? What is it?" Megan snatched the note from her manager's hand.

The message was printed with an ordinary ballpoint pen in big prekindergarten letters.

It read, REAL ANGELS ARE IMMORTAL. YOU'RE NOT.

# *Angel*
## IN THE SENATE

### KRISTEN JOHNSON INGRAM

**PALISADES**

ANGEL IN THE SENATE
published by Palisades
a division of Multnomah Publishers, Inc.

© 1998 by Kristen Johnson Ingram
International Standard Book Number: 1-57673-263-0

Cover illustration by Paul Bachem
Design by Brenda McGee

Scripture quotations are from:
*The Holy Bible,* New King James Version (NKJV)
© 1984 by Thomas Nelson, Inc.

Printed in the United States of America

For information:
MULTNOMAH PUBLISHERS, INC.
POST OFFICE BOX 1720
SISTERS, OREGON 97759

Library of Congress Cataloging-in-Publication Data:

Ingram, Kristen Johnson.
    Angel in the senate/Kristen Johnson Ingram.
        p.  cm.
    ISBN 1-57673-263-0 (alk. paper)
    I. Title.
    PS3559.N435A8 1998
    813'.54—dc21                                    98-9284
                                                         CIP

98 99 00 01 02 03 04 — 10 9 8 7 6 5 4 3 2 1

*For my son, Frank, and for his sons, Victor and Max*

# Acknowledgments

Bobbie Christensen, Linda Shands, and Woodeene Koenig-Bricker pored over the manuscript for me and helped me find loose ends. Dr. Christopher Walton, orthopedic surgeon, and Karen Thorland, ICU nurse, gave me the medical advice I needed. The docents at the National Cathedral and the Town Trolley guides in the nation's capital answered my scores of questions with grace and wit. Senator Ron Wyden's office (D-Oregon) got me tickets to sessions of Congress and dispensed information about the Senate dining room and restaurants on Capitol Hill. And my teenage grandson, Victor Schramm, was kind and patient enough to accompany me on a long plane trip to Washington, D.C. There he sat with real grace through a session of the Senate, a splendid service at the National Cathedral, and several ethnic dinners, and toured the city with me every day, despite snow, sleet, wind, and cab drivers who spoke almost no English.

# ONE

The first sign that anything had changed came as Megan read the morning paper. She saw a dance of light across her own picture on the front page.

"Megan Likely Elected to Senate," the banner read. She looked again and the spatter of light was gone. Maybe it had been a sunbeam, caught by her watch crystal, although the November morning was dark and wet. She didn't think much about it; in fact, soon afterwards, she laid the paper on the bed beside her and slipped back into sleep.

She had made her victory speech shortly after midnight; now the months of campaigning, of living from suitcases, drinking burnt coffee, and gulping fast food as she rushed from one rally to another, had caught up with her. As she drifted to sleep, she thought about her grandmother's phone call last night.

"Are you scared, Megan?" her grandmother had asked.

"Oh, Ceelie, I don't know. I'm too tired right now to feel anything."

"I think you've been chosen," Celia said. She allowed only Megan to call her Ceelie. "And if chosen, watched over. And if watched, protected."

"What?"

And her grandmother had laughed, saying she knew Megan was going to make a difference in Washington.

"I hope so. Now that I've won, I feel overwhelmed."

Megan's only elected public office had been on the Ripon city council. Of course, she had been appointed to the state commission on human rights, and she had served two terms as president of the bar association. Regardless of her experience, or maybe because of the lack of it, the voters apparently believed her campaign speeches that promised Wisconsin a real senator, not a political puppet.

"Nobody can beat Henry Arlow," some party people had told

her. "Corrupt or not, he's too powerful. He initiated legislation that has brought millions into the state. He'll die in office."

But Megan's campaign appearances, awarding ribbons to goats at 4-H fairs, shaking hands at Grange meetings and handing out brochures at women's coffees, her months of making speeches at canneries and insurance centers and cheese-processing plants, had paid off at the polls, first in the primaries and finally in the general election.

"I want to bring light into dark places," she'd said at every rally. She meant it, too. "I want to break up political machinery and represent not the party but the people of Wisconsin."

After she fell back to sleep, Megan didn't hear Iris Millman, her campaign manager, tapping on the hotel-room door and then tiptoeing into the room. But she began to stir when Iris poured a cup of hot, fresh coffee from the carafe she was carrying and set it on the nightstand.

"Meggie?"

"Go away, Iris. I'm sleeping all day. Maybe for a week."

Iris leaned against the closet door and adjusted her jade earrings. "Shall I bring them up here, then?"

"Bring who up?"

"The press. Wire services, networks, they're downstairs in our campaign room, eating a small fortune in pastry and coffee. They want to interview the woman who unseated Henry Arlow."

Megan closed her eyes. "Tell them I have measles."

"Get up, dear. You're a celebrity."

Iris started to pull a blue wool dress off its hanger, but Megan sat up, crying, "Oh, no you don't! I dressed up for the campaign. When I get to Washington, I'll try to observe convention. But today I'm going to be myself."

She pushed the covers back and padded toward the bathroom; at the door she asked, "Iris, are the lamps doing something weird? The light keeps flaring up or something."

Iris shook her head. "Probably just fatigue, Meggie."

"Probably." She headed into the shower. Ten minutes later, she emerged in a pair of jeans and a bottle green sweater, her wet hair drawn into the French braid she'd always worn until the horrified Iris brought in a stylist. He had cut an inch off her hair all the way around and given Megan soft, wispy bangs that made her green-brown eyes look bigger than ever.

"You're not going down like that!"

Megan smiled. "You're right. I can't go barefoot." She pawed through her suitcase for a pair of cotton socks and worked them onto her feet; then she knelt on the floor and rummaged under the bed for her sneakers.

"Okay, I'm ready."

"Megan Likely, you mustn't; you'll wreck your image."

"Iris, that glamour girl you've been peddling isn't my image. I ran for the Senate because I thought somebody should clean up after Arlow, not so I could model for magazine covers. The election's over, and until I go to Washington, the press has to take me as I am."

A tiny circle of lights flicked over her hair as she left the room. Iris didn't see it; she was making a note in her daybook that Megan should see her ophthalmologist.

In a room on the first floor, twenty-one reporters and nine videocam operators were breakfasting at a long table covered in white damask. They were pouring coffee out of silver hotel pots and sampling pastries and scones, all amidst the wreckage of campaign headquarters. One end of the banner that read, "Meg's Likely…to Win!" had come off its anchor nail, so now the slogan was vertical. Her crowd of supporters had thrown confetti and shredded paper around the room after her victory speech; cups, glasses, and aluminum pop cans lay on every table and desk. Megan thought the whole place had a discarded look, like a ruined ball gown or a wilted corsage.

And one important person had been missing at the victory party: Mark Combs, the man she had planned to marry.

She took a last look around, pulled her shoulders back and shouted, "Well, good morning!"

The reporters abandoned their doughnuts and cinnamon rolls, licked their fingers, and grabbed notebooks and tape recorders. Red lights on a dozen video cameras signaled that the national networks and Wisconsin TV stations were ready for her.

"Good morning, Senator!" Most of the faces were familiar; one new man lurked in the shadows with only a notepad.

The *Milwaukee Statesman-Journal* shouted, "Megan, what do you think the people of Wisconsin said by electing you?"

"Senator Likely, will you try to get Arlow's old seat on the Appropriations Committee?"

Finally the man from CBS won. "Senator, is it true you never heard from Senator Arlow?"

Megan shrugged and looked at Iris, who shook her head.

"Look, if he's as tired as I am, he probably isn't thinking about making phone calls."

"Do you have any idea why it was Linderman who made Arlow's concession speech?"

The thought of Bob Linderman, Henry Arlow's campaign chairman, set her teeth on edge. "No idea," she finally said.

Someone from the left side of the room called, "Will you comment on the investigation into Linderman's handling of campaign funds?" That news had broken three days before the election.

"No comment." She really didn't know any facts except those in the newspaper.

The brunet CNN reporter held out a microphone. "Megan, you won by a landslide. Do you think the old-boy establishment is on its way out?"

Megan grinned. "Hey, the campaign's over. Don't you want to know what Meg's Likely to do next?"

The hubbub increased, and the reporters pressed closer, all shouting, "Yes, come on, Senator, tell us...."

She held up her hand. "I'm going to bail my little dog, Ewok, out of the boarding kennel, go home to Ripon, and spend the next three weeks settling my office. At the end of the month we'll drive to my grandmother's house for Thanksgiving." She smiled as the strobes began to flash. The photographer from the *Milwaukee Statesman-Journal* caught the picture that became famous when the wire services picked it up. The photograph showed a finely chiseled profile of Senator Megan Likely, laughing, a thick braid showing over her shoulder, her fingertips just below her naturally rosy cheek, a spatter of reflected light playing around and behind her head like a halo. The picture appeared the next day in the *Milwaukee Statesman-Journal,* with the caption, "Angel in the Senate?" It was picked up by the wire services.

Three weeks later Megan was reclining in an examining chair while the ophthalmologist held a small light near her pupils. He knew her eyes well; he'd started fitting her with contact lenses when she was nineteen.

"I want you to have a CAT scan, Meg."

She blinked and pushed his hand away from her face. "Sit me up, will you? And tell me what you're talking about."

He adjusted the lever with his foot, and the chair slowly raised to a sitting position. "I can't find anything that would explain these flashes of light you're seeing."

"Not really flashes. Sunbeams. Maybe that's all I'm actually seeing, real sunbeams."

The doctor raised his eyebrows. "Well, sometimes older people see things happening to light, and that's usually because—" he paused—"That's nonsense. You're thirty, not sixty-five. You could have, well, something else. Like, um, some obstructive cells."

"You mean a brain tumor?" Meg blinked again. She could hardly see the doctor's face because his intense light bulb, held over her eyes for more than twenty minutes, had left her with circles of darkness shimmering between her and the world.

"Let's see what the scan shows," he muttered. "I'll have my nurse call Madison. They're closed tomorrow, of course, but we might be able to get you in early Friday morning, and—"

"Not Friday, you won't." Megan pulled herself out of the chair. "I'm going up to my grandmother's in Door County for Thanksgiving weekend. I'll call you when I get back."

"But if you do have a serious problem, Meg—"

"If I really have what you call a serious problem, it probably won't change much over a weekend. Look, I'm not seeing blazing light or anything. Just sunbeams." Her vision began to clear. She saw the anxiety in his face and she relented.

"See if they'll take me Monday. I'll call you Friday from Egg Harbor to check."

When she relayed the news to her former-campaign-manager-soon-to-be-a-senatorial-chief-of-staff, Iris was horrified.

"A CAT scan, Meggie? Good grief, do you realize what the press will do with this? And the Arlow people?"

Megan felt tears sting her eyelids. "The campaign is over, Iris. I've been elected. And you're the one that kept nagging me to go to the doctor, remember? Look, I have to get on the road. I'll see you Monday."

Her hands were trembling as she unlocked her car door and let Ewok, her little Shih Tzu dog, leap in. *I wonder if Iris would think of politics immediately if I dropped dead! I don't care about image; I just want to be the best Senator Wisconsin ever had. Even though I have to do it without Mark.*

The drive from Ripon to Egg Harbor took longer than usual because preholiday traffic was heavy and the weather unpredictable. Ewok sat up, puzzled, as snow lashed against the windshield. To make things worse, the freeway that bypassed Green Bay was under repair, and traffic had to be routed through the city.

Soon after she had finally turned her blue Ford Escort onto the Green Bay Peninsula, toward Door County, the right rear tire went flat. And as she maneuvered the car to the roadside, the tire going *ploppity plop,* snow began to plunge to the earth in earnest. And it would soon be dark.

She leaned over the seat back and dragged the three-month collection of books and magazines onto the floor so she could dig out her cellular phone. During the campaign, Iris had scolded her constantly about keeping the phone unplugged: "You're paying for the service, Meggie, so keep it plugged in. What if I need to get in touch with you…?" But Megan had said she needed peace and quiet, if only in her car; she'd bought the phone not for the campaign but for emergencies. For moments like this.

Gently pushing her curious dog aside, she plugged the unit into its battery, then dialed the toll-free AAA number that was stuck on the side of her phone. Busy. She waited, tried twice more, and listened to the rhythmic song of the busy signal. Half of Wisconsin was on the road tonight, and it might be hours before she could get service.

Well, she'd change the tire herself. She knew how to do it. She could do almost anything a man could do—pitch hay, install a faucet washer, run for office….

"You've lived alone too long," Mark had said, that day on the lake, as he ran the striped spinnaker out over his sailboat. "Wouldn't you rather share your life with someone? Me, for instance?"

She unloaded her spare and was pulling the bright yellow jack out of her trunk when a gray Mercedes pulled to a stop behind her. The tall man who climbed out looked familiar. Oh, no! It was Bob Linderman, the smarmy hotshot who'd managed Arlow's campaign and who was now under investigation for campaign-fund irregularities.

Linderman had been sarcastic and patronizing in his remarks about her run for the Senate. Although she had campaigned on a conservative platform, commercials written by Linderman seized on her statement that drug addicts needed treatment, suggesting she was sympathetic to drug dealers. Linderman had smeared her wherever possible, calling her a godless women's libber because she wasn't a churchgoer, making snide comments about the fact that she was still single at thirty, and saying her lack of elective experience made her naive and incompetent.

When Megan won, Linderman broke every tradition when he, not Arlow himself, made the briefest and most condescending of statements to the press. Iris had shrugged off his attitude as campaign theatrics; but Megan sensed something that was… She'd been about to say the word *evil* to herself when he slammed the door of his car and stepped out, leaning forward on the wind, into the swirls of snow.

"If it isn't Senator Likely! But this time, you need a man's help, don't you?"

She gritted her teeth. "Hello, Bob," she said, squatting to slide the jack under the Escort's back bumper and aiming a lug wrench into the socket. "I think I can manage, thanks."

"Don't be a show-off." Linderman knelt beside the wheel and elbowed her aside. Ewok went wild inside the car, barking and clawing the window. The man looked up and snickered. "You call that a real dog? Not much protection. You should have a Rottweiler or a German shepherd," he said.

"I don't need protection." She thought of the odd phrase Ceelie had used: chosen, watched over, protected. From what?

He worked the wrench up and down until the wheel was off the ground, and he turned it deftly to release it. He got all the lug nuts off but one. Megan handed him the small metal mallet she always carried.

"Looks like you're prepared for everything. Who taught you to change a tire? Your daddy?"

"My grandmother," she said, lifting the bad tire into the trunk. "Okay, I can finish up now."

"Hey, I'm glad to help a lady." With a flourish of his wrist he swiveled the wrench to fasten the last nut, then lowered the jack.

Megan tossed her tools into the trunk and slammed it shut, hoping he'd leave quickly. But he didn't.

"There's a restaurant up the road at Dycksville," he said. "Can I buy you a cup of coffee?"

"I'm late now. Thanks anyway."

As he smiled, his teeth gleamed in the lights from passing cars. "I'm sure we'll meet somewhere soon," he said, and she shivered.

"I'm freezing," she said. "And as I said, I'm late." She sprang

**14**

into the car. Ewok licked her cheek as she locked the doors. What was it about Linderman that made her and the dog so nervous?

"I wonder what he's doing up here," she said to Ewok, who now lay on the shelf behind the rear seat, watching out the back window. "Well, maybe even Linderman goes home for Thanksgiving."

The dog didn't answer, but the cellular phone began to ring. She'd forgotten to disconnect it. But who would call? The number was unlisted, and only Iris and Ceelie had it. Ewok yipped at her impatiently and she finally picked up the receiver.

"Hi, Megan," said a smooth voice. "This is Bob Linderman."

# TWO

**M**egan gasped, "How did you get this number?" Linderman said, "I was wondering if we could see each other while we're both on the peninsula."

"Of course not! How did you—"

"I could see the phone in the car when I walked up."

"But how did you get the number? And where are you?"

"If you look out your left window, you'll see where I am."

Sure enough, his car was beside hers; he waved and smiled as she jerked her head to look at him.

"Mr. Linderman, go back to Washington or something."

"I'm headed for Sturgeon Bay. I thought that when life at Grandma's got too boring we could meet for a drink or something."

"I don't drink. Good-bye." She stepped on the gas, then cut to the left lane a few cars ahead of him. Holding the wheel with her left hand, she unplugged the phone; a pickup truck honked loudly as she nearly swerved into it. How had he gotten the number?

"He scares me," she told Ewok. "I hope Ceelie's right, that I'm watched over." Headlamps flashed in her mirror, and the light scattered like tiny goldfish over her face and the backs of her hands.

Suddenly she felt better. She could no longer see the gray Mercedes, tomorrow was Thanksgiving, and she was going to be home with her grandparents in an hour.

Celia held a wooden kitchen match to light each of the seven white tapers in her silver candelabra. Her neighbor, big Ben Tolufson, was seated at Celia's right. Megan sat next to him; across from them was Ben's wife, Ruthie, with Caleb, their nine-year-old son. George Likely, Megan's grandfather was parked at the end of the table in his wheelchair.

George had neither spoken nor walked in the twenty-four years since the accident with a pickup truck. The truck had belonged to a neighbor who came to the Likely farm to pick up six flats of cherries. He had left his pickup parked, running, at the edge of the orchard. Nobody could ever explain how the vehicle suddenly kicked into gear and began to rampage at high speed toward six-year-old Megan and her parents, who were filling wooden lugs with cherries. Megan's grandfather had hurled himself in front of the wheels, trying to stop it, but it was too late: the vehicle shot over his body and then struck Keith and Barbara Likely. Barbara, seeing the face of death, pushed Megan as hard as she could, knocking her out of the truck's path.

Growing up in her grandparents' Egg Harbor home, Megan had frequently dreamed the scene and heard her mother's screams. And she would never forget the sight of her grandmother, straight-backed and tearless, as she sat at the funeral for her son, her only child, and his wife.

Now George could usually shake his head yes or no, and on most days he could feed himself. Often he could point at what he wanted. He minded Celia when she told him, "Put your arms up so I can get your sweater off, honey," or "Take another bite of that cobbler, dear." He usually smiled when his wife or Megan kissed him. Every morning, Celia sat in the kitchen and read the entire newspaper to him while he spooned up his oatmeal.

Ben, a former FBI agent working on his dissertation for his doctorate of divinity, always came in the midmorning to help with George's bath and lunch, sometimes in good weather to convey him in his wheelchair around the neighborhood. On two afternoons each week, Ben's wife, Ruthie, a registered nurse who worked part-time in a doctor's office, came to the Likelys' to stay with George so Celia could go grocery shopping or attend a church guild meeting or make another batch of the cherry jam she sold to Zeigler's big tourist store on the Door County highway.

At night, Ben helped get George into bed. Then Celia sat beside him to read their Bible lesson out loud. She talked to him about whatever was on her mind—their granddaughter or the cherry crop, the latest news or her deepest spiritual concerns.

"I can't tell you what a comfort it is to discuss things with you, dear," she'd say, and then kiss him good night and turn out the light.

After the accident that killed Megan's parents, Celia had forgone small luxuries for herself so she could spend all her jam-and-dried-cherry income on the girl's food and clothing and allowances. Meanwhile she methodically invested Megan's Social Security and insurance payments in blue-chip stocks. By the time the girl was ready for college and then law school, Celia had accumulated a good-sized nest egg to pay board and tuition and buy books.

But Megan had also worked through school as waitress, tutor, and finally law clerk to pay for an apartment where she could study instead of a noisy dorm.

Now as they sat at the table, with the fragrances of Thanksgiving surrounding them, Celia said, "George, will you say grace?"

He lowered his head, and the others bowed with him; after a few moments, he patted the table with his hand.

"Amen," Celia said. "Thank you, George. Megan, I'm sorry Mark Combs isn't here with us."

Megan smiled. "I am too, Ceelie. And I'm also hungry. Start carving, Ben. By now, Mark and I should have been married."

Ben stood to carve the turkey, and the lighted candles reflected on his blade and then the small chandelier overhead, sending lighted rainbows over the table.

"Wow, look at that!" Caleb exclaimed.

"Thank goodness! You see them, too?" Megan said, before she thought.

Celia raised her eyebrows. "Is our Senator having some kind of eye problem?"

"I—I keep seeing sunbeams, that's all. I'm just tired from the campaign, Ceelie."

Ruthie nodded. "My mom says every sunbeam is really an angel in disguise."

"Then I've seen an awful lot of angels lately," Megan said, helping herself to some of Celia's famous creamed onion pie and adding a spoonful to her grandfather's plate. "If they really are angels, I hope they go to Washington with me. That should be a welcome change."

Everyone laughed, but Celia looked at her granddaughter thoughtfully. "Angels are not like us. They're obedient and only go where they're sent," she said, looking back up at the sparkling chandelier. "But of course they'll be sent to Washington with you."

Megan smiled as Caleb sneaked a morsel of dressing under the table to Ewok.

"Caleb, dear, that dog will be sick if you feed him such rich food," Celia said without looking at the boy. At seventy-one, her face bore the honorable signs of age: laugh lines around her eyes and mouth, dark gray waves of hair that now were thinner than the heavy dark mop she'd once tossed, and the vestiges of sorrow, not self-pity but true sorrow, in the depths of her gray eyes and the curve of her throat. "Will you have some cranberry sauce, Ruthie? I bought the berries from Grafton's bog farm."

Ruthie took the ivory crackleware bowl and began ladling cranberries onto her plate. "I don't think an angel could obey God any better than you do, Celia."

Celia smiled again, this time at her husband, who was leaning forward, his forearm resting against the edge of the cherrywood table.

"George could tell you how perverse I really am. He hears my daily confession. Why, Megan, only yesterday I told your grandpa I had a strong leading that I should call you and ask you to check your tires. But I felt foolish, so I didn't call. And look what happened."

"Nothing happened. I just had a flat tire, that was all."

"Was that all?" Celia's black eyebrows crept upward again, but she didn't press her granddaughter. "Well, anyhow, an angel wouldn't have decided whether or not to call."

~ ~ ~ ~ ~

The elderly Likelys had never owned a television. Reception was impossible on their part of the Green Bay Peninsula without a satellite dish, and Celia couldn't have sacrificed her frugal habits for the sake of entertainment. Megan spent the long weekend visiting with her grandmother, watching snow cover the high yellow grasses by the bay, reading the back issues of the magazines collecting in her car, tossing a ball for Ewok, and talking to her grandfather by the fireplace. She sat on the ancient Chesterfield sofa, he in his wheelchair with a blanket over his lap.

"Oh, Grandpa, I wish you could talk to me! I remember Daddy's saying you were the smartest man alive. I'm not sure I'm up to my new job—I could sure use some wisdom right now."

George smiled and patted the arm of his wheelchair; then he nodded toward the kitchen door, where they could see Celia cutting up her home-canned pimentos to make turkey à la king.

"You want to see Ceelie?"

He shook his head.

"Oh, you mean Ceelie is wise. Yes, you're right. In fact, I'd take her to Washington with me, if she'd go."

"Well, I won't," Celia called in. "Who would take care of the cherry orchard? But we'll be there for Christmas. And we'll keep you surrounded in prayer, my dear."

*It's going to take more than prayer to get me through the U.S. Senate,* Megan thought.

"There isn't any more," her grandmother said, coming to the door.

"What?"

"You were thinking it's going to take more than prayer. Well, there isn't anything more than prayer."

"Ceelie, how did you know what I was thinking? Are you clairvoyant or something?"

"Certainly not. What an idea! I've known you all your life, that's all."

20

On Monday morning, as she was rolling into the Ripon General Hospital's CT scanner, Megan wondered if Ceelie was praying for her right then; and then she forgot, because a circle of lights danced before her face, and when the machine started humming, she thought for a moment she heard choral music.

Two days later, the neurologist was smiling. "Everything's fine, Senator Likely. We can't locate anything in your brain that might be causing these sunbeams or whatever they are. But have a checkup in a few months." He shook her hand. "Congratulations on your election. I voted for you."

Megan chuckled. "I hope I don't let you down. But then my grandmother is praying—and she can whomp up a powerful prayer."

He didn't laugh. "You know, grandmothers have a way with God. I don't think I would have made it through medical school if mine hadn't prayed for me."

By the start of the third week in December, the Wisconsin Bar Association had asked for a deeper probe into irregularities in the Arlow campaign, and a "for lease" sign hung in the window of Megan's modest Ripon law office.

After she passed the bar, Megan had worked for district attorney Mark Combs in Fond du Lac for three years. When she left that agency, she opened her own office in Ripon, in the same building where her father had once been senior partner at Likely and Twiss. And Mark remained district attorney of nearby Fond du Lac.

Now the gray steel cabinets of client files were sealed and ready for storage, and her secretary, short, soft-bodied Fern Loftis, had gone shopping. At each store, including the elegant domed shop that had once been the Carnegie Library, she managed to whisper to the saleswoman, "I'll need some really nice things. I'm going to

Washington with the Senator, you know. She wants me for her secretary in Washington, too."

Megan had finally admitted she needed a few clothes. She bought a black suit and two long dresses for receptions: a straight scarlet crepe, and a floor-length black gown whose long-sleeved jacket could close to the neck. She had already taken two suits to a dressmaker for alterations because she'd lost nine pounds during the campaign.

"I think you should have hired a new secretary in Washington," Iris said on December twelfth, as Megan packed her attaché case. "Fern doesn't project the impression you want to make in the Senate office building. And she has no real political experience."

"Iris, dear, the only place I want to make an impression is on the Senate floor. Fern has been with me for ten years, and she keeps my life in order. She stays."

"Why did you hire me if you won't take my advice?"

Megan laughed, turning the lock on her briefcase. "I hired you to talk to the people I'm scared of up there on the hill and to make sure I get where I'm going on time. And at this very moment, you should be advising me to hurry up or I'll miss my plane."

"Good grief, you're right! Okay, Meggie, let's go. I'll arrive a week from tomorrow with your grandparents and the Tolufsons. Did I tell you Celia gave me a very hard time about traveling first class? I finally convinced her that it was the only way George would be really comfortable."

"We're going to have a wonderful Christmas," Megan said almost wistfully as she lifted Ewok's empty animal carrier into Iris's car. The dog himself was already stationed in the front seat.

"So what's the matter?"

"Oh, it's just I can't remember ever having Christmas anyplace but Egg Harbor. Even when my parents were alive, we always went to Ceelie's for Christmas. And in those days my other grandparents came, too."

"They have Christmas in Washington, D.C., too, Megan," Iris said, laughing. "At least I think they do. I'm Jewish, so how would I know?"

"But your parents weren't observant, were they?"

"I don't remember. My parents were divorced, and my mother was an alcoholic. I grew up in a foster home where we weren't allowed to observe anything. Not even birthdays or the Fourth of July."

"Well, this year you'll share holidays with us, Iris," Megan said. "You can call them Christmas or Hanukkah or Kwanza, just so you have a good time."

The two women had met three years earlier at a university conference about real estate law, where they'd both been speakers: Iris as a broker, Megan as an attorney familiar with contracts, capital gains taxes, and inheritance. She'd been impressed with Iris's understanding of the legalities of property, and had invited her to have a cup of coffee in the snack bar. When Megan had mentioned having political aspirations and they discovered they were registered in the same party, Iris had gone into gear promoting Megan's campaign. Much to Mark Combs's despair.

Iris had designed a program and an image that presented Megan as sincere but wise, believing in old-fashioned values while living in the present, a Washington outsider with no political debts but a woman of strong political connections. In other words, she'd created a flawless portrait Megan hated trying to live up to. Thank heaven the campaign was over and she could actually function as a lawmaker now!

At the airlines desk in Appleton, Megan checked Ewok's carrier, trying to ignore her dog's sad expression as she nudged him into the little kennel. He was groggy from the tranquilizer the vet had prescribed, but he still balked at being confined.

She bought a *Green Bay News-Chronicle* and tucked it in the outside pocket of her briefcase. Then she kissed Iris good-bye and climbed the steps to the Chicago shuttle, which took off over Lake

Winnebago; its dark green surface was rippled by the winter wind. Mark had proposed marriage on the lake two years ago while the sails on his neat little sloop lifted with the wind and frisked them across the water.

Besides being district attorney for Fond du Lac county, Mark had also inherited, then slowly added to his holdings by purchase, hundreds of acres of Wisconsin's richest dairy land. He hired managers to oversee most of the Holstein herds and crop fields, while he dwelt near Ripon on one of the loveliest little farms of all, a rolling piece of green turf with a live creek running through it, a pond full of water lilies, and a white-painted covered bridge.

He told Megan he'd fallen in love with her almost as soon as he met her three years after his former fiancée, a doctor at the county hospital, had left to take a job as the dean of a medical school in North Carolina. Mark had been bitter, saying he'd never marry a career woman, until he met Megan.

"Well, at least we can share a career," he'd said. "I'll leave the DA's office, and we can set up a law firm together, Meggie. Say you'll marry me." When Megan had hesitated, he added, "I know you love me."

"You're right. I do. But you want children, Mark. I'm almost thirty, and I'm not sure about starting a family now. Besides, I've got some political plans."

Megan finally accepted Mark's ring soon after that day on the sloop, but they debated for months about whether or not she should run for office. The argument ended when Megan actually went to Madison to file as a candidate for the Senate.

"Come see me when you lose," he'd said bitterly and stamped out the door. She returned her engagement ring by mail. After the election, she left messages at his office, but he'd never called back, and she was left with her memories of the sun shining on the lake, wind puffing against the bright spinnaker sail, and Mark leaning toward her, his eyes full of love.

"Good-bye," she whispered as her plane's shadow fell over the familiar lake. She busied herself checking her tickets and then looking at the schedule in her planner so she wouldn't think any-more of Mark. In a short time she was in Chicago, boarding a 707 stretch for Washington, D.C. She asked the flight attendant to make sure her dog's carrier had been transferred onto her second plane. The attendant said, "The loading crew say he's asleep, Senator, and doing just fine," then hung up Megan's jacket and offered her something to drink.

"Hot tea, no lemon," Megan told her and unfolded the news-paper she'd bought a half hour before. As she opened it, her own face looked back up at her. The headline read, ARLOW ASKS FOR ELECTION PROBE, SAYS MEGAN LIKELY COMMITTED FRAUD.

# THREE

I ris Millman twirled once in front of the mirror to make sure the back pleat in her skirt was centered, pulled her single-strand jade necklace around so the clasp didn't show, and shrugged into her suit jacket. She leaned into the mirror to make sure her makeup concealed her freckles, and smoothed her apricot-colored hair. Then she stepped out onto Megan's front porch, where the herd of reporters was waiting.

"Senator-elect Likely has not been informed of Mr. Linderman's accusations of fraud," she said when the clamor died down. "In fact, she's on a plane to Washington. If any formal charges had been filed, she would have been told."

A correspondent from the *Milwaukee Statesman-Journal* asked, "Did Megan see the papers before she left?"

Iris smiled professionally. "I didn't see the story myself until I got home from Appleton, a few minutes ago. However, Senator Likely was aware that Henry Arlow's election committee and Robert Linderman are under investigation for misuse of funds."

Iris spoke the truth about the fraud story, although with limitations. She hadn't seen the papers until then. What she didn't say was that Megan's secretary, Fern Loftis, had telephoned her about the story two hours ago, while Megan was still packing. Nor did Iris tell them she had decided not to inform Senator-elect Likely because there was no use upsetting her at the start of her trip to Washington. And Iris did not say she had seen Megan buying the evening paper, which meant she probably had read the story on the plane by now.

"Will Senator Likely come back for the hearings?" called a Madison TV reporter.

"What hearings? No charges have been filed. Next question?" She pointed to Guy Lippert, the syndicated political columnist from Fond du Lac, whose company she had learned to enjoy as he traveled with them on one campaign trek after another.

"Ms. Millman, when are you going to Washington? Or will this change your plans?"

"I'm leaving next Saturday. I certainly won't change my plans just because Senator Arlow gets some kind of wild idea," she said, knowing Guy would probably hang around to take her to dinner. "There's absolutely no basis for any accusation of fraud."

"Linderman says the ballot counts were irregular in three counties," a reporter from the local ABC affiliate said, hoping the evening network news would show him in action. "He wants a complete investigation by the election board, or maybe even by the district attorney."

"Isn't District Attorney Combs an old boyfriend of Megan's?" Guy Lippert asked, and Iris glared at him.

"I'm sorry, ladies and gentlemen. I have nothing more to tell you at this time. We'll be issuing a more complete statement when we have some real facts." She stepped inside the front door, her navy blue heels ringing on the cement porch. She shut the front door a little harder than necessary, to let Lippert know that dinner was no longer a possibility. She had started upstairs when the telephone rang in the front hall, and she sprinted to catch it, wondering absently why Megan had lived in this old-fashioned white two-story her parents had left her, when she could have afforded a nice place in a newer section of town.

"Iris?" Megan's voice was accompanied by a deep humming sound.

"Megan? You're not in Washington already, are you?"

"No, I'm on the plane and reading the Green Bay evening paper. Iris, have you seen it?"

Iris used the same evasion she had for the press. "If you're talking about that ridiculous accusation of election fraud, I read the story when I got back to the house, dear. I've just now been talking to the media on your front porch."

"My front porch? Good grief! Maybe I should take the first plane back. Has the election board charged me with—"

"I wouldn't worry. As far as I know, this is just one of Linderman's fantasies, and no actual charges have been filed. Megan, dear, try to relax. Why don't you take a nap on the plane? You could use the extra rest. And call me from Washington, so I know you got there all right."

"Iris, I'm depending on you to run this story down for me. You know it's all a lie."

"Call me when you arrive," Iris said. "By then I should know a little more."

As soon as she hung up, Iris dialed the office of Mark Combs.


Mark was standing in a corner of the outer office, his arms crossed, listening to one of his assistant district attorneys explain why she had lost what looked like an open-and-shut case.

"He tricked me," she said. "I'm going to file a complaint that he didn't make full witness disclosure."

The telephone rang, and Mark picked it up. When he heard it was Iris, he said, "I'll take this in my own office." His heart was beating faster than usual. Breaking up with Megan had been the dumbest move of his life, but pride kept him from returning her calls. Maybe Iris could be the bridge between them.

"Mark, this situation with Linderman is completely out of hand," she said. "You've got to move fast. You know Megan isn't capable of fraud."

"I'll read the complaint this afternoon," he said. "And I'll let you know what's happening."


Megan put her head back and closed her eyes, trying to obey Iris's instructions to nap, but it was no use. After a hard campaign, she had won the election fairly. Hadn't she? Hadn't she? Yes. And the people had spoken, but Arlow and Linderman were still trying to take victory away from her. Probably they were trying to drag attention away from the money probe of Arlow's reelection committee.

She didn't want to begin her job under a cloud. Learning the ropes in the Senate would be hard enough. And if the accusation went to trial, Mark would be involved. Would he have to prosecute her? She thought of him with mixed feelings. Her yearning for the sound of his crackling voice and a glimpse of his dark eyes was mixed with anger at the way he'd treated her. A man who loved her wouldn't reject her just because she found a way to help her country. She would never have done that to him.

She gazed out the plane window at what looked like a vast ocean of whipped cream. Her wristwatch, already set for eastern standard time, read four-fifteen. That meant she'd be down in an hour. She hoped Ewok was faring all right in the cargo hold. Iris had said she was crazy to take the dog with her now; it meant extra plane fare and a pet deposit at the hotel, but until December 20, he was the only family she'd have with her.


Mark Combs was about to speak to Senator Arlow's answering machine when a woman's accented voice interrupted, saying, "Yes?"

"Mrs. Arlow?"

"I sorry. They both gone. I take a message?"

"This is the district attorney for Fond du Lac County. I need to speak to the Senator about a legal election matter."

"I give him your message." The woman's accent was possibly Caribbean.

Mark recited his number. The woman's voice said, "If this about election, you call Mr. Linderman in Oshkosh." And she hung up.

Linderman's wife answered the phone when he called; Mark heard the man yelling, "Ellen, I said I'll take all calls." But his voice was even and charming when he got on the line. "Mr. Combs? I presume you're calling about the complaint we filed."

"I have some questions about it," Mark said.

"Of course, you're undoubtedly prejudiced in favor of Ms.

Likely. Seeing that you have a—" Linderman's voice took on a slick tone—"personal relationship and all that."

Mark felt himself stiffen. "My private life is none of your business."

"It is if it affects my case. Now, how can I help you?"

"Can you be in my office tomorrow?"

"Well, let me look at my book."

*Look at your book, my foot. What does an unemployed campaign manager, whose committee is under investigation, do with his time?*

"I can be there in the afternoon, right after lunch."

"I'll be waiting for you."

As Mark hung up, he wondered if Megan had ever had to deal one-on-one with Linderman.


As she rolled her carry-on bag behind her into the main terminal at Dulles, Megan was startled to see a slender woman with blond hair, waving at her. Because she wasn't expecting anyone to meet her, it took her a second to become oriented. Then she recognized Brenda Penning, the reelected Congresswoman from Wisconsin District 14, standing in the reception area.

"Welcome to Washington, Senator," Brenda said, kissing her on one cheek and then the other. "And congratulations on your election, which you deserved."

"Thanks to people like you," Megan said. Brenda had campaigned hard for her, appearing with her at political rallies all over the state. Brenda's own first election to the House, six years earlier, had startled pundits because she had been a nobody: a soft-spoken, nonpolitical schoolteacher with a determination to tell Congress what her district really wanted. That same gentle resolution had carried her into the powerful Appropriations Committee; now she was respected as a woman with a mission, working hard for her state and helping other women climb into government.

"I didn't expect anyone to be here," Megan said. "Why aren't you in Fond du Lac, trimming your parents' Christmas tree and basking in your success on pushing the fiscal responsibility bill through the House?

"Because I'm spending the holidays in town. With Rick."

"Your fiancé? You're staying with him?" Megan was surprised. She and Brenda had both admitted to feelings about couples who lived together before marriage.

Brenda's soft blue eyes twinkled. "No, I'm staying with my husband. And my name is Samuelson now."

"Brenda Samuelson? Then you finally married him!"

"Four days ago. We went down to Baltimore. Come on, let's walk."

Much had been made in the press about Brenda's being over thirty and, like Megan, single; for a while a couple of the tabloids had implied that perhaps there was something "abnormal" about the relationship between the two women, until they discovered Brenda was engaged to Rick Samuelson, a radio station owner and occasional TV producer from Fairfax, Virginia. The papers then began to work with Rick's and Brenda's hopes of marrying during a Congressional break, printing two-inch-high headlines such as, "RICK FINDS OUT BRENDA'S DARK SECRET!" (The secret was that Brenda had lied about her age to get her first job, when she was fifteen.) Finally the gossip columns gave up and turned their poison on a football team owner who was accused of embezzling and having affairs with the players' wives.

Megan pulled up the handle on her rolling suitcase, and they began walking toward the front of the terminal. "Well, where is the groom?" She glanced around, but didn't see the tall, blond-bearded Virginian whose photograph had run in the papers when they'd announced their engagement.

"Driving around and around the terminal because the press is waiting where I told them to look for you, at gate fourteen." She gestured toward a gate at the far end of the terminal.

Megan laughed. "You lied to the reporters?"

"Why, Meggie! I didn't lie; I just said they should look there. Let's go get your luggage before they find out I sent them on a wild-goose chase."

Megan shifted her coat from her arm to her shoulders. "Iris shipped my things to the hotel. I just brought this carry-on. And Ewok. I'd better bail him out of his prison. Besides, you wouldn't really want to spend the rest of your honeymoon at a baggage carousel, would you?"

Ewok licked her face for a minute after she unlocked his kennel, apparently to make sure she realized how lonely he'd been in the luggage compartment. She fastened his leash and picked up his carrier, while Brenda took over pulling her bag.

"You travel awfully light, lady, for a Senator."

"Campaigning taught me a lot. More clothes will be here tomorrow or the next day. All I have with me are my jeans, my coat, two t-shirts, two blouses, and the suit I'm wearing."

"Which is gorgeous. You look stunning in black, Megan. And I love your sunflower pin." Brenda strode ahead, leading the way out of the terminal to the sidewalk, where she watched for her husband's car.

"I suppose you've seen the papers or heard the story," Megan said.

"Oh, I knew Arlow and Linderman wouldn't let go of the Senate so easily."

"But fraud, Brenda! How can they accuse me of fraud? I haven't done anything."

"Hey, we know that. Ah, there's Rick," she said, waving vigorously at a dark red Taurus.

"Oh, Meggie, you haven't actually met him, so I guess I better warn you."

"Warn me? Does he bite?"

"Some people might think so. He's a born-again Christian."

Megan laughed. "I'm not afraid of Christians. I grew up in a devout home, Brenda. And you married him, so he must be okay. What did you say your new last name is?"

"Samuelson. It's actually the remake of an unpronounceable old Scandinavian name. I was going to just keep going as Penning, but our pastor feels strongly that a Christian woman should take her husband's name. So the state of Wisconsin will just have to get used to my new identity."

Rick pulled his car up to the curb and climbed out. He was lanky and bland-faced, and in fact, he looked familiar. Like an old friend. His smile made Megan feel utterly welcome. *Too bad Brenda saw him first. I could go for a sweetheart like him.* "Welcome, Senator Likely. Jump in quickly, here come the news hounds."

Megan glanced behind her and saw a pack of reporters, some with videocams, cantering down the sidewalk. She picked Ewok up and slipped into the backseat while Brenda explained why they didn't have luggage to load.

"Actually, I guess since I own a radio station I could be classified as a news hound too," he said, shaking hands over his seat back. "But I promise not to ask you a single question. At least not till you've eaten." He turned and started to drive.

"I'm booked at the downtown Embassy Suites," Megan said.

"Let us buy you dinner first," Rick called over his shoulder. "We want you to taste some of the best barbecue in Virginia. And then Brenda has a surprise for you."

In Alexandria, Rick pulled into the parking lot of a red-brick building attached to a wooden mill wheel. A sign over the door outlined with tiny hot-pepper red light bulbs read Old Mill Barbecue.

"A surprise? What kind of surprise?" She maneuvered Ewok back into his kennel and braced herself for the worst. *Is there more news about the fraud story? Do they know more than I do?*

Brenda turned to look over her shoulder. Reflected lights were dancing all over the car. "It'll be a surprise, all right," she laughed. "Hey, look what the lights are doing in here."

Megan took a deep breath. Whatever the surprise was, she had to cope with it. "I've had enough shocks today, what with the headline," she said. "Tell me now."

Brenda looked at Rick and they both shrugged. "Okay," the congresswoman said. "The president wants to see you."

# FOUR

The clear-eyed Marine Corps guard who accompanied Megan was at least a foot taller than she was. He marched through the corridor without looking at her, opened the door to the Oval Office with his left hand, straightened to attention, saluted his Commander-in-Chief, and made a snappy about-face.

Megan stepped inside to face the man whose views she had openly opposed all through her campaign. After all, the president represented the other side, the wrong side of politics. *And now I've been accused of election fraud, and he's going to let me know what he thinks of me and my party.* She waited for his verbal attack. He was probably going to tell her she was unfit for the Senate, what with these charges. *I'm actually standing in the Oval Office, looking at—*

"Senator Likely!" the president roared, grinning, and thrust out his hand. His football-player shoulders, exuberant voice, and warm smile were famous all over the country. "Welcome to Washington! Please, sit down and be comfortable."

She shook his hand, noting the firm grip. President Jackson had been an athlete before he became a congressman and then senator from New Mexico. He was famous for his daily workouts in the White House gym, and he swam thirty laps every noon with two members of his staff.

"You're not exactly the kind of senator I'm used to talking to," he said as she sat on the edge of the sofa.

*Uh-oh. Here it comes. He's going to say I have better legs than most of them or that I'm younger and prettier or—*"In what way?" she asked, stiffening.

"Most of them are longtime politicians. I want to tell you it's really refreshing to meet a woman of principle who has no political debts to pay."

Megan tried not to look surprised at his reply. "Well, according to this evening's papers, I have no principles and may have to pay in court. My opponent claims—"

"Yes, that's why I called Representative Penning. When I found out you were coming in today, I asked her to bring you here. I wanted to talk to you about the charges." He paused and grinned again. "Half the people in public office today have been accused of fraud at one time or another, and only a tiny percentage are ever convicted. In fact, most never see a courtroom. Ten years ago when I was running for the Senate, my opponent tried to accuse me of election fraud. Can you believe that?"

*Well, maybe.*

"Now. I'm concerned that because you just arrived in Washington, you don't have a lot of connections yet. Do you have a good lawyer in Wisconsin? If not, we need to get the senior senator from your state to assist you right away. His wife is a fine trial attorney, and she has several investigators working for her. She'd probably be happy to defend you if this ever gets to court."

The senior senator from her state was Luke Callon, a man she had admired for years. He was ethical, wise, and highly respected by his colleagues on both sides of the aisle. He had briefly spoken at three rallies for Megan, but it had never occurred to her to try to know him or his wife better. Now the president was telling her to call on Callon, the president's own political enemy, for help.

"I've met him several times, but I don't really know Senator Callon," she began, and the President chuckled.

"Of course you don't," he thundered. "You really got here on your own, didn't you, Megan? Can I call you Megan? And you call me Jerry."

She smiled and nodded, almost unable to breathe. Good grief! Is this how she was going to act on the Senate floor, too? Like a mute, starstruck young girl at a rock concert? President Jerry Jackson was just a man, after all. *And now he's dialing a phone number, probably calling a mental hospital to come and get me.*

"Priscilla? Pris, this is Jerry Jackson. I've got Senator Likely in my office and—Yes, she got in late this afternoon and yes, she's read the papers. That's why I'm calling you…. Uh-huh…. Uh-huh…. You've already lined up a possible lawyer for her? Uh-huh…. Gee, I don't know. Let me ask her." He put his hand over the mouthpiece and said, "Now I've done it. Can you possibly have dinner with the Callons tomorrow evening? Priscilla says it's nothing huge, just a little pre-Christmas late supper party."

"I—Yes, of course," Megan said, finally remembering she was a lawyer, used to public pressure even if she wasn't used to being a senator. "Could I speak to her, please?" He handed her the phone and she said, "Mrs. Callon?"

"Oh, no you don't. You call me Pris like everyone else. Megan, I've already left a message at the Embassy Suites, asking you to dinner tomorrow. The Samuelsons are coming. It's black-tie, dear, but if you didn't bring a long dress, wear your blue jeans. And I want you to know we're going to kick butt with dear ex-Senator Arlow. I've already got one of my people on it. Good-bye, Senator, and kiss the president for me, will you?"

Sure. In a pig's eye, she thought as she hung up the phone. The heady, hearty atmosphere of social Washington was almost too much; she felt as if she were back on the campaign trail, rushing from one rally to another and hearing otherwise genteel women use crude phrases like "Kick butt."


The stack of file folders on Mark Combs's desk was getting higher, and he sighed, knowing he'd have to get to all of them eventually. But first, he had to attend to the fraud charges against Megan Likely.

Looking down at her name on the complaint papers lying in front of him, he suddenly thought of Megan's fondness for the lakes and green hills of Wisconsin. How would she get along in the heady, busy atmosphere of the Beltway? He wanted to call her, to say, "Megan, you're not a big-city girl. Come on home."

But then he remembered the times she'd had to oppose him in court, the brilliance with which she'd fought for her clients, and the way she knew how to ferret out the truth. She'd get along fine in D.C. And that was what bothered him. He wanted a woman who needed him, and although he was sure Megan loved him, he also knew she didn't really need anybody. Had she committed election fraud? As he read through the complaint, he felt certain that this was just someone's revenge.

The president glanced at his watch. "Good grief!" he bellowed. "Luyin will kill me! We have to be at the Kennedy Center in less than an hour."

"And you haven't even shaved," said a slightly accented voice from the other end of the room. The president's small, elegant Chinese-born wife stood in the doorway, her hands resting on her slender, pale-green-satin hips. She smiled at Megan, then stepped forward, holding out her hand. Her handshake was firm, too, but it was cool and delicate.

"Senator Likely, welcome to Washington. I hope this giant buffalo hasn't crushed you with his shouting. He forgets how overpowering he can be." She smiled, a little wickedly. "I'm Tan Luyin, as I'm sure you know. Let's see, we're going to meet your grandparents on the thirtieth, at the Senate reception."

Once more, Megan was stunned and speechless. "How—I mean—"

"My secretary spoke with your campaign manager a few days ago. Oh, look! You really do have a halo, don't you? The lights are dancing on your hair. Like the picture."

Megan's hand shot up to her temple, and then she laughed. "I hope the president thinks I'm angelic after the new session begins," she said.

"He'll be watching," Luyin said. "But I think he's in for some surprises. And now that he has thoroughly addled you, I hope you'll excuse us. We really do have to get to the Billy Graham rally. Jerome, dear, the limousine is waiting at the door."

The president pressed a buzzer on his desk, and the same young, serious Marine appeared at the door to escort her downstairs, where Brenda and Rick waited in the reception area. "See you soon, Megan," the president barked as she marched away with her guard.

"Jerome, stop yelling like that. You'll scare that lovely young woman to death," Megan heard Luyin say.

So that was the enemy, Megan thought. In Washington, the lines certainly weren't clear.


"We're going to ask for a special prosecutor." The recently defeated senator from Wisconsin was speaking to a group of journalists who stood in the rain at the Federal Building in Madison. "We won't leave one stone in Megan Likely's life unturned. We're going to open the whole can of worms here, gentlemen. And, ah, ladies. We're going to find the bad apple in this barrel."

The CNN reporter turned to her camerawoman. "That must be some kind of record, even for Arlow," she muttered. "Three clichés in one paragraph."

"We already have evidence of the worst kind of fraud," Arlow added. "Votes were bought; other votes went into Lake Winnebago."

Bob Linderman began to edge up to Arlow. "It wouldn't be appropriate for us to talk more about it right now while it's under investigation," he said, assuming charge of the microphone. "Suffice it to say that the governor's office is aware of our investigation. Senator Likely may never even take the oath of office."

When the questions from the press turned to the story of illegal funds being funneled from Arlow's reelection campaign to other accounts, Linderman closed the conference.


"The president and his wife are going to the Billy Graham rally," Megan told Brenda and Rick as they drove away, with Ewok skulking in his carrier. "I thought, I mean, they're politically extremely liberal, and she kept her maiden name when they got married. Well, I didn't figure them for being religious."

"I'm not convinced they're seeking conversion. A public official has to be good at making appearances at places like that," Rick said.

"You think that's all it is? Just an appearance?"

Rick shrugged, glanced at Brenda, then looked back at the road. "I don't really know President Jackson, though I disagree strongly with his political stance. Be very careful, Megan. We Christians have to stick together in Washington."

Brenda turned to smile at Megan over her shoulder. "You may think Rick sounds like a religious fanatic, but when you get to know him better, you'll be sure of it." She winked, and then the car was on the red-tiled Embassy Suites entry.

Rick was out of the car and had the back door open before she could reach for the handle. When he started to pick up the animal carrier, the usually peaceful Ewok suddenly went berserk, snarling and growling just as he had when they had encountered Bob Linderman on the road to Egg Harbor. Megan took the kennel and peered in at the dog. Maybe he was just upset by all the travel and changes of the past few months. She'd certainly never seen him so aggressive.

Rick ignored the barking beast. "You've got the pup? Okay, here's your temporary home, Senator. We'll help you with your bag, and you can get your dog settled in your suite." Megan had never felt so tired, or so eager to be alone. She looked at her watch. It was now eight-twenty.

"It's been a long day, Rick. I think I'll just hang up my clothes and crawl in bed."

Brenda stepped out of the car and gave her a hug. "We'll pick you up for the Callons' dinner tomorrow night," she murmured. "And after Christmas, we'd like to invite you to our Bible study. Rick leads it. The Callons come, and the vice president." She kissed Megan, then slipped into the car.

Rick started to carry Megan's small suitcase into the hotel, but she pulled it away. "Come on, Rick, I can manage that. It has wheels, and you two have done enough for me tonight." He started to argue, but a car trying to pull into the curved drive honked several times, and he reluctantly climbed back behind the wheel.

"Tomorrow," Brenda called out her open window. Then a gust of cold wind made her close it, and they were gone.

"Do you wish help, madame?" the valet asked, touching the bill of his cap. His coat was rimmed with frost and snow. Megan shook her head, smiled, and hooked her briefcase over the pull-on handle. She trudged into the bright lobby, her weary feet almost shuffling over the berry-colored carpeting, and she looked around.

The hotel was built around a skylighted atrium, where trees in boxes bowed gracefully over tables and chairs. A waterfall rushing over high black stone walls and surrounded by green plants provided a constant musical background. All the rooms opened to the atrium, clear to the top floor.

As she approached the registration area, she worked her credit card out of her wallet and laid it on the desk.

"Hi. I'm—"

"Welcome to Washington, Senator Likely," the smiling young black man behind the desk said. "I'm Jeff, and your suite is all ready." He slid the registration form across the faux-marble counter top.

"How did you know who I was?" she asked, signing her name on the form.

"Know who you were?" He ran her credit card through his machine. "Senator, you have one of the best-known faces in the country. You're our famous angel." He handed her a plastic keycard, explaining how to unlock her room door with it.

*He means famous former angel. The fraud story is probably all over the city....* She turned and started toward the elevator, but Jeff called her.

"Senator Likely, I'm sorry. I forgot to give you these messages.

One was delivered this afternoon, and this one came in by phone, about an hour ago." He leaned over the desk to give her an envelope and a folded sheet of pale green paper. The envelope contained the note from Priscilla Callon, asking her to the dinner party. The other message, typed on a hotel memo sheet, read: "Megan, dear, I'm glad you arrived safely. But please be careful about angels of light. Love, Ceelie."

# FIVE

Bob Linderman smiled at his own face on the noon news. If he hadn't interrupted the press conference, that clown Arlow would still be mouthing clichés and saying nothing. And they had to proceed carefully at this point: the evidence against Megan Likely was really nonexistent, and if Arlow were turned loose, they'd end up being sued for libel.

"Robert?" Linderman's wife held a candlestick; she stood in the doorway, rubbing the candlestick with a cloth, not looking at her husband. Her lank hair lay in damp strands against her neck.

"What?" The usual waves of irritation swept over him.

"Robert, there's this women's retreat at the church next weekend, and I was wondering if now that the election is over and you're home if you could take care of Bobby so I could—"

"Ellen, you know we've got this fraud investigation going. I haven't got time to do your job while you traipse off with a bunch of silly religious women." His distaste for his wife's appearance and personality was almost as strong as his aversion to their six-year-old son, Bobby, who was slouched in his stroller by the TV. Bobby, his only child, in whom he'd once had such hope, would never walk or speak....

Ellen said, "Robert, honey, I've never asked you before, and it would just be for two days. Bobby's doctor says I should get away once in a while. I just thought you—"

"Well, you thought wrong. I have important work to do. Maybe if you'd given me a real kid, one who could run and play, I'd be interested. Or if you'd be willing to put him in the state home, where he belongs."

They'd had that discussion before. Ellen slumped more than usual as she turned back toward the kitchen.

Linderman looked back at the television and was annoyed to

discover that the picture of his face was gone, the story was over, and the narrow-cheeked anchorwoman was talking about the French helicopter that had been shot down in Sudan. He'd missed the brief interview with Senator-elect Megan Likely.... *Hmmph. Too bad Ellen doesn't have the style Megan Likely has. If that young woman hadn't given me the brush-off on the highway, I'd never have tried the fraud thing.* He looked at his watch. The drive to Mark Combs's office was twenty-five miles. He'd leave as soon as he called his pal in Washington about his Egyptian oil stock.

Megan knew she couldn't wear a suit to a black-tie event. After asking the desk clerk for shopping advice, she hiked from the hotel to the Georgetown Mall. In a shop there she bought a straight, ankle-length white wool dress, whose soft fabric was shot through with silver threads. It cost much more than her natural prudence judged proper, but it would be okay for New Year's dinner, and she could dress it down all winter with her boots and Black Watch plaid shawl.

"This will do," she told the mirror, fastening her mother's heavy silver Navajo necklace at the back of her neck. She tried holding her hair up behind her neck; no, she'd let it fall on her shoulders. She pushed her feet into her red leather pumps and was ready to go until she thought of the president's wife, standing in the door of the oval office in her slim, silk Chinese gown. Megan suddenly felt frumpy and gaudy.

"I'm not going," she told Ewok, who was lying on the bedspread, his head cocked quizzically. She was about to fling herself down beside him like a frustrated adolescent when the phone chimed.

Linderman was almost shaking with rage. "What do you mean, you don't find enough evidence to call a grand jury? It's all right there in front of you."

Mark shook his head. "Mr. Linderman, what's in front of me are a lot of accusations and implications but not a solid piece of evidence. If you really believe Megan Likely committed fraud, you've got to give me more than this."

"I told you I had a call about votes at the bottom of Lake Winnebago. Why haven't you followed that up?

"It's not my job to follow your tips. I've discussed this case with the state district attorney, and he agrees with me. I've got to go by the letter of the law, Mr. Linderman, not hunches. There's no reason to continue with this case. I've already announced that to the press."

Linderman stood up. "This isn't the end of it," he said.

"Fine. Bring me something solid to work on, and we'll talk."

Linderman put both his hands down on the edge of Mark's desk and leaned forward. "You'd better start watching your back," he said. "I can expose your life, too. We could even discuss the summer of 1985."

Mark was suddenly warm all over. He stood until Linderman was out of the building. Then he sat down and wiped the sweat off his brow and upper lip. Linderman was dangerous, and Mark had to take steps to do something about him.


"Megan, don't forget what I told you," Celia said as soon as Megan answered.

"Ceelie, hello!"

"Did you get my note yesterday, dear? About the angels of light?"

"You said to beware or something. Of an angel? Does that mean me?"

"No, dear, it means folks in Washington who seem to be from heaven. How is the hotel? Are you going to any Christmas parties?"

"As a matter of fact, I'm going to the Callons' party tonight. Ceelie, last night I met the president and his wife, Dr. Tan."

"A notable woman," Celia said. "You will be watchful, won't you, my dear?"

"Watchful? I don't understand."

"Be sober, be watchful," Celia quoted. "We'll see you next Saturday." And she was gone.

Be sober, be watchful.... Sober? She didn't even drink! The words sounded familiar, but she couldn't quite place them. Wasn't that one of Ceelie's Bible verses?

She looked in the mirror again and decided she didn't look bad after all. Tan Luyin was probably a size one, if that, but then, it was no disgrace to be a six, was it? And the First Lady wouldn't be at the party anyway.

Brenda and Rick would, though. In fact, they were probably already parked in front of the hotel, waiting for her, because now it was four minutes until nine. She grabbed her red coat and evening bag, crammed her room security card into her pocket, then dashed to the elevator. She didn't hear her phone ringing as she raced down the hall.


While Celia washed up the cider cups, Ben Tolufson pushed the wheelchair toward the bedroom the Likelys had shared for fifty-one years. Celia watched thoughtfully. George had choked twice during dinner. On top of that, she'd been worrying about Megan. *Be sober, be watchful, Megan,* she repeated in her mind. The devil prowls around, looking for someone to devour. She closed her eyes and asked God to surround her granddaughter with angels.


The Callons had lived in their tall, narrow, two-hundred-year-old Georgetown brick house ever since the people of Wisconsin had sent Luke to Capitol Hill, first for three terms in the House, and then for two to the Senate. Friends urged Luke to go back to Wisconsin to run for governor, but he said he felt called to Congress.

But this was the first time they hadn't spent Christmas with relatives and old friends in Wisconsin. Priscilla Callon was going to argue before the Supreme Court in January, and she had to stay near her law library.

"The Supreme Court! I've really got a humdinger of a wife. Next you'll be nominated to a federal judgeship or something," Luke said, touching his wife's silver-blond hair.

"I don't want to be a judge unless it's in some warm place like Hawaii," Priscilla said, brushing any possible lint off her burgundy dress and looking around at the hors d'oeuvres and punch bowl. The caterer's assistant was ready to open the door and take coats. A tall, young man in a tuxedo shirt with black pants and vest stood discreetly behind the table.

"What do you think, Bryan? Draperies open or closed?"

Bryan turned his dark head toward the windows. "With the new storm windows, it doesn't seem to make a difference as far as the cold is concerned. Aha, Mom, I hear footsteps thudding through the snow. The party is starting."

As Rick rang the doorbell something beeped loudly.

"My pager," he sighed. He pulled it off his belt, then nodded his head. "I'm going to have to go see what's wrong at the transmitter."

"Clear to Fairfax?" Megan cried.

"No," Brenda said. "The transmitter is right over the bridge. Rick, you will hurry back, won't you?"

He kissed her and plodded back to the car. Several people had arrived behind them; soon they were all shaking snow off umbrellas and giving their wraps to the young woman in a dark blue uniform. Megan handed over her red coat and walked up the oak stairway to greet her hostess, hoping she wouldn't have to talk about the fraud charges with this Washington crowd. "Welcome," Priscilla said, kissing both cheeks of each person who came in. "And thank you so much for coming out in this storm."

"As if we would have missed the party," Brenda said, and apologized for Rick's absence. Brenda wore a Christmas-red dress that Megan thought made her fair complexion look pale, even washed-out. "Luke, Pris, you've met Megan Likely, haven't you?"

"Only briefly," Priscilla said. "We talked yesterday on the phone, thanks to the president. We're honored she could come on such short notice," she added. "What a stunning dress, Megan! And congratulations on your election."

"Yes, congratulations," Luke Callon said. "And thanks for getting Henry Arlow out of my hair. He was the last of the old-time politicians, I hope!"

"I'm the one who's honored," Megan said, looking around the elegant room and wondering if she'd stepped through the looking glass. It was nine-fifteen. By ten-thirty, when they sat down to eat, Megan had talked with some of Washington's brightest luminaries, including General Rudy Martinez, chairman of the Joint Chiefs, and Ladonna "Donnie" Thurmond, city editor at the *Washington Window*, a biweekly liberal political magazine. The Callons made friends on both sides of politics: Martinez was thoroughly conservative, a possible presidential candidate in four years, and Donnie Thurmond was ultraliberal. Megan liked the tall woman, though in fact, Donnie looked rather like a younger Celia Lively.

"I'd like to talk to you, Senator," Donnie had said, jingling the ice in her Perrier.

"Okay, here I am."

"No, I mean—" Donnie glanced over her shoulder and lowered her voice—"I mean, really talk. Alone. Perhaps we could have lunch this week?"

"Well, I hope I'll be working on my new office. And my grandparents, their neighbors, and Iris Millman are flying in Thursday, Miss Thurmond. Maybe we could make it after Christmas? Although I don't know what I could tell you about myself that you don't already know."

"Call me Donnie. First of all, I want to know how you beat an old warhorse like Henry Arlow. Were his fraud accusations true?"

Megan flushed the color of autumn maple leaves. "Of course not," she said hotly. *Be sober, be watchful,* her mind said, and she took a deep breath. "And," she added in her best lawyer voice, "you know I can't discuss the investigation while it's ongoing."

"You didn't hear? It's not."

"Not what?"

"It's not ongoing. I heard it on NPR on the way over here. The district attorney for your county has declined a grand jury hearing. So the investigation is probably over, unless, of course, Arlow goes for some other charge."

*Thanks, Mark.* Megan tried not to imagine his face as Donnie continued. Rick Samuelson joined them, towering over even the willowy, gray-haired Donnie.

"Rick! When did you get back?"

"Oh, I just took care of a small problem. I've been here awhile. Evenin', Ms. Thurmond," he said, exaggerating his easy Virginia drawl. "Forgive me for interrupting. Brenda would like for Megan to meet someone."

"Sorry. I don't remember your name," Donnie told Rick with a cool glance.

"Rick Samuelson. I'm—"

"Oh, yes, now I remember. You're the preacher who married Congresswoman Penning, aren't you?"

"Not a preacher. Just a Bible study leader. I actually own a radio station in Fairfax." Rick's face was big and bland, and he smiled patiently at Donnie. "I'm the station's news producer."

"Producer? I'll bet you are," Donnie said. "You'll take a beating on the oil stock you own if Libya annexes that Sudan corridor, won't you?"

Rick's cheekbones flushed dark red for a moment, and then he said, "Oh, I might lose a dollar or two. But it's all in a day's work."

Donnie whispered to Megan, "I need to talk to you about something important when we meet." Aloud, she said over her shoulder, "I'll call you, Senator Likely."

The room was too warm, and for an instant Megan wished she

were home, in the crackling-cold Wisconsin night. Maybe on a sleigh ride where she could snuggle with Mark as the horse trotted over the quiet, snow-covered terrain, with jingling bells the only sound.... Finally she realized Rick was looking at her.

"What an odd woman!" she murmured, gazing at Donnie's back, now across the room.

"Donnie Thurmond is dynamite," Rick said, with a touch of sadness in his voice. "Too bad she chose the political far left. I could use an editor like her in my newsroom. Come on, this way, Megan. Brenda's holding on to Senator Jim Ruthwell for you."

Ruthwell, majority whip of the Senate, was a wiry, graying redhead whose benign appearance had fooled a number of junior senators. His stinging wit and political savagery were famous all over the country. In fact, one commentator on TV's *Capital Gang* referred to him as "Senator Ruthless."

"Brenda wants me to meet him? Stand by, Rick, I may need CPR when he gets through with me."

She was saved from the encounter by Pris Callon's announcement that dinner was ready if they were. As they drifted through the Georgian archway and into the dining room, the handsome young man who had served hors d'oeuvres began picking up the used glasses and placing them on a tray.

"Senator Likely?" he whispered as she passed. She raised her eyebrows but kept walking. "Please, Senator, can I talk to you for just a minute?"

She waited to see what senatorial favor the young waiter wanted.

"Welcome to the Beltway," he said. "I'm Bryan Callon, the Callons' son."

Megan's lips parted in shock. "They make you wait on their guests?"

He chuckled, discreetly retrieving someone's half-eaten cheese crisp from the corner of a Sheraton desk. "Most everyone here has known me all my life. My parents have always let me help at their parties. When I was five, I was allowed to start taking coats."

"What do you do now, besides serve appetizers?"

"I'm in law school. The reason I stopped you was to ask if you'd hire me. You're entitled to a couple of aides, and besides, I've never met an angel before." He lowered his voice. "And I need to talk to you about something else, something important."

Only a few moments before, Donnie Thurmond had said the same words. And this young man was smooth and engaging.

"I haven't made any decisions yet," she said. "In fact, I haven't even seen my office."

"What? In that case, let me escort you. I could pick you up tomorrow at your hotel. You are still in Embassy Suites, aren't you?"

"Megan? Are you coming to dinner?" Pris Callon appeared in the arched doorway. "Oh, you've met my son, Bryan. Isn't he wonderful? I made him myself. With some help. Come on, Senator, we're waiting for you."

Megan flushed and followed her hostess. Her first Washington party, and she'd held up dinner!

"I'll call you tomorrow," Bryan said, flashing his beguiling smile. "Enjoy your dinner."

"Don't be out late tonight, will you, Bryan, dear?" Pris said as they left the room. "The streets are like an ice rink." Turning to Megan, she whispered, "He's hoping to work for you. We'll all talk about it later. And there's another matter, too. I'll call you tomorrow."

*Three people now want to talk to me privately about something important,* Megan thought as she started on the clear soup. *And apparently each one about something mysterious. This town is humming with intrigue.* She was seated, as a guest of honor, on Luke Callon's right. To her right was the formidable Jim Ruthwell, who scrutinized her face, said, "Oh, you're the angel," and then turned to his food.

By the time she had eaten her Wisconsin cheese soufflé, and the maid was bringing in the green salad that preceded the baked salmon, Ruthwell had only asked her for the salt and muttered that the salad dressing was too spicy for him. So she jumped when he said, "Well, Little Miss Angel of the Senate, what's the first thing you want to change in Washington?"

She swallowed her mouthful of hot bread, smiled, and said, "Senator, my reputation for being angelic is exaggerated. I actually have a strong devilish streak."

The people at their end of the table hooted with laughter, and Luke Callon said, "Maybe you've met your match, Jim."

Ruthwell grinned. "You're all right, Senator Likely. Likely: What kind of name is that?"

"Scot. I understand it was actually Lochlea once. From the Highlands, in the far north of Scotland."

"That must mean you've got Viking blood." Ruthwell was beginning to warm up for a jousting match.

"Well, you can't have it both ways, Senator Ruthwell. Either I have the wings of an angel or the horns of a Valkyrie."

As the others laughed again, Ruthwell muttered, "Glad to have you in Washington, Senator."

"Me too," Bryan Callon said from the doorway. He was now in jeans and a dark red sweater, with his down jacket over his arm. "I just came in to say good night and to ask Senator Likely if I can pick her up in the morning. To go see her office."

"Oh, but we were planning to come up to take her to church," Brenda said from the other side of the candelabra. Megan stiffened. She hoped Brenda wouldn't become another in the line of people who tried unsuccessfully to manage her life.

"I think I need to spend a lazy morning," she said, smiling so her irritation wouldn't show. "I've only been in Washington twenty-four hours, and already I've met the president, the editor at the *Window*, and the most menacing senator in the chamber. To say nothing of a host and hostess I've revered for years," she added.

"I see how she got elected," General Martinez laughed from Priscilla's end of the table. "Senator Likely, are you sure you're new to politics?"

By the time they got to the flaming cherries jubilee and a discussion about the poverty alleviation bill pending in the Senate, fatigue began to overtake her; after a few bites she laid her spoon on the table and sipped her coffee, hoping it would wake her up.

"You can drink coffee all night, folks," Priscilla told them. "This is decaf."

*Oh, great. I hope I don't nod off into my dessert.*

Mercifully, at eleven-thirty, Rick Samuelson told his hosts it was snowing hard outside, it was a long way to Fairfax, and they needed to take Megan home. He waved the caterer's assistant aside and fetched Priscilla's and Megan's coats and evening bags from the closet himself. Megan kissed her hostess good-bye, promising to call her when she found out more about any remaining fraud charge. She was pleased when Luke Callon planted a fatherly kiss on her forehead. In spite of their friendliness, though, she was glad to get away; somehow she'd have to learn to cope with a steady diet of statecraft at every social event.

Rick hurried the two women through the snowstorm to his car. Several inches of snow already lay on the car top, and he had to scrape the windshield.

"Well, they didn't serve Roast President," she said as she fastened her seat belt.

"The Callons are not gossipmongers," Brenda said. "They're very dedicated Christians."

"Nice people," Rick said. "And what a nice place they have! I just hope Senator Callon isn't a radical in sheep's clothing." He began backing the car, his eyes on the rearview mirror.

"Oh, nonsense," Megan said before she thought. "Luke Callon has voted for every important conservative measure in the past sixteen years. He's one of the best men in the Senate, and clean as a laundered towel."

Rick paused a moment, then said, "You're right, of course. I wonder about his wife, though." They pulled onto M Street. "You'll have to admit she keeps some strange company."

"Tell me more about Donnie Thurmond."

"I wish I had one reporter that could grab a story the way she does," he said. "But her opinions are 100 percent bleeding heart. She's a government scandal junkie, on the prowl for someone in Congress who took home a paper clip or something."

"I think members of Congress should be scrutinized. We have to be like Caesar's wife. Beyond reproach," Megan said, trying to see Brenda's face. Brenda wasn't this silent in the House of Representatives; she'd been in Congress for six years and was just reelected. Was she so much in love with Rick she was dumbstruck?

"Do you two go to church in Washington?" Megan asked, eager to get off government for a minute.

Brenda said, "We found a Bible church across the river, in Alexandria. We hope you'll go with us soon."

"My grandmother wants to attend the Christmas services at the National Cathedral."

Rick smiled over his shoulder. "They put on a beautiful ritual," he said. "Great choir. An organ that rivals any in the world. But there are people who say you can't find a real believer in the place."

"But surely—" Megan bit her lip and stopped. She knew, in fact probably everyone in the District knew, the Callons always attended Sunday services at the Cathedral, even though they also participated faithfully in Rick's Bible study.

*Be careful about angels of light.* Celia Likely's note danced before her eyes. Maybe Rick was right. About many things. He was opinionated, sometimes even overbearing, but he was also obviously sincere. He'd treated her kindly, and he appeared to love Brenda. The Callons must be the dangerous "angels of light" Ceelie had mentioned!

They followed a snowplow back to the hotel, with Megan sleepy and transfixed by the slow, rhythmic sound and by watching the snow fly into piles at the sides of the road. She was so tired she could barely climb out of the car when they pulled up in front. The valet, wearing his black cape and snow boots and holding an umbrella for her, opened the car door and said, "Good evening, Senator."

"I'll phone tomorrow," Brenda called, and then closed her window quickly to shut out the cold.

Megan waved and walked with a crunching step through the snow that had blown under the awning onto the red tiles. She hurried through the revolving door into the hotel, glad for the rush of warm air that rose up to meet her. She took the elevator to her suite, where she could hear Ewok barking furiously inside, and as she pushed her key card into the slot, she leaned her head against her door.

She almost fell down as the door, already unlatched, swung open and Ewok rushed into the hall. Megan grabbed the doorjamb to regain her balance and surveyed the scene in her room. Every drawer was open, her underclothes and shirts were flung about, her good suit lay on the floor, and the contents of her briefcase had been emptied onto the table.

# SIX

The police were in her rooms until two-thirty, with the hotel night manager fluttering in the background like a disorganized bat. And because Megan was a senator-elect, the FBI had sent an agent to check the disorder. He waited until the police were gone to ask another long set of questions.

Finally he said, "You're sure you can't think of anything a thief would want? Jewelry? Money? Secret government documents?" At that point, Megan, punchy with fatigue, began to laugh.

Special Agent Warburton fixed her with cool blue eyes. "This is no laughing matter, Senator," he said firmly.

"Well, how could I have any secret government documents? I was just elected a month ago, and I've only been in Washington about thirty hours."

"Perhaps you were working for the government before that."

Megan sank into a chair, smothering the laughter that kept trying to break through. "Hardly, Mr. Warburton. Someone who thought I had something they wanted broke into my room. My question is, why would they think so? And my second question is, what are you going to do to find him? Beyond asking me about secret documents?"

"The police dusted everything," he said, looking around at the gray powder that was left on every surface despite efforts to clean up. "They only found a few fingerprints that weren't yours, and even those may be from housekeeping. So until we get some idea what the thief was looking for, we won't know who to suspect. Do you have any enemies, Senator Likely?"

Linderman's repulsive smile leapt into her mind. But he wouldn't stoop this low, would he? His fight with her had been just political. And besides, he was in Wisconsin. She hesitated; if she mentioned him to the FBI, they'd probably think she was seeking revenge for the phony fraud charge. "No enemies to speak of," she said. "You know, I'm awfully tired, and I have this mess to clean up. If you don't mind?"

Warburton smiled, and she realized for the first time how attractive he was. And about her age.

"Here's my phone number," he said, writing on a business card. "And I've given you my pager number, too, just in case you think of something important, or if you're harassed again."

Her travel alarm read four-ten by the time she got the suite put to rights, shampooed the hair spray out of her hair, and climbed into bed. A good thing she'd refused Rick's invitation to attend church in the morning, she thought as she fell asleep, with Ewok on the bedspread nestled in the curve of her knees.

Bells ringing in a church somewhere woke her at ten the next morning, a faint sound through the snowstorm. She'd planned to sleep even later, but a combination of tension and excitement made her leave the bed and head for the shower. After she braided her hair and dressed in jeans and the black turtleneck she'd worn on the plane, she crumpled Ewok's newspaper and stuffed it into the wastebasket. The dog began whining for his breakfast, so she poured dry kibble into his dish and thought about her own morning meal.

Outside her window was a blizzard; she didn't want to try to walk anywhere in the wind and snow. The suite had a microwave, a small refrigerator, and a coffeepot with premeasured packets of Folgers coffee. But no food, not even a cracker. So after leaving a note for the maid to be sure to clean up the fingerprint powder, she took the glass elevator downstairs to eat in the hotel's garden atrium.

She poured herself a cup of coffee and grabbed a copy of the *Washington Post* from the free stack. She found the fraud story; in fact, she didn't have to look for it. It was on the front page, next to small headlines about the record snowfall, and it was illustrated by the famous "halo" picture from the morning after the election.

"No Probe Yet of Angel Election," the headline read. The story said Fond du Lac County District Attorney Mark Combs had refused to convene the grand jury to consider irregularities in the recent senatorial election in Wisconsin. The state attorney general hadn't commented, however, and an official from the election board had said, "We'll continue to explore the matter to decide whether former senator Arlow's charges have any merit." Whatever that meant.

*I'm not home free yet,* she thought. *Arlow—no, it's Linderman—really will never give up. Should I have told the FBI about him?* For a moment she wished, as she had the night before, that she was home in Ripon. This time last year she'd been cross-country skiing with Mark and several other friends on the trails in Chequamegon National Forest, near Lake Superior. The world had looked perfect, that day: the sun had gleamed on the soft powdery snow that covered everything except the tall pines and hemlocks. The sun also caught the light from the diamond in her new engagement ring. She felt her cheeks glowing as Mark stopped on the trail to say, "I never expected to love anyone this way—"

"Good morning, Senator." She looked up, startled out of her reverie, to see Bryan Callon standing by her table. He was wearing the same maroon sweater she'd seen him in the night before when he left his parents' party.

"I was in the neighborhood," he said, laughing, and she continued to stare at him: people weren't in any neighborhoods but their own this morning. The blizzard was raging, roads and bridges were closed, and most public transportation was out of service. Only the Metro was running on its tracks below ground, and its nearest stop was seven blocks from here.

"Bryan, isn't it? How on earth did you get here?"

"Actually, I've been here at Embassy Suites all night. I was at the Young Conservatives Caucus in the conference room until about one-thirty, and then the storm got too fierce to get home."

He'd been on these premises when her room was being ransacked. "How are you?" she asked. *Surely Senator Callon's son wouldn't rifle my hotel room! And what would he have been looking for, anyway?*

"Please sit down," she added finally, her manners overcoming her dismay.

He stepped to the buffet, poured a cup of coffee, and slid into the wicker chair across from her. "This place makes great coffee," he said. His blue eyes were wide and innocent. "How do you like your suite?"

If she told him about the break-in, he might think she suspected him, especially if he really was the intruder. On the other hand, if she didn't tell him, he'd wonder why later. "Actually, my suite was ransacked last night, while I was at your parents' house," she finally said. "Nothing was taken and, thank goodness, my dog was unhurt. But they sure messed my things up and I felt invaded. I'll be glad when my business manager gets here and we move into our apartment."

"They ransacked your rooms? Here at Embassy Suites?" He yanked a cellular phone out of the holster on his belt and said as he punched in a few numbers, "We've got to get you into a safer place."

"Well, I think I'll be fine "

"Mom? Mom, Senator Likely's suite was broken into last night. Yes, while she was at our house." He waited a few moments, listening, and then said, "Senator, my mother wants to talk to you." He handed her the phone and went toward the breakfast buffet.

Reluctantly, Megan again recited the story of Ewok's wild barking, the open door, the rifled drawers.

"Well, that settles it," Pris said. "The storm is letting up. As soon as the roads clear, Luke will go over there and pick you up. I've got to leave overnight, but the housekeeper will be here, and I'll be back tomorrow. You can stay at our house until your family comes on Saturday. We should have invited you to stay last night when the weather was so bad."

"I'm very grateful, Pris, but I need to be here in case my grandmother or my campaign manager calls. And if the snow lets up, I need to see about my office. I'll be moving into my own place next week."

"That's right, you're going to be in Dupont Circle, aren't you? Washington House?"

"Why yes. How did you know that?"

"You mentioned it last night at dinner. All right, then, dear, but you let Bryan stay with you for a while today. If someone's after you, Megan, you shouldn't be alone for a minute. This isn't peaceful little Ripon, Wisconsin, you know."

*If someone's after you...* Why would anyone be after her?

Bryan came back with his plate heaped, and he methodically began working his way through waffles, sausage, bacon, an omelet, fruit, and muffins. How did he stay thin, eating like that? When his cell phone rang and he began talking to someone about a House bill, Megan went over the facts: first, Priscilla Callon had insisted that she come to their party; next her son had turned up at the hotel under circumstances that were unusual, to say the least; and now she was trying to move Megan into their home. And Megan was certain she hadn't mentioned leasing the apartment at Washington House....

"If this snow keeps retreating, we'll be able to slog over to the Senate Office Building," Bryan said after he hung up. "I hope you're remembering what I asked you last night, about maybe being on your staff?"

"I haven't really had time to think about it, Bryan." She'd have to be careful. Be sober, be watchful, Ceelie had said. Maybe "sober" meant not getting carried away by people's charm. She glanced across the table at the young man's brilliant white smile and wondered what she would do with him all day.

"Well," he said, "could I come up to your suite after breakfast? I've got some propaganda to lay on you, but I think I'm going to order another omelet first."

"Now, which are you? A law student or a lobbyist?" she teased, trying to bring back the light mood she'd been in before he came.

"Law student now, planning to be a lobbyist after I graduate," he said. "I'll show you my concerns when I come up."

Megan sighed. Well, wasn't this why she'd flown in early? To find an aide, see her office, and check out the apartment? "I'll go on up," she said. "You eat breakfast, and I'll see you in a little while."

Her door was ajar again as she started to slide her card into the slot. She froze: Someone was in her room again. But the manager stepped out, along with a workman in a blue jumpsuit. "We just changed the locks," the manager said, handing her a new key card. "Whoever broke in here last night will have a hard time if they try it again. Senator, please turn the deadbolt and the clip lock when you're inside. By the way, housekeeping is in there too, just finishing up."

She pushed the door open to find two maids cleaning the suite. They smiled, but they softly chattered to each other in a language Megan had never heard before. Ewok, who hadn't gone near a vacuum cleaner since the day Megan nearly sucked up one of his ears, was in the bedroom on the newly made bed, slowly wagging his tail and holding a dog biscuit in his mouth. A small gold box of chocolates and a ribbon-tied stack of biscuits rested beside the clock on the night table, with the computer-generated note, "Embassy Suites welcomes Senator Likely and Ewok."

"Toto, I don't think we're in Wisconsin anymore," she said, and dropped onto the bed. Ewok immediately curled against her. The maids' gentle murmurs, the whirring sound of the vacuum, and relief at being safe let her drift into sleep laced with dreams about thieves in the White House.

Knocking at the door woke her. It was twelve-fifteen, and she couldn't remember for a moment where she was. The knock sounded again. The maids had left, so she got up and peeked through the door peephole.

It was Bryan, holding his coat over his shoulder and toting a briefcase. He came in and clicked the briefcase open, saying, "I told you last night I had something important to talk to you about. Dad wanted to discuss this with you too, but because of the snow, I'll have to do it."

He handed her a copy of SB7738, a Senate bill left over from the previous session, and one with which she was more than familiar. It was known as the poverty alleviation bill, and as far as she was concerned, it was a scam, originated by two senators on the other side of the aisle: a wild-eyed former actor from California, and the chubby, gray-haired woman from New York.

"You don't have to tell me a thing about this," she said. "It's an effort to double the size of the welfare bureaucracy. And it will cripple the people it's supposed to benefit."

Bryan looked up from his papers, his face showing dismay. "Dad feels that with a certain amendment, the bill would be acceptable. In fact, more than that. He plans to introduce the amendment when you go back into session. He's hoping you'll be in favor."

She stared at him in disbelief. "As if I could vote for anything from that pair. Surely your father's not going through with this."

Bryan slipped on reading glasses and looked more like the twenty-three-year-old he was than the callow boy she'd breakfasted with. "Senator Likely, just take a look here at clause 13B. Dad says if you reword it to say…"

They read and debated for more than two hours, Bryan working over the bill clause by clause, and Megan wondering how she could ever agree to even one phrase. Finally she took Ewok out for a half-block walk; when she came back she made coffee and called room service to send up some cookies.

"Those cookies will cost you about a hundred dollars apiece," Bryan said, grinning. "Just wait till you get your bill."

"Who pays your hotel bill? Your parents?"

"Are you kidding? My father would croak if he saw it. His Wisconsin ancestors would also croak if they weren't already dead. No, I've been working as a waiter and usually saving my money. Sometimes I get a choice tutoring job. And my grandmother left me a small fund."

"Do your parents pay you for serving at their parties?"

Bryan's fresh, boyish face turned dark. "Of course not," he said, in a voice edged with anger. He stacked up his folders and shoved them into his briefcase. "After all they've done for me? And besides, I usually like meeting their friends."

Megan answered the door and received a plate of cookies on a cloth-covered tray. When she signed the tab, she noted that the cookies were not a hundred dollars apiece, but they were incredibly expensive. She wanted to joke with Bryan about it, but his face was still tense. Apparently he had a temper, one he was trying to hold under control. Who was he, really? Maybe he'd lied about his father's being interested in the poverty alleviation bill. Maybe he'd broken into her room last night, just to frighten her.... Maybe his mother—

Bryan's eyes widened. "Wow!" he said. "Look at that!" He was pointing at her hair, and she glanced into the ornate mirror over the desk.

The faint crown of little lights danced over her head. Whatever these lights were, she was getting used to them. "It's just a reflection of sunlight from the window," she said. "See? The blizzard is breaking. I can see a patch of blue out there."

"Great!" Bryan ate two cookies, then stood up and drained his coffee. The anger was gone from his face. "It's only a little after four. Put on your boots, Senator, and let's go see your office."

While she gave Ewok fresh water in his plastic bowl and found her briefcase, he paced around the front room of her suite, chattering about the best places to eat, walk, and get information in Washington.

"You'd better wear a heavy coat," he called as she knelt on the floor of her bedroom closet, pulling out her fleece-lined rubber boots. As she started to rise, light from the bedroom lamp glimmered on something. And this time she wasn't seeing sunbeams, but the glint of metal on the closet's back wall, near the floor. Her hand closed over it: a round, disk-shaped object, somewhat smaller than a doorknob, with perforations. Instinctively, she pulled, and it dropped to the floor with a soft *thirk* as suction cups let go.

What in the world? Frowning, she picked it up to examine it more closely. Then she grabbed her purse and retreated into the front room, where she placed the object on the coffee table. With her finger on her lips to keep Bryan from speaking, she opened the front door and pointed out to the gallery.

The ash trees were bare, and a few snowflakes danced in the Wisconsin sky like ashes in wood smoke. Looking through the window, Mark knew winter was really here, and he wished for weather warm enough to take his sloop out on the lake. Sailing was probably the best thing in his life, now that Megan was gone.

They could have had a nice life, living on his farm, maybe practicing law together in Ripon or Fond du Lac, sailing on Green Lake or Winnebago, skiing in the wintertime. Sundays were hard for him. The office was closed, he'd read all the papers, fed the animals, and watched part of a football game. He switched off the television and sat down at his desk to sort through the stack of notes his assistant had handed him on Friday evening as he left work.

At the bottom of the stack was a picture postcard from Robert Linderman. The scene on the front was Lake Superior, with a fisherman holding up his record catch. The message, scrawled on the back asked, "Have you been fishing lately? I'll call you soon. Linderman." *He knows. He knows about Gail and me and the summer she disappeared. And if Linderman knows, no telling what he'll do with it. The man is a menace. For that matter, so is Henry Arlow, his boss. There has to be a way to get them out of my hair.*

# SEVEN

Robert Linderman glanced at his watch. Bobby had cried for at least an hour, and Ellen was, as usual, unable to do anything about it. He was tempted to hire someone to help her, but he had Ellen thinking they were poor. No use telling her yet about the money.

"Shut that kid up, or I'll give him a reason to cry," he yelled. He had to get Bobby into an institution. Maybe then Ellen would come out of her trance. She was no better at child rearing than she was at making a man feel like a man. He could hardly remember why he'd married her, except that his mother had kept pushing him to take that nice young woman out on a date. Back in those days, Ellen had been bouncy and fun; now she was a limp dishrag. She kept a good house, he had to give her that. But it just wasn't enough. And she was always complaining about money. It was probably time to knock her around again, to make her appreciate what she had. He decided to take a walk. He could forget for an hour about his party's national committee asking for a special prosecutor to find out whether he'd really funneled four million dollars of Arlow's campaign money into his own funds. Sure he had. But he'd laundered it carefully. They'd never find it.

He started to put his coat on and then remembered he'd wanted to write one more postcard to that stupid district attorney in Fond du Lac. What a stroke of luck it had been, finding out that one of Arlow's precinct workers had been Mark Combs's college roommate. He opened his desk drawer and noticed that Megan Likely's cell phone number was still there, scrawled on the slip of paper he'd had in the car on the way to Sturgeon Bay. The Oshkosh police chief had given it to him when he called, probably not buying his story that he needed to make sure of debate arrangements. But Chief Busch owed Linderman more than one favor.

He sorted through the picture postcards he'd bought and

stashed in his desk drawer. A picture of the big Paul Bunyan statue up in the North Woods. Yeah, that was it. He circled Bunyan's ax, then on the other side scrawled, "Is this how you got rid of her? Linderman" and addressed it to Mark Combs. That so-and-so would be sorry he hadn't gone on and prosecuted Megan Likely for election fraud.

He licked a stamp and stuck it on, but before he could leave, someone rang the doorbell.

"I'm pretty sure it's some kind of transmitting device," Megan whispered when she and Bryan were outside her door.

"A bug?" Bryan looked shocked. "What are we going to do?"

"Actually Bryan, *we're* not going to do anything. I am. I'll go downstairs to call the FBI. They were here last night, and the agent left me a card. But I wonder why someone is so curious about what I do here? First I'm ransacked, now I'm bugged. Go back in and get your things. You can go down with me."

Calling from the lobby, she reached Warburton, who said, "Be right over," in his terse way. She then persuaded a reluctant Bryan to leave, saying her meeting with the FBI would probably end too late for her to look at her office or talk any more about Senate business today.

"I should stay and keep an eye on you, at least till the agent gets here," he protested, but she insisted she'd be fine, and he finally left.

At five-forty, the distinguished conservative senator, Luke Callon, was standing on a stepladder in the living room, trying to estimate the number of square feet of wallpaper they'd need. He had to admit Priscilla was right. The old stuff was looking a little shabby. At noon she had plodded through the snow to a taxi. She was heading for Oshkosh, Wisconsin, to speak at...what was it she was supposed to speak at? She'd said she'd be back the next afternoon, and he wanted to get at least one wall finished, to surprise her.

"What in the world?" Bryan sauntered into the room and set his briefcase on the floor. "Dad, come down from there. It you want to learn to fly, I'll take you to the airport."

"Very funny. Hand me that tape measure on the desk, will you?"

Bryan picked up the tape and handed it to his father. "You're not going to wallpaper, are you, Dad? Remember the last time, when you didn't match it right in the bathroom? You'd better let Mom do it."

"Your mom is in Wisconsin," he said, checking his watch. "In fact, she's been there for two hours. And I want to surprise her."

"I spent the morning with Senator Likely. Did Mom tell you the senator had her room ransacked last night? While she was at the party here?"

Luke straightened, his lips parted in shock. "Good grief! Is she okay?"

"Yeah, and whoever it was didn't hurt her little dog. But I—" The telephone rang and Bryan picked it up.

"Oh, hi, Jim," he said to Senator Ruthwell. Then it was his turn to look shocked, as he handed the telephone to Luke and turned on the TV, as Ruthwell had suggested. He stood rooted to the spot as he listened to the news about Robert Linderman, Henry Arlow's campaign chairman.


Megan met Special Agent Warburton in the lobby. She sat down on a dark red wing-backed chair, and he perched on the edge of the one facing her.

"You're sure it's a listening device?" He rubbed his finger absently over the cleft in his chin.

"Well, I mean, I've never seen one before except in the movies." She laughed nervously, hoping he hadn't plodded here through piles of snow just to discover she'd pulled something like a thermostat off the wall. "I'd better take you upstairs and show you," she added.

"Wait a minute. Did you see any others? Did you take your telephone apart?"

"Why, no. I figured whoever planted it probably left just one. Hey, maybe it had something to do with whoever had that suite before me. That has to be it."

"That's easy enough to find out." He strode over to the registration desk and showed the clerk his identification. The young woman nodded and went through the door behind her; in a minute she emerged with the manager. Megan couldn't hear their conversation, but she saw the manager pull a computer printout from a file drawer. He and Warburton pored over it for a minute, the manager's finger jabbing the paper. Warburton nodded and spoke briefly, then came back to Megan.

"The room was empty for a week before you got here. And the last occupants were a family from Salem, Oregon, a mother and three little girls. Probably not a group anyone would want to bug. Let's go on up."

He was silent in the elevator. She wondered if he were that quiet at home. "Do you have a family?" she asked.

"My wife died three years ago."

"I'm sorry." She was surprised he was still single; he was an attractive man, cool blue eyes notwithstanding, and many women liked a rather taciturn male. That thought gave in to the image of Mark, laughing as he drew her close....

"Here's your floor," Warburton said as the elevator stopped, and they walked in silence to her room. Ewok gave them a few perfunctory barks, with the plume of his tail waving. Warburton scooped the listening device off the oak coffee table and nodded, his finger to his lips. Using a small screwdriver that clipped onto his shirt pocket like a pen, he opened the object and yanked the wires loose. Then he snapped the cover back in place and said softly, "I'd better search for any others."

He pulled an electronics detector from his coat pocket and

walked slowly through the suite. He found two more transmitters: one in the bedroom telephone and one under the television cabinet in the front room.

"Someone's curious about you, Senator. They wanted to hear every word you said," he told her after he had dismantled both bugs. Have you seen a van or truck parked around here?"

"In the snowstorm we were having? I haven't even seen the store windows across the street! Mr. Warburton, why didn't you or the police find these last night?"

"We weren't looking for them. Maybe they weren't here."

"Not here? Then how—"

"Who has been in here besides you, since I left last night?"

"Well, the maids, two maids, that I know of, and then—" *Bryan! I took Ewok outside while Bryan was reading the Senate bill.*

"The maids and who else?"

"Bryan Callon. Senator Luke Callon's son was here alone for maybe half an hour this afternoon," she said finally and, with a knot in her stomach, watched as Warburton wrote the name in his notebook and put a question mark after it. Then he glanced around the room one more time.

"Let's see your purse," he said.

"I rarely carry one. In fact, I didn't bring one to Washington."

"Where do you carry your stuff?"

She grinned. "Probably the same place you do, Mr. Warburton. I put my wallet and keys either in my briefcase or my inside pocket." She stopped. "Wait. There's—"

"What?"

"Yesterday. I bought a little evening bag. Very small. For the Callons' party." She opened a dresser drawer and pulled out the white brocade purse.

"Did you look in it after you got home? For your keys or anything?"

"No. In fact, I don't think I opened it at all. My key card was in my coat pocket." She opened it, and he extracted another listening device from the tiny zippered compartment, this bug about the size

69

of a small stud earring. It looked almost like a small wood screw.

"But that means the ransacker didn't plant the bugs! My bag wasn't here when he broke in."

"No, it might mean whoever did this was also at the party."

"Oh, sure. The chairman of the Joint Chiefs or the Majority Whip. They were with me at Senator Callon's residence for a party. And then the Samuelsons brought me home." He dismantled the bug. She asked, "How about my briefcase?" She retrieved the black leather attaché from her bedroom. He sat down on the sofa, setting the briefcase on the coffee table. When he snapped it open, he grunted softly and pulled a fifth transmitter, this one also tiny, from one of the inside pockets.

"They wanted to be sure they heard you, all right." He was deft with the screwdriver; he quickly had the wires disconnected. "Senator, there's something you haven't told me, isn't there?"

Sighing, she sat down at the other end of the sofa and told him about Robert Linderman's trailing her to Egg Harbor, the tire change, the cell phone call. "It all sounds silly when I say it out loud," she said. "But he was threatening. And then there is that phony accusation of fraud."

"Somebody wants to hear every word you say. I'll check on this Linderman character and also get somebody to scour the neighborhood for a sound truck."

*Good grief! Listening devices, sound trucks, the FBI. I feel like I'm in a movie about Washington. One starring Clint Eastwood.* "I thought I was coming here to make the world a better place," she said.

"There's no reason you can't," Warburton said. He shuffled a moment. "Say, Senator, I wonder if you could do me a favor." He took from his coat pocket a folded copy of a newspaper bearing her "angel" picture. Holding out the paper, he asked, "Can you tell me the name of the photographer who took this picture? The credit just says United Wire Service."

"I don't remember. It was in the *Milwaukee Statesman-Journal* first, I'm sure. They could tell you. Why?" She sat down, relieved that his request was a professional one. Ewok snuggled against her, facing out, as if he could protect her from unknown enemies.

"Look in the background. There's the silhouette of a man back there."

She peered at the shadowy setting in the photograph. "I can barely see it."

"Next time I come up I'll bring a magnifying glass. I want to know who it is."

"Probably a reporter. And I hope there isn't a next time," she said, and added quickly, "I mean, another emergency."

"Well, actually, tomorrow I'll want to check again for bugs. Who knows? Someone may have bribed a maid to stick them up here. The placements looked pretty professional." He looked around the room. "Senator Likely, don't let anyone in here while you're gone. Including the cleaning people. Stay here when the maids come tomorrow so you can watch what they do."

After he left, Megan decided to eat an early dinner in her room. She gave Ewok another handful of kibble, then put away her briefcase and the small white evening bag. After forty minutes, Room Service brought the turkey sandwich and salad she'd ordered. At no time did she take her eyes off the waiter who brought her food, and when he left, she lifted every item on the tray to hunt for listening devices. Before she ate, she hung the Do Not Disturb sign on her doorknob, turned the deadbolt latch on her door, and checked the windows.

*After all the years I slept in Ripon with the windows wide open! I've never had to be cautious before, not even when I worked in the attorney general's office and was dealing with criminals. Now I'm edgy in one of the biggest, most secure hotels in Washington. And this is only Sunday. I'll be by myself for five more days.*

She turned on CNN and found to her concern that Egypt was massing troops on the Sudanese border. The U.S. secretary of state had left for Cairo at noon to confer with the Egyptian president. She made an entry about it in her spiral-bound notebook, then switched to the Weather Channel and got news that the storm had abated. Tuesday daytime temperatures would rise, and snow

71

would change to rain and freezing rain followed by sun; but more snow was expected by the weekend.

"And they say our Wisconsin weather is fierce," she told her dog. He yawned and closed his eyes, and Megan remembered how little sleep she'd had herself. She switched back to the news channel and tried to stay awake, but in a few moments she was asleep. She didn't hear the report that campaign manager Robert Linderman, who was the focus of an election probe, had been slashed to death by an unknown assailant.

# EIGHT

The videocam zoomed in on Ellen Linderman's face as the reporter from the local ABC affiliate stuck out a microphone.

"Mrs. Linderman, how did you find out your husband was dead?"

"I was putting my boy to bed, and I heard the doorbell ring. Well, I couldn't go, what with Bobby crying and trying to roll off the bed where I was changing him, you know; he might get hurt if I went away for even a minute and—"

"So your husband went to the door?" Time was fleeting. The newsman raised his eyebrows, looking concerned and sympathetic, so his interruption didn't sound harsh.

"I guess so, I mean, like I told the police, I didn't see Robert go to the door, but when I got back into the living room, he was there—he was—he was lying there on the floor, in all that—all that—" She stopped talking and stared, her lips parted and her eyes confused like those of a suffering animal; and then she started to sob. "All that blood," she blurted, her eyes and nose running. "All that blood, that blood."

The reporter stepped away and motioned with his head for the camera. Marsha, the videocam operator, put him in a tight shot. "We've been talking to Ellen Linderman, wife of the man who was slain this afternoon by an unknown assailant. According to police, the fatal slash wounds to his carotid artery were inflicted by a long knife. Linderman was campaign manager for Henry Arlow, who recently lost his Senate seat to Megan Likely, the so-called angel of the Senate. Linderman was recently accused of siphoning campaign funds into his own account. I'm Scott Lacey, from WOSH in Oshkosh, Wisconsin. Back to you, Ron."

Lacey shifted his weight from foot to foot, and finally muttered to the camerawoman, "Do you think we should just leave her

73

here?" Ellen Linderman was still sobbing, still creating a flood of tears. She didn't try to mop her eyes; she stood in her kitchen with her arms hanging down, her head bowed, tears ruining the front of her unbecoming gray print dress. Lacey finally offered her his handkerchief.

"I'm sorry. I ruined your news show. Robert always told me I was a stupid motormouth." She blew her nose but then began sobbing again. "What will I do now? I haven't worked since I got pregnant with Bobby. Robert wanted me to put him in the state home and go with him to live in Washington, but I—" She looked toward the living room, where a large area of the beige carpet was stained with blood.

The police had finished with the crime scene and the coroner had taken Linderman's body away an hour earlier. The officer who had searched the house tried to escort Ellen somewhere, and being repeatedly refused, had finally left. Ellen told the detective in charge of the case that her car was in the driveway and she would leave when he did. But when the TV crew arrived, having waited around the corner in their van until they saw the cops leave, Ellen was still standing in the kitchen, and Bobby was screaming in the bedroom. They'd known that if they taped right then, they could make the ABC Evening News. It was Lacey's big chance.

"Is there someone we can call for you?" Lacey asked. He was uneasy at the thought of leaving the woman with her husband's blood on the floor. "Do you have relatives?"

"Just my mother. She lives in a nursing home in Milwaukee. She's only sixty-five but she had a severe stroke last year after my dad died, and Robert's folks live up in Sturgeon Bay, but they're in Florida right now, so I don't even know how to tell them about—"

"How about someone here in Oshkosh? A friend, or—"

"My pastor, I guess," she said, no longer crying. The child kept screaming from the bedroom. Ellen Linderman's eyes were dull, she spoke in a monotone, and she put her hands to her ears as if to shut out the sound of her child's screams. "Robert didn't like

Pastor, in fact he didn't want me going to that church. He said churches just wanted our money. Not that we had much, with Robert in Washington most of the year and us here.... So maybe it wouldn't be right for Pastor to come here. I mean with Robert's memory and—" She looked close to a breakdown.

Lacey leaned close to her and said firmly, "The pastor's name. What's his name?"

"Pastor Jim. Jim Davies. At Knott Avenue Christian Center. He's—"

Marsha was already pulling her phone out of her pack. "Do you know his number?"

"I-I mean, no, I'm not real active. Robert didn't like baby-sitting. I mean, if Bobby was sick sometimes on Sundays and couldn't go to the nursery when Robert was in town, I'd ask him to watch the boy for an hour—and it made him really mad, so I—"

It took several minutes for Marsha to look up the number of the church; when she dialed, she got the answering machine and went back to the directory for the pastor's home number. Ellen was still standing in the middle of the kitchen floor, staring down at the green vinyl tile. "Grace and peace to you," the voice on the answering machine said. "I'm away from my phone right now—" Marsha shook her head and clicked off. She called the police department, asking them to send somebody to take the woman to a motel or somewhere. Then she and Lacey packed up their equipment and drove away in the white WOSH van, rushing through the rain to make the late news. When they left, Bobby was still screaming. They didn't notice the long, slender piece of glass in the gutter a block away, with the rain washing its blood-stain into the storm drain.

Forty minutes later a pair of police officers knocked several times. Ellen Linderman had to be nearby unless someone had come to get her. Her ten-year-old Stanza was still in the driveway, and her husband's Mercedes was in the garage. Finally they tried the door. It was unlocked. Except for the supper dishes stacked by the sink and the dark red stain on the living room floor, the house was immaculate, but they smelled gas. Ellen Linderman, holding her son close in her arms, had laid her head on the open door of the gas oven. She and the boy were both dead.


"Dead? Murdered? By whom?" Megan stood in the doorway of her suite in her bathrobe, staring at Special Agent Tom Warburton. Ewok was between her ankles, barking only halfheartedly, with his tail wagging. He knew Warburton by now.

"We don't know yet. Maybe his wife. I know it's early, but could I come in?"

She pulled her robe together at the throat and stepped back so he could enter. She glanced at her watch: it was six o'clock. She would have been up soon anyway. When did this happen?"

"Yesterday in Oshkosh."

"Senator Arlow must be out of his mind with shock!"

"Well, that's a problem. We can't find him."

"You can't find him?"

"We checked late last night with the housekeeper, who said Arlow went to Wisconsin for the holidays. And Senator Callon— Mrs. Callon is Mindora Arlow's friend—also thought Arlow had gone to Madison and then he and his wife were heading to their place on Lake Superior."

Megan sank onto the sofa. "Is Senator Arlow a suspect in the murder?"

"Not officially. But that's why I'm here. Have you heard from him?"

She smiled. "I'm afraid I haven't ever heard from him, before the election or after. I've never actually spoken to the man except during our debates and a town meeting."

"You're kidding. Well, that's another dead end. I just thought maybe…I'm sorry I disturbed you so early. The Bureau chief in Wisconsin was in a swivet about it and called me an hour ago." He stood and was about to leave, then turned. "Senator, could I at least buy you some breakfast? I haven't eaten either."

It would be silly to refuse; she was famished, as she always was in the morning. "I'll meet you down in the atrium in fifteen minutes," she said, and locked the door after he left.

Standing in the shower, she lathered her body and mused over the facts. One, Robert Linderman was dead. Two, Henry Arlow was missing. Three, so was his wife. Four, Priscilla Callon was Mindora Arlow's friend, but she didn't know where they were. Or did she? The phone rang just as she stepped from the shower. It was Brenda, calling to say she'd just seen the news about Linderman on CNN.

"Oh, Brenda, I just heard. That FBI agent came to tell me."

"And now there's the awful thing with his wife and their boy."

"What about them?"

Brenda told her about Ellen's suicide with her son. Before Megan could comment, Brenda added, "I'm sorry, Meg. Rick just walked in off the train from New York, and he's inviting me to go out for breakfast. See you later." And she was gone.

Preoccupation with the Lindermans' deaths slowed her getting dressed. Linderman was an awful man, sleazy and untruthful. But so were a lot of political figures, and they weren't murdered. Had Henry Arlow killed his campaign manager? Maybe it had to do with missing millions.

She caught the concierge as he strode along the walkway near the elevator and asked him to put Warburton's breakfast on her bill and not to send the housekeepers up till she called. Warburton was in the atrium, drinking a cup of coffee at the same table beside the waterfall where she'd eaten the day before with Bryan Callon.

"Sorry I took so long. I had a phone call. Mr. Warburton, you didn't tell me about Linderman's wife and son."

"Please, call me Tom. Well, I didn't want to hit you with all of it at six in the morning. The Bureau is very interested in Mrs. Linderman's death, too, but first we have to let the Oshkosh police take a stab at the case.... I was going to get some coffee for you, but I wasn't sure."

"I'll get it." She headed for the counter, where she picked up a blueberry bagel and poured herself a cup of coffee. The woman in the pass-through window beamed. "Why it's our angel! I've been telling everyone I was here when you ate breakfast on Sunday. Is your coffee okay, hon?"

Megan nodded, looking at the selections. She skipped the eggs and sausages and dished up grits, toast, and fruit, the same breakfast she would have had at home in Ripon, except the grits would have been oatmeal. She hoped she'd be able to eat; she was sickened by the thought of someone slashing Robert Linderman to death and leaving him in his own blood for his wife to find.

As she slid into the wicker chair, balancing her tray, she asked, "I understand the Linderman boy was physically challenged?"

"Totally helpless is my information. In fact, the police investigated the Lindermans several years ago. Apparently the kid was born normal, but when he was about a year old, Ellen took the baby to the pediatrician because he was listless. The doctor thought the baby had been shaken so hard it damaged his brain. But the locals couldn't get the definitive evidence they needed to prove Linderman was abusing both his wife and the baby."

"I wonder why she stayed."

"The current theory at the Bureau is that she murdered Linderman, then killed herself and the boy."

"If they suspected her, why did the police leave her there? Why didn't they arrest her?"

"Nobody suspected her until she was dead." He hesitated and finally said, "There's a knife. Everything was rinsed and stacked by the sink, including a long skinny knife, one of those curved jobbies you see advertised in TV commercials, you know, 'Now how much would you pay?'"

"A knife? Was it bloodstained?"

"It was washed off, but they took the knife to the lab to test it for blood. It's pretty hard to get rid of some blood evidence, no matter how carefully you wash it."

The sleepwalking scene from *Macbeth* flashed into her mind, with Lady Macbeth washing her hands over and over, crying, "Yet here's a spot...." She banished the picture and looked around the atrium; only one other person was eating. "I guess we're early birds," she said.

"I apologize again for waking you up. I was all for waiting until later, but orders came from higher up. And I'm sort of glad they did; it gives me a chance to see you again."

She wanted to say, "I'm sorry. I'm engaged to Mark," but instead she smiled. He was a nice guy, after all. And good-looking, in a short-haired, blue-eyed way. She held her coffee cup with both hands for a moment to warm her fingers. "You don't think Henry Arlow did it? Then why is he missing?"

Before Tom could answer, the concierge appeared beside her chair. "Senator, there's a call for you. You can take it in the lobby if you like. The person said it was urgent."

"I've got to go anyhow," Tom said.

When she got to the phone, a hoarse voice said, "Megan Likely? Don't say my name out loud. This is Henry Arlow."

# NINE

S he had intended to spend the morning at her new office; instead, she walked over to Farragut Square, wishing as the cold wind licked at her face that she'd grabbed a cab to ride the nine blocks. The street was busy with people going early to their shops and offices. She rode the "down" escalator to the Metro station, as Arlow had asked, and she waited near one of the ticket machines. She was cold and impatient, and she began to wonder if he'd really come. But after ten minutes he got off the subway looking hunted, almost frantic.

"You've got to help me," he said without any other greeting.

*Help you? Why should I help after the underhanded way you campaigned against me?* "What do you want?"

"Tell the police you met with me last night."

"What? I don't tell lies, especially not for you. Besides, I've talked to the FBI, and they know I haven't seen you."

The wind was holding a newspaper against the escalator wall. Had this man murdered Robert Linderman? "Where were you really, Senator Arlow?"

"My wife and I decided to spend the week at our lodge in Ashland, up near Lake Superior, and then we planned to go to our kids' house for Christmas."

"Then tell the police your wife was with you."

Arlow shook his head. "She wasn't. She left a day early, to shop for Christmas at those outlet stores in Oshkosh. So we took both cars."

"And?" Megan stared at the man she'd run against. He didn't look formidable now; in fact, he looked downright terrified.

"I was partway there when I heard the news on the car radio about Linderman, and that the police were looking for me. I got off the highway in Appleton and grabbed a shuttle to Chicago, and from there I took the red-eye here—" He broke off, looking over his shoulder at a man in the crowd waiting for the Metro. "That guy's looking at me. Let's go up to the street." He grabbed her wrist and pulled her toward the escalator. A wind laced with fresh snowflakes whipped her coat and found its way into her sleeves and buttonholes.

"Wait a minute! Wait a minute!" Megan said, yanking her arm away. She began walking fast, away from him, up the moving stairs; at the top she kept walking, even though Arlow had caught up and begun to tug at her wrist again. "I don't know what you think you're doing, Senator, but you're not going to do it with me. If the police are looking for you, I suggest you call your lawyer and turn yourself in."

"But the police must think I killed Robert Linderman."

"Probably," she said. "I heard your last meeting was hostile. Didn't you threaten to beat him up?"

Arlow looked almost normal for a minute. "Linderman stole three million dollars, maybe more, from my campaign fund. I threatened to punch him. But I don't murder people."

"Well, why in the world did you want me to vouch for you? Which I won't."

"Look." His eyes were beginning to narrow again, to search the streets again. "I came to Washington to find someone who knew I wouldn't kill someone. But everyone's out of town for the holidays. Even the one businessman I know well is in New York. So who would the police believe? Not my friends. You. My, ah, opponent."

*Enemy, you mean,* she thought. "Oh, come now. That's a pretty big reach, Senator. And does your wife know where you are?"

He looked around again, his eyes red-rimmed and suspicious. "No," he croaked. "I called her from Chicago but I didn't want anyone, not even her, to know what I was doing."

"Okay, let's say for the sake of the argument you didn't do it. Who did?"

He thrust his face close to her ear. "They did it. They're after me," he muttered. "There's a conspiracy at work. It's universal. A whole underground government. They'll get you too; they're trying to—"

Megan tried to hide her shiver. "Senator Arlow, I'm not your attorney, and I don't want to hear about any crazy secret system or whatever it is. Go to the police." She headed back down the avenue, her back ramrod straight, toward a knot of early-bird shoppers.

A courier speeding down the sidewalk on a bicycle was aimed straight at her, and she couldn't figure out which way to dodge. She was going to be injured! Suddenly the wind swept her against a building. A little girl in a down suit cried, "Mommy, look at that lady in the red coat. She has Christmas lights in her hair!"

After Megan had walked a block, she looked back and saw Arlow standing alone, his jacket flapping wildly in the wind. When she glimpsed a taxi weaving through the traffic, she forced her eyes away from the agitated man and hailed the cab. It was time to see her office. "The Russell Senate Office Building," she said to the turbaned driver as she climbed in. He nodded silently and the car started forward. She looked back through the rear window, but Arlow was gone, either back down to the Metro or around a corner.

Watching traffic and pedestrian zones full of people that had braved slick, snowy sidewalks and fierce winds, she suddenly saw the Capitol. It was her first real look at it since she had arrived. She'd had a twilight glimpse through the bare trees as Rick and Brenda brought her in from the airport, but that was all. The Capitol! She'd be working in the building for the next six years. Impulsively she said, "Let me out here," and paid the fare.

A line of people was waiting to enter the building, so she took her place at the rear and gazed up at the massive white dome. There was something comforting about it; it was immensely strange and yet completely familiar. A building she'd seen on every…what? Was it a twenty-dollar bill? a ten? She didn't know. In spite of the freezing cold, she felt a warm flush of embarrassment as she dug through her wallet. I'm a United States Senator-elect, and I don't even know what's on my money! Finally she found the building's picture on the only fifty-dollar bill in her wallet. It was a broad view of the Capitol, its columns lifting toward the nine hundred ton cast-iron dome.

"Please stay to the right of the rope," a security officer said, walking down the line. He stopped in front of her; fresh from her encounter with Arlow, she was nervous and wondered if he would ask her if she had a ticket or something. Maybe you had to have an appointment to go into the Capitol.

"Senator?" he said, his face unbelieving. "Aren't you that new Senator from Minnesota or wherever? You had your picture in the *Post* yesterday. What are you doing out here in the cold?"

"I-I want to go inside," she said. "To see the rotunda, at least. I've only been in Washington two days and I haven't been here yet."

"Well you don't have to stand in line, for crying out loud. Follow me."

"No, I'll wait. That wouldn't be fair to these other people."

The woman in front of her turned. "You're a senator? Go on ahead. You ought to get something out of being in office."

Megan smiled and followed the security guard. He led her up the steps, commenting that the thirty-six columns represented all the states in the Union at the time they were built. And then they were inside the Capitol rotunda. She stared up at the dome, tears trying to spring to her eyes. A young woman with short dark hair approached her.

"Good morning, Senator. The security guard told me you were here. I'm Jackie, and I'll be your guide, if you want one." As she continued, her voice took on a chirping quality. "The painting you're looking at, on the inside of the dome, is called *The Apotheosis of Washington,* and it was painted by Constantine Brumidi to glorify the nation's capital city. Most of our hall friezes and all but a small portion of the historical frieze below the dome were also executed by Brumidi, but he died before it was finished."

Dizzy either from looking up too long or from being overwhelmed in the heady atmosphere of history, she reeled for a moment and then decided to follow the tour guide. They looked at all the statues in their mute circle in the rotunda. She saw the empty House chamber, the door to the Speaker's office and that of the majority leader of the Senate. She was about to look into the Senate room, even though it was not in session, when she saw Bryan Callon, standing nearby, grinning.

"Bryan?"

"Mom said I should look for you here."

"Your mother knew I'd be in here? I didn't even know it."

"She said you'd go to your office today but when you saw the Capitol, you'd have to come in and look."

*That woman is either psychic or spying. And I don't believe in psychics.*

"Senator? Should I leave you here?" the tour guide asked.

"I guess so. We'll be going out to the Russell office building in a minute."

"Oh, you don't have to go out in the cold. Just take the elevator downstairs and follow the signs. There's a Senate subway to transport you."

"A subway?"

"I'll show her," Bryan said. "My dad works over there. Follow me, ma'am."

Megan hesitated a moment, then walked back toward the rotunda. Again, she stopped to look up into the dome.

"It's pretty impressive," Bryan said. "When I was a kid I used to come here every chance I got, just to look at the dome. And ride the subway, of course."

In the basement crypt of the building they traveled through a maze of mustard yellow halls and finally emerged in a brightly lighted tunnel full of train tracks. In a moment, an open tram with red vinyl seats pulled up, and they stepped aboard, along with two women carrying file folders. The tram was fast; although they were underground, Megan felt her hair blowing around her face. In a moment, the driver said, "Russell," and everyone got off; in another moment, the tram was gone.

"Okay," Bryan said. "Your office will be on the list hanging in the hall of the first floor."

"Already? But I haven't even been sworn in."

"Well, someone knows you're here, Senator," Bryan said, laughing. Megan didn't laugh. Yes, someone knew. Someone had bugged her hotel rooms. Someone knew she'd be at the Capitol.

Bryan was striding ahead of her. The hallway was dimly lighted; to make things worse, the abundant woodwork was stained dark walnut, and the passage was piled high with desks, carpet rolls, file cabinets, and other rejected office items. New senators had arrived, discarding the props of a previous government.

"Second floor. Room 219," Bryan said, pointing to the list hanging on the wall. Sure enough, there it was: M. Likely, Wisconsin, 219. She was actually on a list of United States senators! And she had an office.

In the elevator to the second floor, Bryan said, "I can't tell you how much I want to work for you, Senator. I have classes only a few hours a day, and I think I could be really helpful. I was a Senate page when I was fifteen, and my dad has let me work as his aide for years. It was his suggestion that I work for you."

She had idolized Luke Callon for years. In the doorway to her office, she looked past the reception desk and out the window, where she could see the Capitol. If Luke wanted his son in her office, that had to be good enough. "All right," she said with misgiving. "Let's go to work."

Mark came out of the courtroom exhausted. He'd arrived in town late yesterday afternoon and had hurried to the Justice Building to see what was happening in a rape case his assistant had tried. He found her standing in the hall, talking to another lawyer; the jury had then taken the rest of that day and all night to convict a rapist who was patently guilty but whose lawyers put up a clever defense.

Now it was just past 9:00 A.M. He stopped on the second

floor to file a set of instruction petitions for a case in another court; at the first floor at the espresso bar he treated himself to a tall latte. He dawdled to read the morning's headlines through the window of the newspaper rack and saw ARLOW MANAGER SLAIN BY SLASHER.

He inserted three quarters and took a paper, then perched on the edge of a bench, setting his coffee cup beside him as he read. The story said police were investigating a number of leads and would not state whether they thought Ellen Linderman had killed her husband.

Mark had been composing letters in his mind. One would have said, "Mr. Linderman, if it will give you some joy to expose the tragic death of Gail Combs, go ahead." That might have stopped the sleazy so-and-so, but probably not. Linderman was too slick to be conned. Another version could have said something like, "If you bring this story to public notice, I will sue you for libel." And a third would have simply threatened to indict the campaign manager for filing phony fraud charges against Megan Likely.

But he hadn't written any letters because he'd been too busy, and now it was over. He didn't have to relive the horrible mess about Gail. And Henry Arlow would never pursue the fraud charge against Megan. Arlow couldn't function without a manager, and now his manager was no longer a threat. Mark was sorry about the wife and son. He hadn't been prepared for that. But he sighed and opened his Daytimer, placing into it a stick-on reminder to write a thank-you note to Priscilla Callon, his bar association speaker. And he began to drink the latte.


Ruthie Tolufson looked up from her sewing machine and smiled. Caleb was building a model on the other end of the kitchen table, and the pink tip of his tongue had protruded over the edge of his lip. She loved to see him concentrating like that, partly because when he did, he looked exactly like Ben.

She'd fallen in love with Ben when she was working on a degree in nursing and he was a young FBI agent; he'd confessed to her that he really wasn't very interested in law enforcement but wanted to go into the ministry. After she graduated and they were married, they lived in Chicago seminary housing while he attended classes and she worked at Cook County Hospital. Caleb was born just after Ben took his M.Div. and went to work as the assistant pastor at a good-sized Milwaukee church. A year ago, after they'd prayed together about it for months, Ben had resigned his position, and they'd moved to the outskirts of Egg Harbor while he finished his doctorate. Ruthie worked part-time in a doctor's office, but she was always home by the time her son got off the school bus.

Now Ben was the interim pastor at Egg Harbor Community. Probably they would call him to be permanent pastor after he finished his doctorate, and Ben hadn't decided whether to take the job or head for a bigger city and a bigger salary.

Ruthie wasn't sure what she loved best about Ben: his gentleness, unexpected in a man his size, or his love for God.

"How's it coming, Caleb?"

He looked up at his mother, startled. "I forgot you were here," he said, grinning. "I just put the ailerons on the wings. What do you think?"

"I think you know a lot more about that—" she glanced at the model box— "about that Cessna than I do. Okay, honey, when you have a minute I want you to wash all that gunky glue off your hands and try on this shirt."

Ruthie made almost every article of clothing the three of them wore, except for their jeans and underwear and the beautiful garments their parents sent them for birthdays. She had painstakingly tailored a wool tweed jacket for Ben's Christmas gift; it was wrapped and under her bed, waiting to go to Washington. Celia Likely had helped her with the lapels and the buttonholes, and she'd prayed her way through the lining. She had also remodeled an eight-year-old dark green dress by giving it new brass buttons and raising the hemline an inch to follow current fashion. Its color set off her auburn hair, and she had never even thought of buying a new dress. Shopping for shopping's sake just wasn't in her experience.

Ben came in from the Likelys' and lounged against the door frame, chatting for a few minutes with Caleb about his model. Then he kissed his wife, remarking that she was both beautiful and a sewing genius, and headed into the bedroom where his aging computer and stacks of books sat on a card table. They were managing to live on savings, their small salaries, and occasional unexpected gifts from relatives.

Ruthie watched Ben as he left the room. *I love my life,* she thought, looking at his straight back and powerful shoulders.


Celia Likely was sewing, too, but not on a machine. She was embroidering her husband's monogram on a white linen handkerchief; seven others like it were done. The set would be one of her Christmas gifts to him.

George was dozing in his chair, so when she leaned over to turn on her favorite classical music station on the radio, she kept the volume low. After she had sewn the last stitch, she folded the handkerchief into her sewing basket and opened her Bible. Every afternoon she spent an hour or two studying the Bible and praying. Today she read Psalm 91, keeping her finger on the line, "He shall give his angels charge over you...."

*Keep her surrounded, Lord,* she prayed. *Keep Megan safe and surrounded by armies of your angels.* With her eyes closed she recalled a painting she'd seen of the ranks of angels, archangels, thrones, principalities, dominions, powers, cherubim and seraphim, all in a great circle around a light so brilliant that it obscured its own center. *As many as you can spare, Lord. I think she's in danger.*

# TEN

Megan limped into her bedroom and fell over on the bed. Ewok leapt up to sniff her ears and lick her chin before he settled beside her. In a few minutes she had enough strength to remove her sneakers, but then she stretched out flat again.

What had possessed her to run all the way to the White House and back, in this chilly weather? She'd been unpacking her recently arrived trunk full of clothing when her eyes fell on a set of black sweats, so she'd donned them and her running shoes and gone racing down the sidewalks, jogging in place when she had to stop for traffic lights. Not that the distance was so great. She'd often run five or six miles a morning in Ripon, but the weather outside was frigid, and she had traveled straight down a hill. And not only had she gone as far as the White House, racing past the wooden and cement barriers now blocking access; she had cut across Lafayette Park at sunset, trying not to see the clusters of ragged men with black garbage bags full of their belongings, men who would sleep that night in the freezing outdoors. She slowed down long enough to look up at the gilded dome of St. John's Church, where, according to the sign in front, every president since John Adams had at some time sat in pew 54; and she shook her head at two panhandlers who tried to approach her for money.

Then she began the uphill trip home. By the time she hit M Street, her muscles were full of lactic acid, and she wondered for a moment if she might just pitch into a gutter and die there in the frigid twilight.

She lay on her bed until she could walk again, then got a bottle of water from the refrigerator and guzzled most of it. She looked at herself in the mirror and sighed. She never ran at twilight, even in Ripon, and that city was safe. She hadn't stretched or warmed up her muscles before she dashed out into the cold. But her cheeks were rosy, and her body had lost the stiff posture it had assumed during the last week. *I needed that run. If I don't get more exercise I'm going to turn fat and mean.*

"Fat and mean," she repeated aloud to Ewok, filling his dish with kibble, and he offered a short bark in response. "Well, tomorrow Iris will be here, and she'll keep me hopping."

She tried again to telephone Tom Warburton, but she only reached his answering machine. She wanted to tell him about her meeting with Henry Arlow, among other things. In fact, she almost missed having him around.

As she stood under the shower, pouring shampoo onto her hair, she thought again about the Lindermans and their terrible deaths. What, what could convince a mother to kill herself and her child? Several years ago, she had prosecuted a woman in Madison who had smothered her baby with a pillow; the woman was found not guilty by reason of temporary insanity. She had been sent to the state hospital in Appleton for a year and then was released as cured. The verdict was probably just, although at the time Megan had been disappointed.

Had Ellen Linderman killed her husband? If she hadn't, would the police assume she was guilty and fail to look for the real murderer? What about Henry Arlow? If he murdered Linderman, he didn't seem to know it.

She put on her gray terry-cloth robe and curled up with her "suspect" list. Bryan could have planted the listening devices when she was walking Ewok. He had been alone here for nearly half an hour, which gave him time. She jotted down, "Tell Tom that Bryan could have put the bug in my evening bag."

Laying the yellow legal pad on the coffee table, she switched on the news and watched with increasing concern the report that Egyptian troops had crossed over the Sudanese border. She jotted down a few notes, deciding the next time she was at a party with General Martinez, she'd pick his brain for real information. One of these days she might have to make a major decision about the conflict over there.

Her last thought as she fell asleep that night was, *Ceelie is coming. Then it will be Christmas.*

In Oshkosh, Wisconsin, the harried police chief was finally getting his day's mail opened. He put in a separate stack things like the letter in the white, official FBI envelope.

"That'll be another notice of their interest in the Linderman case," he told the female dispatcher, who was across the room.

Why did they keep sending him these notices? He already had Agent Warburton breathing down his neck. He tossed his rejected stack of mail onto Hanniford's desk. The kid was out with a leg he'd fractured when he tried to get a kitten out of a tree. He could answer all the letters, including the one from Washington, when he came back to a temporary desk job.

"What a wonderful dinner this is going to be! All of us together again," Celia Likely said, smiling up and down the table. Megan smiled back, but her mind was elsewhere. Today had been busy. She'd been trying to sort out her new office, but she'd had trouble getting in and out her door because ladders and paint cans had joined the desks and carpet rolls lining the hall. She had taken a walk to the building's small rotunda to see the late Senator Russell's statue, only to discover that repainting was going on there, too, and the statue was covered with a canvas drop cloth. Bryan was taking tort exams today, so she had to cope alone with the herds of lobbyists who stopped by. The junior senator from Minnesota had shown up to discuss a water project that would affect both their states. She'd lunched with Luke Callon to talk about—actually, to listen with dismay as he talked about—his amendments for the poverty alleviation bill. And at the airport, where she picked up her family, she'd had to dodge the press. Her face had even been in the tabloids, as if she were royalty or a rock star. *Next they'll have absolute proof I'm an alien from outer space.*

She deliberately turned her mind to their dinner. A few moments ago Rick and Brenda had arrived; as they came to the table, Ben Tolufson had stood up saying, "Greg Dobbins, isn't it?"

"Not me," Rick said, smiling as he pulled Brenda's chair out for her.

"I could have sworn…" Ben shook his head and sat down. Megan noticed that every few moments, he stole a glance at Rick. They were seated at a large, round table in Georgia Brown's, an upscale soul-food restaurant in downtown Washington. Nine-year-old Caleb Tolufson could hardly sit still.

"Do you think we might see the president?" he asked, twisting in his chair to scan the room. "Hey, they've got pecan pie. Can I have some?"

"After you eat your dinner," Ruthie Tolufson said.

"Aw, c'mon, Mom. I ate lunch on the plane, just a little while ago."

"About five hours ago," Ben said, looking at his watch. "Mr. Samuelson, I understand you conduct a Bible study for people in high places."

"Not just for bigwigs, although a few of them are kind enough to come. Our little group is for anyone who wants to study the Word." His genial face was long, almost horsy, and his pale blond hair, beard and eyebrows broadcast his Scandinavian roots. He turned to his left. "Ben, I understand you're a former FBI agent and a candidate for ordination? What Bible college are you attending?"

"Actually, I'm already ordained. I'm working on my doctoral dissertation for Woodfield, a seminary in Wisconsin. And right now I'm the interim pastor at Egg Harbor Community Church."

"God will bless your work. And I trust you're preaching straight from the Bible." Rick stopped to order Maryland fried chicken from the hovering waiter.

George Likely cleared his throat, and Megan saw a twinkle in her grandfather's eye.

"George is right," Celia said. "Ben not only preaches the gospel, he lives it. Now, Brenda, didn't you say the pan-browned catfish was wonderful here? That's what I'm ordering."

*Thank you for changing the subject, Ceelie! As much as I like Rick, I know he can be stubborn about religion.* The Senate would offer enough opportunities for debate. She could hardly wait to be sworn in, to be part of the 109th Congress, to take her seat in the Chamber....

"Are you wool-gathering, dearest?" Celia said, and Megan came back to the present.

"I'm sorry, Ceelie. I've just had a weird week." She smiled over at her manager, who was perusing the slick, spiral-bound menu. "Now that Iris is here, maybe I can accomplish something."

"The first thing we're going to accomplish is to finish getting your office set up." Iris sounded crisp.

"And you're going to love it. The woodwork is horribly dark, but the windows look right through the trees at the Capitol. I think the trees are cherries, although they're bare right now."

"We'll get that woodwork painted," Iris said.

"Rick, should we consecrate the office like you did mine?" Brenda asked.

Celia lifted her eyebrows but said nothing. Iris snorted softly and looked at her plate.

Rick shrugged, looked at Brenda and said, "Sure, if Megan wants. We could go over there and have a prayer circle with some other Christians we know."

Megan began to flick the ends of her fork tines, making a faint musical sound. "I'm afraid that might be construed as a church-state conflict, if anyone saw us consecrating."

"You're right," Rick said. "We'll just pray for you."

Celia said, "Megan's work is already blessed anyway. In fact, I feel certain she's surrounded by God's angels. Now where is that waiter? I'll have another glass of that delicious peach iced tea. I want to know what spices are in it."

"And I want to know what Megan's going to wear to the Senate reception," Iris asked.

"Probably the white wool dress I bought for the Callons' party."

"But haven't several people already seen you in that? Remember your trunks are here now. How about that beautiful red gown? You look very glamorous and professional in it."

"I want to wear the red dress for Christmas." Megan grinned. "Come on, Iris, don't—"

"The white dress is perfect," Brenda said. "And it looks beautiful on her, Iris. The only people that saw it were a few crusty old senators who won't remember, and the Callons. Pris Callon wears the same clothes over and over."

Iris shook her head. "Now look, people, don't sabotage my efforts to upgrade Megan's image."

"Simplicity is a sign of godliness," Ben said with mock piety. "And I've got my mouth all ready for those short ribs. Where is our food?"

"Right behind you," the waiter said, bearing a large tray. "Okay, the pan-browned catfish here, the chicken Maryland over here, and the crab cakes for Senator Likely. Glad to have you with us, Senator," he added as he started unloading the others' dinners. He put a ground beef patty and vegetables down in front of George. Celia began cutting up the meat as the waiter bent down to quietly tell George, "Enjoy your dinner, sir."

"God bless that waiter," Celia said as the man left for another table. "The world could use more decent human beings who will speak to someone in a wheelchair."

Ben and Ruthie were nodding, and Brenda said, "He was certainly kind. I wonder if he's a Christian."

"I think the man's decency and good works are a sign of his salvation," Ben said.

"Spoken like a true hyper-Calvinist." Rick said, laughing, and began carving his chicken.

"All right, that's it," Megan said firmly. "There will be no further discussions involving religion while we're in this restaurant. I wonder how the waiter knew who I was?"

"You've got a famous face," Brenda said. "How's that catfish, Mrs. Likely?"

Ben said, "Speaking of famous faces, Rick, were you ever in the FBI?"

Rick shook his head. "Never even got acquainted with an agent. Wait a minute, our station interviewed one on a news report. But I didn't do the interview."

They settled into small talk about the meal until Rick brought up the tense situation between Egypt and Sudan. "I think there's going to be a war in that region," he said. "Maybe Megan can give us some senatorial insight."

Megan looked up. "Hey, I haven't even been sworn in yet," she said. "But in my personal opinion, I think we should stay out of Sudan. If we go in there with armed forces or just with military advisors, Ethiopia and Libya will immediately declare war on us."

"Now can I have some pecan pie?" Caleb said. His eyes were still bright. He'd eaten most of his fried shrimp and part of his salad.

"Well, let me see," Ruthie said, and then George cleared his throat again. Ruthie smiled at George and said, "All right, Caleb. It is a special occasion. Ben, wave down our waiter, will you?"

Rick kept on talking. "Then maybe we should go into Ethiopia and Libya before they get a chance."

Megan was shocked. "Rick, how can you say that? It sounds like you're in favor of war."

"In this case I think we need to make a preemptive strike," Rick said. "Libya is one of the most dangerous countries on the globe, and Egypt is crucial in God's scheme of things. Oops, I'm heading into forbidden territory. Brenda, are you about finished, honey? We've got to get to Bible study."

"In fact, we're almost late," Brenda said, looking at her watch. She drank her coffee and kissed Megan and Celia.

Rick pulled a hundred-dollar bill out of his wallet. "This will help with our part of the tariff," he said, and he and Megan argued good-naturedly about it.

"Dinner is on me," Megan kept insisting, and Rick finally gave in, saying he'd get even by paying the check next time and that he was delighted to have met Megan's family and friends. Then he and Brenda were gone out into the evening.

"Rick and Brenda have been helpful and kind," Megan said, hoping her grandmother liked them.

Caleb said, "This pie isn't as good as yours, Mom. It has some kind of weird stuff in it. It tastes more like lick'rish." He had laid his spoon down after one mouthful.

"Well, eat it anyway. It probably cost twelve bucks," Ben said. "However, I will say the short ribs and these braised collard greens are worth whatever they cost. I just hope we can afford to stay in Washington until Christmas."

"I told you dinner and dessert are absolutely on me," Megan said, blushing. She'd grown up poor; how could she have brought them to such an expensive place? She'd wanted them to taste the delicious Southern food, but had she forgotten what it was like to pinch pennies? "And that includes a different dessert for Caleb if he doesn't like his pie." She grinned at the boy. "Pass it over here, Caleb. I'll finish it for you. Iris, you love Black Forest cake, and this place is famous for it. Waiter? Can we see the desserts?"

They lingered for a few moments over the dessert tray, with Caleb finally deciding to have plain chocolate ice cream. Ben said, "Rick sure looks like an agent I knew once."

"And why was he picking your brains about the Sudan?" Iris asked.

"He has a religious interest." Megan took a forkful of pie and decided the flavor Caleb hadn't liked but she did was cardamom. Iris was not distracted, even by her cake.

"Megan, you can't be led astray by people who want to know Senate business."

"Did you see me showing signs of being led astray? I wouldn't discuss Senate secrets if I knew any. Which I don't. Now, let's talk about that office of mine. Do you think pink-checked ruffled curtains trimmed with lace would be too, too Wisconsin?"

Iris had just taken a bite of cake. She had to put her hand over her lips as she laughed. "You're trying to make me choke to death, aren't you?"

"Murder at Georgia Brown's!" Ben crowed. "Somebody alert Margaret Truman. That sounds like one of her titles."

"Is she in here too, Dad?" Caleb said, looking wildly around the room. "She's famous, isn't she? Mom read one of her books about the CIA. Is she a spy?"

A spy! Henry Arlow's voice rang in Megan's ears. *You don't understand. There's a whole underground system working....*

It took the valet a few minutes to unload the luggage into the three suites. When he was finished, Celia peeped into Megan's room. "Isn't this great? We practically have the whole wing to ourselves."

*I hope so!* Megan had been nervous ever since Tom Warburton had shown up before daybreak last Monday. In fact, she'd been jumpy since...since when? Was it when Bryan Callon was up here, or when she'd heard about the Lindermans, or when Henry Arlow grabbed her arm on Pennsylvania Avenue? Or when Priscilla Callon had known where her apartment was going to be? Or back when Bob Linderman had known her cell phone number? Or—

*I'm getting downright spooky. Maybe I caught Henry Arlow's paranoia.* She kicked off her shoes and collapsed onto her bed. Iris was quietly putting things away in the closet, and Megan was glad her friends and family were nearby. Now maybe she could get to her work as senator and let Henry Arlow's underground forces fade from her mind. In fact, although she herself never prayed anymore, just knowing her grandmother was praying for her made her feel safe. Warm. Protected.

After Iris got into bed, Megan hung up her clothes, noticing that scraps of bright rainbow light beams were dancing in the door mirror.

# ELEVEN

S he was lingering on the far edge of sleep when the phone rang. She sat up too fast, and her blood thrummed in her ears as she reached in the darkness for the phone. *What could be wrong now? My whole family is right here. Who could be—*

She was relieved when Tom Warburton's voice said, "Did I wake you? I forgot about the time difference. It's an hour earlier out here."

"I wasn't asleep yet. Out where?"

"I'm in Oshkosh, doing a follow-up on the Linderman murder."

Iris was breathing softly and regularly. Megan said, "Let me go in the other room."

As soon as she picked up the living-room phone, she said, "First, did you ever hear of an FBI agent named, ah, let's see…Dobbins? I believe it's Greg Dobbins? He might not be with the Bureau now."

"No. Why? Is it important?"

"It may be. I don't know for sure. Tom, last Monday after you left, Henry Arlow showed up here in Washington."

"Right. He just turned himself in to the FBI about two hours ago. The Bureau called me."

"How did you get to Wisconsin? The last time I saw you, you were leaving the restaurant downstairs."

"After I left you, I went to the office, got my orders and transportation, and flew out here. But I'll be home tomorrow."

"Well, wait. You need to hear this. Remember the phone call I got when we were having breakfast? That was Henry Arlow. You had already left the hotel, and when I called your office later, you were out of town. Anyway, Arlow had taken the red-eye to get to D.C. after Linderman's body was discovered. He wanted me to meet him at the Farragut North Metro stop."

"And of course you told him no."

"Well, actually, I went." She hadn't known Tom Warburton long; she had never heard him sound angry before.

"Megan! He could have killed you!"

"He didn't," she said. "Tom, I can take care of myself. It was a public place. And in fact, he looked scared. He was babbling about underground systems and forces beyond our control. I think he's cracked up, because he insisted there was a universal plot or something. I told him to go to the police."

Tom's voice was calmer. "Please don't ever do anything like that again. Especially when I'm out of town."

"I've been out of town myself for thirty years, Tom. I didn't have an FBI agent to protect me, but I've managed just fine." She took a deep breath. "I'm going to bed now. I'll see you soon, I'm sure. Will you look up Dobbins, please?"

As she settled under the covers, she thought, *Men! You meet one you kind of like and the next thing you know, he's managing your life for you.* She imagined Mark's angry face, saying, "Come see me when you lose the election...." *I'm not over Mark yet,* she thought, as she settled into the comforter and Ewok snuggled against her knees. *I wonder if I'll ever be over him....*

Sunlight was filtering between the slats of her vertical blinds when she woke. She heard Iris saying thank you to someone, then shutting the door. The fragrance of fresh coffee wafted into her room.

"Iris?" she called, sitting up. She drew her robe from the foot of the bed. "Do I smell coffee?"

"Uh-huh. Want me to bring some in there?"

"I'll be right out. It's—" she glanced at her watch—"Good grief, it's eight o' clock." She pulled on her slippers. "I didn't mean to sleep so late." As she dressed, she flipped open the blinds and looked out the hotel window. Sunshine was gleaming on ice and snow. Icicles hung from the window's outer frame, and the city beyond looked like a holiday card. She shivered, but this time not because of murder or any other horror; for the first time since the night her room was ransacked, she was excited because she was in Washington. And because it was almost Christmas, with her family and friends here.

Iris, in a navy robe but wearing her jade earrings and with her amazing apricot hair perfectly combed, was standing beside a small table covered with a white cloth, pouring coffee from a silver pot into heavy china cups.

"Your grandparents and the Tolufsons went down for breakfast," she said. "I thought you looked tired last night, so I told them I'd let you sleep and call room service." She lifted the silver dome cover off a platter of scrambled eggs and fried potatoes. "Are you hungry? I could eat a whale, myself."

"Oh, sure. You who hardly eat enough to stay alive! You picked at your dinner, and you ate maybe four bites of your cake. I'd like to see you eat even the fin of whale." Megan took the proffered cup of coffee and sank onto the sofa. "And I was tired last night. I had a really busy day. I'll be glad when Fern gets here after Christmas."

"She's excited about coming," Iris said, handing her a plate of food.

"I had not one but two discussions about SB7738 yesterday— the upcoming poverty alleviation bill. Can you believe Luke Callon thinks he can insert an amendment that makes the bill acceptable to conservatives?" Megan looked down and realized that in less than a minute, she'd already eaten more than half her eggs. "Did you hear the phone last night? It was Tom Warburton, the FBI agent I told you I met. He called from Oshkosh to say Arlow had turned himself in."

"In Oshkosh?"

"No, to the FBI here in Washington." She didn't mention her meeting with the former senator.

Iris used the tip of her knife to scrape a flake of parsley off a potato chunk. "Arlow is undoubtedly aware that Linderman has been named in the funneling of campaign funds. And he took losing the election badly, maybe enough to kill Linderman."

"But what about the wife and little boy? Iris, when I think of that poor woman, killing herself and her child—"

Iris reached over to the coffee table. "It's in here," she said, unfolding the day's newspaper. "A TV reporter in Oshkosh said the police left her alone in that house, so the paper did a feature on it. Here, read it."

The article, headed, "Widow's Last Hours," included a statement from the Reverend James Davies of Oshkosh. The pastor was outraged, he said, first, that a highly regarded professional man could be murdered in his home and, second, that the police would abandon the distraught widow alone to end her own life.

Pictures of all three Lindermans were interspersed with the text. As she read the article, Megan thought about Ellen Linderman, with her child in the house where her husband was murdered. How could anybody leave her there?

"It says she told the television people that she had no income," Iris said. "But she would have had Social Security for her son, wouldn't she?"

"And widows' benefits. But maybe she couldn't face the present."

"Hmmph." Iris set her coffee cup down. "My husband walked out and left me with three kids to bring up. And you don't get Social Security when your husband disappears. I didn't even apply for welfare. I went to work as a market checker and moonlighted as a waitress."

"Who took care of your kids?"

"They did. My oldest was eleven, and she baby-sat all evening. I called home every hour. Okay, enough about me. What are you going to tell the press?"

"Tell them? About what? I haven't even been sworn into the Senate yet, so I doubt if I'll be making statements about anything."

"About Linderman and his family. Haven't any reporters asked you about what you thought?"

"Oh, sure. They were at my office the next afternoon and were looking for me yesterday at the airport. I said I was deeply saddened by the brutal murder and the other deaths and I couldn't add anything to what they already knew."

"Perfect. The press came after me, too. They wanted a sort of campaign manager's insight about a campaign manager's murder. I told them essentially the same thing you did. Now that Linderman is dead, I hate to say it, but he was a slimy, repulsive slug who thought he was God's gift to women."

"Speaking of God, are my grandparents in church this morning?"

"They had their own service in their living room. I guess Ben preached a little sermon and they sang a hymn. Celia said she wanted to go on the cathedral tour at twelve-thirty." She took Megan's empty plate and heaped more eggs on it. "Megan, I know you don't usually go to church. But do you believe?"

"Oh, sort of. I can't completely ignore Ceelie's training. But I don't really buy Christianity. All religions are probably good. Why?"

"Well—" Iris rose from the hassock where she was sitting and brushed the skirt of her robe—"Oh, nothing. I just wonder about it sometimes, that's all."

"Ceelie could tell you more than I can. Or Rick and Brenda."

The phone rang and Iris reached for it. In a moment she covered the mouthpiece. "Do you want to speak with Donnie Thurmond, from the *Washington Window?*"


Ben Tolufson was also discussing God at breakfast. He and Ruthie had taken Caleb and the Likelys down to the hotel atrium for breakfast; now he was eating a no-fat, egg-substitute veggie omelet and saying Rick Samuelson's Bible study might not be his cup of tea, even if he were staying long enough to attend it.

"But Dad, you don't drink tea." Caleb had chosen pancakes and was devouring them with the same speed Megan was eating her breakfast upstairs.

"I just mean Mr. Samuelson and I may not look at God the

same way." He glanced up at a large woman who was hovering over the table.

"Hello?"

The woman beamed, not at him but at Ruthie, who was sitting farthest away. "I just wanted to tell you I recognized you and I think you're wonderful."

Ruthie looked perplexed. "I'm sorry, I don't remember meeting—"

"Oh, no, of course you didn't. But I know yoo-oou!" she trilled, waggling her forefinger at Ruthie. "I told my husband, he's up in the gift shop, I told him, even with that auburn wig, I'd know anywhere that you were—" She named the popular blond assistant on an evening game show.

Caleb's mouth fell open. "She isn't on TV. She's just my mom."

The woman beamed again. "It's all right, dear. I know you have to hide your identity in public. This will just be our little secret." She turned away, toward the atrium door.


Tom Warburton had been surprised when he got off the plane in Oshkosh to hear someone say, "Thanks and good-bye, Mrs. Callon." He recognized the attractive blond woman from news photos and remembered Megan's suspicions. He made a mental note to find out what Priscilla Callon had been doing in Wisconsin.

The police called him at his Oshkosh motel when Mindora Arlow, for whom they'd combed Madison without success, came to the police station. She had probably arrived on some signal from her husband, who turned himself in at the same time in Washington.

The detective said on the phone, "Well, we couldn't locate Henry Arlow for you, but you can sit in on our interview with his wife. She just showed up."

Mindora Arlow was a pediatrician in Madison, which explained why Henry Arlow had lived alone in a condominium in

Washington during the Senate sessions. She was wearing a slate blue ski jacket and a cap on her gray-streaked, dark pageboy. She explained about starting for the lodge in two cars and stopping at the outlet stores to buy gifts. When she got to the cabin, where they had a satellite dish, she'd been wrapping presents when she heard about Bob Linderman on the news. She'd called Senator Arlow's pager, leaving their car-phone number. And then she had simply got back into her car and gone to a hotel in, well, she'd rather not say where. But she'd paged Henry again, to let him know where she was. Yes, he had voice mail on his pager.

"When did she last hear from her husband?" Tom muttered to the chief, who repeated the question.

Mrs. Arlow looked down at her hands. "I talked to Henry about an hour ago," she said finally. "He said he was going to turn himself in."

"Where was he when he called?"

"You can't believe Henry would commit a brutal murder like this. He's still a United States senator! And he's a kind husband and father."

"Where did you say your husband is now?"

She glanced at her watch. "He's in Washington," she'd told them, with a wintry smile. "He and his lawyer should be at FBI headquarters right now."

*This case has tentacles in funny directions,* Tom thought as his plane began the flight to Dulles. *I wonder where they'll end up.*


The National Cathedral docent, or tour guide, said they wore purple choir robes and square purple caps because a cathedral was the *cathedra,* or chair, of a bishop. And bishops wore purple. She also told them the great sanctuary room they were standing in was called a nave.

As she led the group up the chancel steps at the end of the long aisle, she said, "It's a tenth of a mile from the doorway to the high altar." Megan glanced at her grandfather's face. Ben was pushing his wheelchair up a side ramp, and Celia bent over now and then to whisper a comment to him. *He's showing his age,* Megan thought, with a skip of her heart. *I won't have him forever.*

The docent stopped by a huge, carved white stone chair with a stone kneeler. "This is the Glastonbury cathedra," she said with enthusiasm. "The stone was sent here from the ruins of a monastery in Glastonbury, England. Tradition tells us the monastery was founded in A.D. forty-three by Joseph of Arimathea, the man who gave Jesus his own tomb." Megan tried to remember her Sunday school lessons as the group moved toward the high altar.

"The altar is made from stone quarried at Jerusalem, so we call it the Jerusalem altar. The carved stone screen behind it is called a reredos, and it contains a hundred and ten apostles, martyrs, saints, faithful Christians, and—" she stopped for a moment and grinned at Megan—"angels."

*I'll be really glad when everyone forgets that angel nonsense about me,* Megan thought. She sidled up beside Ruthie and whispered, "How tall did she say the reredos thing is?"

"I think thirty feet," Ruthie murmured. "But everything in here is so big, I feel like Jack in the giant's house."

Megan looked over at Celia, whose face was transformed. Her eyes were shining. *Ceelie doesn't need any rainbow lights. She's the real angel here.*

"Besides the main church, the cathedral contains eight chapels where services are celebrated every day." The docent pointed out the round stained-glass windows, called rose windows because they were shaped like flowers. "On the north side, you're looking at the Last Judgment, and on the south, the Church Triumphant." Christ, crowned as King, was seated in the center of both windows, his hand raised in judgment in one, and in blessing in the other. Megan stood gazing at the Church Triumphant: the window was almost speaking to her. But she brushed that feeling away. *There's too much religion here,* she decided. She felt smothered. Resurrection, judgment, heaven! She hadn't felt that way, growing up in the little church at Egg Harbor that had no stained glass, no angels or gargoyles, no altar or carvings. But here the whole business was suffocating. She thought about walking outside, but the wind was brisk and the air icy. Impatient, she whispered to Ruthie, "I'll meet you in the gift shop when you're through."

She turned and left the nave, walking down the stone stairs to look at the basement shop's hundreds of items. She finally decided on a gargoyle wind chime for Caleb. The shop was dim, but she pawed through the racks of books and found a leather-bound Greek Bible for Ben. Then she sat down in a chair near a leaded-glass window.

"Megan? Are you all right?" Celia was standing beside her, looking solicitous.

"Ceelie! What are you doing here? Go finish your tour."

"I saw everything I came for," her grandmother said. "And I was concerned about you. You looked very uncomfortable."

"I'm just not very religious, Ceelie. But the cathedral is beautiful. A little forbidding, maybe."

"Forbidding?" Celia raised her dark brows. "I've never felt more welcome anywhere in my life. The very stones acknowledged my salvation."

Megan wished Iris were here; maybe Ceelie would answer some of her questions about God. But Iris had begged off, saying she needed to iron all her clothes, that they'd been wrinkled in the suitcase.

In a few more moments, Ruthie and Caleb appeared. Ben was waiting upstairs with George. Caleb looked longingly at a wicker basket of assorted small gargoyles.

"Maybe you'll get a gargoyle for Christmas," Megan said. "Do you know what they're used for on a building?"

"Sure. They're water-drains," Caleb said with a smug smile. "I listened to the woman upstairs."

Celia said, "If we're going to see the Lincoln Memorial today, we'd better go find a taxi."

~ ~ ~ ~ ~

Iris hung up a pale yellow silk blouse, the last garment she'd had to iron. Then she took a look at Megan's side of the closet. Sure enough, some of her clothes were rumpled. She carried an armful of garments into the bedroom. As she started to press a black suit jacket, she removed the topaz sunflower pin Megan had said had belonged to her mother. Then she heard something rustle in the pocket and pulled out a slip of paper, something apparently torn from a larger sheet. It contained a handwritten name and address: Robert Linderman, 2461 Braddock Lane, Oshkosh, WI.

# TWELVE

On Christmas Eve, the city warmed up, and streets were suddenly full of last-minute shoppers. At a quarter to three that afternoon, a thermometer set into a lavender wooden elephant in the south window of the Shalimar Boutique read forty-eight degrees.

Megan had lunched with Donnie Thurmond at the Starbuck's coffee shop in one of the Smithsonian museums. Donnie ate fast, devouring a small salad while she wrote in a spiral notebook. Megan had ordered a ham sandwich and a cup of coffee, but she had barely sipped the dark brew when Donnie began firing questions at her: How had she beaten Henry Arlow? And had she seen Arlow since she came to Washington?

Megan rarely lied and wasn't good at it. She tried to parry. "Why would I see Arlow in Washington when he never even spoke to me in Wisconsin?"

"A little bird told me you might know something about the Linderman murder. Something the police didn't know."

"What?"

Donnie leaned forward. "Senator, or may I call you Megan? Robert Linderman was a scumbag. A sleazeball. He was a womanizer, a liar, and a purely political animal. Probably a thief, if the campaign money went into his bank. And anything else you can think of to call him. I think someone from Washington murdered him."

"Like who?"

"I want you to tell me. Who, besides you, had reason to think he was evil?"

*Evil!* Wasn't that the word she'd thought of, the day he'd changed her tire? Once more, she tried to parry. "How did you know him?"

"Are you kidding?" Donnie touched her mouth with her napkin. "He insinuated himself into Washington society at every possible moment. Turned up at every party, every political event. He spent more time in society than he did in Arlow's office. I thought Arlow's first campaign manager was bad, but Linderman was worse. I don't know what the people of your state were thinking before you came on the scene. They kept voting for true-blue Luke Callon, and at the same time kept sending Arlow back to the Senate."

Eager to keep the conversation off herself, Megan asked, "Who was his old manager?"

"A guy from Madison or somewhere. He committed suicide about six years ago. I think there was a flurry about it at the time. He shot himself over in the Russell building, but he had an unexplained skull fracture. And no one could find a reason for him to kill himself. Linderman came in on the campaign before this one, after the other guy was dead."

Megan nodded. "I remember now. I thought it was probably murder."

"So did the D.C. police, but they never closed the case." Donnie moved her tongue over her front teeth. "Now. Did the same murderer kill Linderman? And was it Henry Arlow?" She stared at Megan.

"You want me to answer that?"

"You may not have the answer right now, Megan, but you will. You're one of the few honest people in the Beltway, and your instincts will force you to ferret out the truth. Now: When you figure it all out and the murderer is arrested, will you give me an exclusive?"

Megan laughed, but Donnie Thurmond's face was serious.

"Okay, Donnie. If I solve the murder—maybe two murders—I'll call you right after I call the police." She took a bite out of her sandwich, thinking, *This woman is out of her mind! I'm having enough trouble figuring out how to be a senator, without becoming a sleuth, too.*

"The second thing I wanted to see you about is—"

"Ladonna Thurmond! And the Senate angel! Now, what do you two have your heads together about?" Rick Samuelson was grinning down at them.

"The question is," Donnie said with iron lips, "what you're doing in the Museum of American History?"

"I'm here to interview the American Revolution curator for my radio station. I'm early, so I stopped in here for a cup of that wonderful coffee." He smiled down at Megan, and she felt utter relief. Donnie Thurmond's conversation had made her anxious and edgy, but Rick's presence was wholesome and calming.

Megan touched the chair beside her. "Sit down, Rick, and have coffee with us." She ate the corner of her sandwich, suddenly hungry and eager to get through with lunch so she could finish her Christmas shopping.

"Well, thanks, if I'm not interrupting." Rick dropped onto one of the curved wooden chairs and waved at a waiter. "I think I'll have a scoop of ice cream, too," he said, stretching his long legs in front of him.


Two hours after their lunch, Megan shifted her bundles and opened the door to the Shalimar Boutique. A dark-skinned young woman wearing a long, pink gauze skirt, and with a jewel in her nose, placed her palms together and bowed slightly as Megan entered the warm, scented room.

"A happy holiday. How I can help you?"

"Something jade. Jade jewelry." She wanted a special gift for Iris, one that would express her appreciation for her loyalty and hard work. She had been to several jewelry stores, but everything had looked commercial and ordinary. Then she'd noticed the Shalimar.

"Ah." The girl reached into the counter and removed a willow basket of jade rings and other ornaments. Megan immediately reached in for a pale green bracelet with tiny elephants carved into it. It would be lovely on Iris's slender wrist. She turned toward the window to look at it in natural light and was startled to see Bryan Callon, hunched into his camel's-hair topcoat, staring in at her.

"Just a moment," she said, dropping the bracelet into the young woman's hand and dashing to open the door. "Bryan!" she called, but he was gone. She couldn't see anyone in tan except a large woman carrying a red tote bag, her head scarf fluttering behind her. Megan stood on the sidewalk a moment, turning to look in three directions.

Nonplussed—how could Bryan disappear on the street?—she stepped back into the boutique and decided on the bracelet, wincing slightly at the price on its tiny tag. But Iris was worth it, and Megan wanted all her gifts to be special. Now, gazing around the boutique, Megan found an old-fashioned blue topaz pin set in silver filigree for the lapel of Ceelie's blue coat. "This very old, Victorian," the girl said, nodding her smooth head and an antique silver spoon from India for Ruthie.

She wanted one more small gift for Caleb, so after paying for everything she walked back toward the hotel gift shop where she'd seen a kit for a Tyrannosaurus rex that walked, powered by a tiny motor.

Drops of rain began to make indentations in the snow. She tried to walk faster, but in a few moments she was overtaken by a heavy shower. By the time she reached the hotel door, her hair and shoulders were soaked, and she was protecting her purchases by holding them under her coat.

"Well, it'll at least melt the snow," the doorman said by way of greeting. She nodded and dashed inside, where she handed her coat to the valet and asked him to have it dried and pressed by ten o'clock. Then she stepped inside the gift shop and found the dinosaur kit gone.

"We could have sold one of those to every guest in this hotel, I think," the young blond man behind the register said. He was counting cash receipts, tossing the too-long front of his hair back every few minutes.

"Are you closing?"

"Not until you're through, ma'am. I can wait." His eyes sparkled. "I'm giving my girlfriend her engagement ring tonight, and then we're going to dinner."

Megan tried to hurry, and finally settled for a small electronic game Caleb could play alone; perhaps it would entertain him on the plane going home.

"Well, have a nice Christmas. And good luck. Does your girlfriend live in the Beltway?"

"We have an apartment in Rosslyn, across the bridge. She's a nurse's aide, and she gets off at three. And I'm leaving right now. We're going to get married on Valentine's Day, if we have the money." His Adam's apple bobbed as he talked.

*If you have the money to live together, what more do you need to get married?*

As if he'd read her mind, he said, "She wants a really big Polish wedding. She's paying now on the dress in layaway. It's gonna cost five thousand dollars."

He looked no older than twenty. She said good luck again and headed to the elevator.

The lobby was crowded; as she entered the elevator, she thought she saw Bryan Callon getting off the adjacent car. That was twice today! Was he following her? She wanted to chase him, but she couldn't get off quickly: two large men with suitcases and laptop cases had got on, and the elevator was starting to rise. She turned to the glass side of the car, hoping to see him in the atrium, but he wasn't there.

She did see the young man locking the gift shop, and thought about the couple scrimping in a tiny, dark apartment so the girl could have a wedding gown encrusted with pearls or something. Five thousand dollars! When she and Mark were planning to marry, they'd hardly talked about the wedding itself except to decide it would be in the little Egg Harbor church she'd attended as a child. When the elevator stopped, she blinked back the tears that formed as she thought of Mark.

*It's Christmas,* she told herself. *Wear a Christmas face.* When she opened the door to her suite, Ewok barked joyfully and turned in three circles to show how glad he was to see her. Iris was on her knees, stowing gifts beneath a six-foot Christmas tree in the suite's living room. The presents were all wrapped in dark burgundy paper and tied with gold ribbon.

"Iris! Where did the tree come from?"

"Surprise! Santa brought it."

"You did this, didn't you?"

"I bought it at a lot about two blocks away," Iris said, her eyes dancing. "I had the florist here at the hotel decorate it and deliver it. If you're going to celebrate Christmas, it should at least look like it."

"I love Christmas," Megan said. "I can't thank you enough."

"I've got to put the angel back on the top. It slipped off when they delivered it."

"I'll help. But first let me chuck these. They still need to be wrapped." When she was at the door to her bedroom, she turned. "Iris, was Bryan Callon up here today? I thought I saw him on the street and again down in the lobby."

"Why no. Why would he be here? We told him to take the day off, remember? In fact, we gave him the week off. Which is just as well, since the painters are coming Friday to start on your office."

"I hope I like all that ivory and gray."

"Don't forget about the old rose carpet," Iris said.

"How could I forget anything as exciting as old rose?" She took the sacks into her room and dropped them on the bed, hiding the jade bracelet in her dresser drawer. When she went back out, Iris was standing on a chair to adjust the angel at the top of the tree. Steadying the chair, Megan gazed at the dark green branches and realized that all the ornaments were angels of varying sizes.

"All angels?"

Iris stepped down and dusted her hands. "I didn't think any other symbol would be appropriate here," she said. "Oh, Meg, Fern Loftis phoned from Ripon. She'll be here the day after

**113**

tomorrow. She said to wish you a happy holiday." She slid the chair back under the small round table.

"Thank goodness! But that doesn't give her long for the holiday with her family."

"I think she's more excited about coming here than having Christmas." Iris stepped back to look at the tree. "I hope she can do the job." She motioned at the tree. "Well, what do you think?"

"About Fern or the tree? The tree is..." she surveyed all the angels and smiled wickedly. "The tree is heavenly."

Iris chuckled. "A bad pun, spoken by the angel herself. Also, Priscilla Callon called to wish us all a good Christmas. She said they'd be at the Cathedral tonight and they'd watch for you. And Brenda called. They said they'd be over about eleven tomorrow to bring their gifts, unless we're all going to be gone."

"I'm sure we'll be here. Since the service at the Cathedral won't be over until after midnight, we'll probably just be getting up. And Ceelie doesn't let anyone open presents until morning." She closed her eyes and breathed the aroma of the decorated tree. The fragrance brought back scraps of memory, snatches of holidays in Egg Harbor.

Ceelie had usually put up a tall northern pine tree, draped with silver icicles and antique ornaments, and Megan had opened her gifts on Christmas morning. Those mornings had been perfumed with the scent of ham, glazed with brown sugar and studded with cloves, baking along with yams and hot rolls in Ceelie's kitchen....

"My gosh!" Megan said, her eyes flying open. "We didn't do anything about Christmas dinner! I'd better get a reservation."

"Your grandmother said she ordered dinner from somewhere," Iris said. "They'll deliver it here at one-thirty tomorrow afternoon."

"Dinner? What are they getting?"

"Celia said ham, and I don't know what all else. Megan, how was your lunch with that editor?"

"All she wanted to talk about was Linderman's murder.

**114**

Fortunately, Rick showed up to bail me out. Where is Ceelie?"

"Resting in her suite. We're eating tonight across the street at Blackie's before church, right? I made the reservation last week at the office."

They were interrupted by a tap at the door. Megan peered through the peephole to see Brenda's face, so she flung the door open.

"Brenda! I thought you were coming over tomorrow."

"I am, with Rick." She held out a foil-wrapped package. "But I wanted to drop this off so you could nibble on it tonight or have it for breakfast." She pulled the foil back to reveal three loaves of braided, iced Christmas bread. "I was coming into town to pick up some things from my office, so I thought I'd bake some stollen. Oh, and here's a pound of coffee from Starbucks. I had it ground for you."

"You baked?" Megan asked, dumbfounded.

"I love to bake. It's how I caught my husband," Brenda said as she set the bread on the counter above the little refrigerator. "I took a Linzer torte to a barbecue at some friends' house in Fairfax, and there Rick was. He scarfed it up like he hadn't eaten in a week, and he called me the next day. Now, can I visit your powder room?"

"Of course. Through there," Megan said, gesturing down the hall. Brenda returned in a few minutes, planted a quick kiss on each of their cheeks, and whirled toward the door.

"Merry Christmas, you two. Iris, your tree came out gorgeous! I wish I had a tree this year. We'll see you tomorrow." And then she was gone, waving and smiling.

They were silent for a minute after she left. "That's the most animated I've seen Brenda since I got here," Iris said finally.

"She wishes she had a Christmas tree? Oh, Iris, why don't we send her one? I wonder if that florist of yours would deliver to Fairfax."

"That florist of mine, as you call the place downstairs, closed at three-thirty today. Which was ten minutes ago. And those two make enough money between them to buy a redwood if they

**115**

wanted one. Maybe they just didn't have time to put a tree up."

"But if she had time to bake bread, surely—" Megan broke off, shaking her head. "Well, I'd better get my gifts wrapped. Come see what I got." In the bedroom she took the presents out of their sacks and arrayed them on her bed. At a rare-and-used bookstore she'd found a set of signed Audubon bird prints for her grandfather. She bought another leather Bible for Brenda and Rick, this a new one labeled as a "couples devotional Bible"; it was the translation Rick said he preferred.

Iris picked up Ceelie's antique brooch, making sounds of appreciation. "Let me help. I love to wrap," she said. Megan turned on the built-in stereo and found a station with Christmas carols.

"You were right," she said, taping bright paper around Ben's Bible.

"I'm always right," Iris said. "But about what this time?"

"You said they have Christmas in Washington, and they do. Or, at least, we do." She looked out the window, where the sun was setting. "Although it's not Wisconsin weather."

"Thank goodness." Iris tied the last bow.

"Is that all?" Megan said. "You helped me make short work of it."

Iris ducked her head to acknowledge Megan's thanks, and then said, "Oh, what's this?"

A square, cream-colored envelope lay on Megan's pillow, holiday greetings from the hotel, no doubt. Iris picked it up. "A special card for someone?"

"It's probably from the maids. Open it, if you want. They're probably inviting us to enjoy the tree in the lobby or something."

Iris used one blade of her scissors to open the thick envelope. The paper inside was white, with a torn top edge, and Iris turned almost as pale as the paper. In fact, she looked as if she might fall down.

"Iris, what? What is it?" Megan snatched the note from her manager's hand.

The message was printed with an ordinary ballpoint pen in big prekindergarten letters.

It read, REAL ANGELS ARE IMMORTAL. YOU'RE NOT.

# THIRTEEN

Tom Warburton leaned back on Megan's sofa and typed into his laptop the latest information about Megan. He was trying to profile the intruder who kept invading her suite. He'd started several short lists, the first an index of anyone who might want to threaten Megan. One possibility was someone she'd convicted years ago when she worked for the DA's office. But why hadn't he come out of the woodwork till now? Second, possible political rivals. But Linderman was now dead, and Henry Arlow was in custody, about to be extradited to Wisconsin. Megan didn't have any other enemies he could think of. And although he jotted down her name, he could find no reasonable connection to Priscilla Callon; Megan had told him she felt vaguely uneasy about the senator's wife.

"She knows too much about where I'll be," Megan had said.

And Tom had seen her leaving Oshkosh the morning after the murder. So maybe she had opportunity, but she had no apparent motive. Nor did Bryan, who was working part-time as Megan's new assistant, but the young man had been in the hotel the night her suite was ransacked and bugged. Tom needed more information about Bryan and Priscilla.

His next list included those who could get into the rooms legally: that roster included the hotel management, who had a master key card, of course. He found no link to management or housekeeping in his investigation, although the maids could have been hired to leave the envelope on Megan's pillow. Next, Celia and George Likely: after briefly interviewing them, he knew they weren't believable candidates. Nor were the Tolufsons. Iris Millman had a key card because she was Megan's suite mate, and Iris was either the world's best actress or she was really close to shock. She kept putting her slender, multiringed hand to her chest and blowing her cheeks out while he was talking to her about the note.

Iris looked even more horrified when Megan revealed the suite had been ransacked and bugged.

"That happened the second night after you got here? Why didn't you call me? Or at least tell me after I arrived?" she'd demanded, standing in front of Megan with her arms crossed. Celia, who was making coffee in the kitchenette, had turned toward her with a questioning look, and Megan lifted her brows.

"I did what I thought was best."

"Best for you, maybe, although I doubt even that. Did you forget I had to share this suite with you? And that your grandparents might be in danger too?"

"I didn't think any of our lives were in danger. "

Iris turned to Tom Warburton. "What do you think?"

"I haven't felt Senator Likely was threatened until now," he said. "Would you feel better if I asked the Bureau to post a guard out in the hall?"

The question in Megan's eyes penetrated through his skin and skull, and he nodded involuntarily. *Yes, you could be in some danger,* he answered silently. A guard would be a good idea. Tom cared more than might be wise about Senator Megan Likely, and the thought of any harm coming to her...

"Where did you say you're going to Christmas Eve service tonight?" he asked.

"At the National Cathedral," Megan said, looking over at Iris. "Why?"

"I'll ask for an agent to accompany you." He took his folding telephone out of his satchel and dialed the Bureau.

As he waited for his department head to answer, Celia Likely, who had been silent until then, asked Megan, "When your suite was rifled, Megan, did you think it was done by Senator Arlow?"

"Well, I actually thought it was more likely to be someone connected to Robert Linderman. Maybe someone Linderman had hired to scare me or spy on me. That was before he was murdered, of course."

Iris's eyes were smoldering. "After Linderman was dead, you had no way of knowing Arlow would turn himself in. Nobody even knew where he was until after we got here."

"I did," Megan said.

Iris's cheeks and her neck were mottled with pink splotches. "How? Did an angel tell you?"

With almost exaggerated patience, Megan explained about her Metro-stop meeting with Arlow. It was the same technique she'd used in courtrooms with a difficult witness: She spoke softly and slowly, looking directly into Iris's eyes. "After I talked to him, I knew he was confused, possibly even deranged, but not threatening to me."

"I hope you prayed for him," Celia said.

Iris whirled to face Celia. "You people are all crazy!" she cried. "There are murderers out there! We could be killed! If neither Arlow nor Linderman could threaten Megan today, who could? Are you praying for whoever that is?" She fled to the bedroom and shut the door.

"Kinkaid," a terse voice said in Tom's ear. He had been so absorbed in the discussion he'd almost forgotten he was holding his telephone.

"This is Tom Warburton. Say, we need to get a guard over here. Senator Likely has had what amounts to a threat on her life." He told Kinkaid about the note and explained that there were three suites on the fourth floor, all connected. One hall guard would be appropriate; plus, someone needed to accompany the senator herself to public places. Megan was a member of the government, after all.

"You want to stay there awhile?" Kinkaid said in his soft Tennessee accent. "I can't get anyone over there for at least an hour. In fact, I've only got one man available. You'll have to go to church with them."

"No problem," Tom said, smiling as he hung up.

∼∼∼∼∼

Ruthie buttoned an embroidered Christmas vest over her dark green dress and twirled around like the game show hostess. "Guess what famous TV star I really am?"

"I dunno. But I'm going be dead pretty soon, because you guys are starving me. Can I order a pizza or something?"

"We're going to dinner, right now," Ben said, coming out of the bedroom carrying his jacket. "Caleb's right, it is late. Let's go over to Megan's and jack everybody up." He slipped into his weather-beaten jacket and Ruthie got her coat, smiling to herself because the next morning he would have a new jacket to wear.

"Caleb, can you carry Megan's present?" Ben asked. "Mom has the others in her tote bag."

"Oh, boy, are we going to open presents tonight?"

"No, we're going to put them under Megan's tree. And if the FBI is finished, we'll go eat. Which is what you were complaining about not doing."

Caleb picked up the Christmas-wrapped package containing a hinged frame of photographs, one of Celia and George, sitting in front of their fireplace, and one of Ewok, wearing a bright blue bow. Ben had shot the pictures Thanksgiving week and processed them in the bathroom that doubled as his photo lab. Ruthie had found the frames at a garage sale and had sanded and lacquered them carefully.

"Be careful," Ben and Ruthie said to Caleb together, and they smiled at each other.

"I'm glad you're here," Ruthie said. "Life would be awfully meager without you and Caleb."

"I'm not sorry you're here either," Ben said, and put his arms around her. "Mmmm," he added, as he kissed her lips. "We'll celebrate later."

He gave her a squeeze around the waist, and she whispered, "I don't even need Christmas presents. You're the gift God gave me, Ben."

"Oh, no!" Caleb said, grabbing his throat and pretending to lurch into the wall. "They'll let me starve to death while they do goo-goo-ga-ga." He rolled his eyes wildly.

"We won't let you starve to death, but we might feed you nothing but liver," Ruthie said, rubbing the close-cut top of her son's head. "Okay. Everything turned off? Let's go."

Tom folded his phone back up and dropped it into his satchel.

"Okay, Megan, you'll have a guard in the hall, starting right away, whether you're home or not. And an agent will accompany you to the Cathedral. What time is your church service?"

"Eleven," Megan said. She looked toward Iris's room. "I'm sorry, Ceelie. Iris didn't mean to be rude, I'm sure."

"She wasn't rude; she's just frightened." Celia lifted the foil cover on Brenda's Christmas stollen. "Oh, this looks delicious. Too bad we have no butter to add a few thousand calories."

"We might." Megan bent to open the little refrigerator and peered in. "Yes. I was sure she'd do it here, too." Smiling, she held up several silver-wrapped square pats of butter, the kind served with bread in restaurants.

"Iris?" She walked to her campaign manager's door and tapped. "Iris, is this your butter? Can we use some? And are you coming out?"

Iris thrust her head out the door. Her mascara had run, as if she had been crying. "Help yourself. Megan, I—"

Megan kissed Iris's cheek. "You gave us this beautiful Christmas tree," she said, pulling on Iris's manicured hand and leading her into the room. "Come out and enjoy it." She smiled at her grandparents. "Iris eats no fats. Not even a smidge of margarine on her toast. But she's too frugal to leave those butter pats in the restaurant, because she's paid for them."

"It's a leftover from childhood poverty," Iris said, sheepish. "I'm sorry for my outburst, everyone. I'm just not used to all this cloak-and-dagger stuff."

"Oh, good grief," Megan said, still holding the butter but staring into space. "Wait, Tom, don't go. I just remembered something. Something awful," she added.

Tom waited. He knew that look. He'd seen it before, on the faces of men and women who were able to dig into their memories. Megan looked reluctant to speak, so he remained absolutely silent. That way she wouldn't be distracted.

"Brenda," she said.

"Oh, no!" Iris clapped both her palms to her face. "You're right."

"But it's impossible," Megan said.

"Megan, dear, tell Mr. Warburton what you mean," Celia said, pouring coffee into mugs.

Megan sighed. "Brenda. Congresswoman Penning, I mean Samuelson. She went down the hall to the bathroom this afternoon. Right next to my bedroom. We were out here, decorating the tree, so I don't know whether she went in my room or not."

Warburton looked at Iris and Megan for a minute. Then he unzipped the carrying case for his laptop and turned the computer on. In a moment he was into his Lotus database, and he typed into the "Legal Access" list the name of Brenda Samuelson, congresswoman.

"Any idea why she would want to leave that note on your bed?"

"Of course not. As I said, that's impossible."

The Tolufsons were knocking on the door, and Celia let them in. "We're just finishing up," she said. "Caleb, you're probably starving. Can he have some sweet bread and butter, Ruthie? Brenda baked us some stollen."

"If I don't get something, I'll eat the doorknobs," Caleb said, nearly inhaling the slice of the Christmas bread spread with Iris's butter. "Aren't we going pretty soon?"

"Right now," Tom said. He collected his things and put on his coat. "You have to put up with me, too. I'm your official escort."

"You're welcome, of course, Tom, but it's just catercornered across the street."

"Sorry. From now on, you're escorted everywhere outside this suite."

"Okay. We'll come back here and dress for church, I guess." They pulled on coats and scarves and left the suite, with Tom bringing up the rear.

When the headwaiter at Blackie's House of Beef saw that one of the dinner guests was in a wheelchair, he removed a chair. Then he counted the number in the party and scooped an extra place setting from the next table.

"Your table is ready now, sir," he said to Ben Tolufson. After making sure everyone had ice water, he said, "Your waiter will be here in a moment."

"The FBI is paying for my dinner," Tom announced. "And I know what I'm having: the baby back ribs."

"You must have been here before," Megan said. "Are they really good?"

"Wonderful. I live close by, in Dupont Circle. That's how I get here so fast, early mornings and holidays."

"Sounds like we'll have our own personal FBI agent," Iris said. "We're moving into Dupont Circle too."

"Really? Where?"

"Washington House," Megan said. "It's an apartment complex on Sixteenth Street."

"I know where it is," Tom said. "I live about two blocks from there. We'll be neighbors. Ah, here comes our waiter."

A dark-haired young man in tuxedo pants, ruffled pink shirt, and black vest emerged from the back room. He was carrying an order pad and smiling like a jack-o'-lantern. It was Bryan Callon.

# FOURTEEN

I still can't believe it," Megan said over her shoulder. "Bryan never told me he was moonlighting at Blackie's. That's across the street, for crying out loud. Don't you think he would have said something?"

"He was probably afraid that if you knew he already had one part-timer, you wouldn't hire him for your office," Celia said from behind her, buttoning Megan's blouse. "His face was quite a picture when he realized who was sitting at his table."

"I don't see how he does it. He goes to school all morning, works every afternoon for me, and waits tables on weekends and holidays? What a schedule."

"Apparently he has lots of energy," Celia said. "Okay, your buttons are fastened. That's a lovely blouse, dear." She headed out to the living room, where Tom Warburton was reading through his notes; after offering him coffee, she went back to her own suite.

Because it was raining again, Megan had decided against wearing her red dress to church. She stepped into her black suit skirt, zipped it up, and reached for the jacket, still hanging in the closet.

"Oh, no! My pin! My sunflower pin!" she cried as she took the garment from its hanger. "It must have fallen off somewhere!"

"It's here," Iris called from the front room. "I'm sorry, Meg. I took it off on Sunday to press your suit and left it on top of the TV." She appeared in the doorway, holding out the topaz sunburst.

"You pressed my suit? I thought it looked awfully good. But you shouldn't have, Iris. You're not the maid." She fastened the pin onto her jacket, then peered into her closet. "Iris, you pressed all my clothes, didn't you?"

Iris pretended not to hear the question. She hesitated, then said, "Meggie, there was something else in the jacket." She held up a scrap of paper torn from a longer piece, a slip of paper with a raised blue border on three sides. "I found this in your pocket."

Megan took the slip and read Robert Linderman's name and address. "What? Iris? What is this?"

"I told you. I found it in the pocket of your black suit."

"But why in the world would I have Linderman's address?" She stared at the paper as if it might reveal its source to her. "You said it was in my new suit?" She picked up her jacket and took the address out to Tom, with Iris following.

"Tom, this was in my jacket pocket," she said, handing him the scrap and putting on her jacket. Tom read it, then looked up at Megan.

"What do you mean, it was in your pocket?"

"Iris found it. She was pressing my clothes."

"I'll have to turn this in as evidence, you know."

"Well, I hope you do. This might be—" She broke off. "You mean, you'll have to turn it in as evidence against me?"

He shrugged. "It may not be important. This address is in the Madison phone book. But the fact of your having it is strange. Think back, Megan. Did you ever write it down? Maybe during the campaign, to mail him an announcement or something?"

"Never. I had no real contact with Linderman before the election. We spoke to each other at the debates, of course, and at a town meeting in Kaukauna. And then I told you about his changing my tire when I was on my way to Egg Harbor."

"Could he have handed you the address then? Or even have slipped it into your pocket?"

"I didn't own the black suit until after Thanksgiving."

"Well, if you didn't write it down, someone laid that on you. And that brings up two questions. Who and why. Do you recognize the paper?"

She shook her head, thinking back. "Tom, I bought this suit just before I left Wisconsin, and I've only worn it once before. That was on the plane to come here. The rest of the time, it was in my closet." She shook her head. "I've had about enough shocks for one evening. First it was Bryan Callon, showing up as a waiter in the restaurant. That was downright spooky, and he acted odd

126

all through dinner. Now it's Linderman's address in my pocket. I wonder what will be next?"

Tom looked at his watch. "It's almost ten o'clock. We better get everyone rounded up."

Megan hesitated, standing in the living room, staring toward the slip of paper in Tom Warburton's hands. But Iris said, "Okay, I'm ready except for my coat." She darted back into the bedroom and emerged carrying her navy blue coat and Megan's red one, still with the hotel's valet strip across the collar.

"Christmas isn't a day I really celebrate," Iris said. "I used to have a little tree and presents for my kids, but the day never meant anything to me."

"Well, you needed Ceelie to make it Christmas. As soon as I got elected, she started talking about going to church at the National Cathedral on Christmas Eve." She opened the door to find her grandparents and the Tolufson family already in the gallery, talking to a tall man in a brown suit.

"Hey, there's your guard," Tom said, nodding to the man. "How are you, Ferguson? Keep your eyes on these three suites, whatever you do. Okay, Megan, you and your grandmother can get in my front seat, and we'll get everybody else into the back."

"Your car? You're coming with us?"

"I said you'd have an escort to church. And Kinkaid hasn't found anyone else, so it's me, and I've got a nine-passenger van."

He herded the two women into his vehicle and helped Ben lift George Likely inside. When the lighted spires of the Cathedral came into view, Megan tried to get into the spirit of Christmas. How can Ceelie stay so calm and cheerful, with murder and threat and heaven only knows what else going on? And Brenda! Did she put that horrible note on my bed? Why would she? This can't be Christmas; it's some kind of a bad dream.

Although the service didn't begin until eleven, the choir and congregation were singing Christmas carols.

"Let earth receive her king," they sang. "Let e-ev'ry heart prepare him room, and heav'n and nature sing...."

As they filed into a row of seats halfway back in the long cathedral, Megan found herself singing along with the carol. In fact, she discovered she knew all the words to that hymn, and also to the next, "O Little Town of Bethlehem." She smiled at Celia, who was singing with vigor, and glanced across Iris, Ruthie, and Ben to nod at her grandfather. The Callons were sitting across the aisle, a few rows ahead; Priscilla turned and waved. Megan waved back, wishing she didn't get such a knot in her stomach when she saw the senator's wife.

On her left, Tom was singing the words from a hymnal. She wished she could fall madly in love with Tom; he was obviously interested in her. He was easygoing and solid as a rock. She liked him. She liked him a great deal. But something was missing. Or rather, *someone* was missing, and his name was Mark.

At five till eleven, the choir left the chancel steps, where they'd stood for the carol sing, filed behind the altar, then disappeared. An air of expectation lay over the congregation. A few programs rustled, and occasionally someone coughed, but the church was very quiet as they dimmed the lights, and Megan thought, *It really is Christmas after all.*

Henry Arlow lay on the bunk in his cell, wrapped in the dark red velour blanket Mindora had sent him, along with a tiny, artificial Christmas tree. She would have come to Washington, she said when he called her collect, but she thought he'd be in Wisconsin by now. What was going on with the extradition procedure?

He told her he and his lawyer, a man who'd served two terms in the House before deciding the real money was in private practice, were fighting to have him tried in Washington instead of Wisconsin. Because the Feds wanted to prosecute the case, he had a good chance.

"Why?" Mindora asked. "I've been waiting for you to get here and be out on bail."

"I don't want our children and grandchildren to watch me

being tried for murder," Arlow gasped. His breath was getting more labored. "I've got to lie down," he said. "I'll talk to you in the morning."

"But Henry—"

"Tomorrow, Mindora," he said, rubbing his breastbone. "I'll call you tomorrow at Linda's house. Tell her I love her, will you?" He slid the receiver onto the hook and presented himself to the officer at the desk, who escorted him back to his cell. He rolled up in the new blanket and wondered if he'd ever have a normal life again.

When he lost the election to Megan Likely, he had almost been relieved. He could go back to Madison and prune his rosebushes, play pinochle with his old-time friends, and catch up on his reading. Of course, it had been ignominious to lose to a thirty-year-old small-town lawyer, a woman to boot. And when he was ready to make his concession speech, Linderman said, "Don't concede a thing yet. We may be able to prove fraud here."

"What? That innocent kid wouldn't know fraud if it jumped up and slapped her in the face. Look, I want to get this concession over with."

Linderman had insisted, and Henry was half scared of the man. So he let his campaign manager make the brief concession speech. Linderman could go back to his job as a railroad lobbyist on the Hill soon and be out of Henry's hair.

But Linderman hadn't returned to his former work. He'd hung around, calling Henry at all hours. It soon became clear to the former senator that Linderman was working for someone else.

"Our cause is universal," Linderman said once. "We're going to win."

*I hope I win. If I live to get to court, that is.* He fell asleep with his hand pressing against his ribs.


The organ thundered the processional carol, and the bishop started the Christmas Communion service. After twenty minutes, George

Lively started coughing and choking. Ben rubbed the older man's back, slapped him between the shoulder blades, and finally whispered, "We'll go get a drink." He wheeled George out through the columned cloister at the right end of their row and headed for the entry hall.

Megan tried to concentrate on the service, but the heady atmosphere of the huge church was overwhelming. She kept gazing up at the central arch in the Gothic ceiling, remembering the docent had said the high point inside was ten stories high. And then she forgot the church and the sermon and even Christmas because the sound of a gunshot rang against the stone walls.

# FIFTEEN

H e's shot! A man is shot! The guy who was pushing the wheelchair!"

Megan wanted to put her hands over her ears to shut out the voice. She wanted someone to say it was a mistake. But instead she heard Ruthie screaming and screaming.

As she and Tom ran toward the door, she glanced back toward the altar at the bishop, who'd been holding out the silver plate of Communion bread in invitation. He set it down, shook his head with sorrow and said, "Let us attend quickly to the need of our fallen brother."

Several were yelling, "Call 911!" Others simply surged toward the bloody body on the floor. A man in a black suit shouted, "I'm a doctor. Let me through, I'm a doctor." Megan edged her way through the crowd until she glimpsed Ben Tolufson, bleeding from a massive chest wound onto the stones in the cathedral floor. George Likely, in his wheelchair, was still coughing; now tears also streamed down his cheeks, and his shoulders shook.

Megan whispered, "Tom, quickly. Take Ruthie to Ben." She held tightly onto Caleb's wriggling shoulders so he couldn't get closer to his father.

Tom, with Ruthie in tow, pushed through the crowd, his badge raised. "FBI. Coming through, please." Just as they got to Ben's side, the doctor, kneeling beside him, looked up, his face grim.

It was seven the next morning when they returned to the hotel. In the lobby, valets were wheeling luggage carts toward the elevators, and hotel guests, many of them families with children who carried new toys, were hurrying toward the atrium for breakfast. It was

Christmas morning for them; they would spend the day as families are supposed to, by celebrating.

Nobody had seen the murderer. The distraught usher, twisting the stem of his silk carnation, said, Yes, he'd noticed the older gentleman appeared to be choking and that the other man, the one now lying on the floor, had taken him out to the drinking fountain. Security patrol people said they had not been guarding the doors carefully; they were inside the nave and had really been hired only for crowd control.

With the ushers' help and finally that of the bishop himself, Tom had managed to get most of the crowd back into the church. A number of people left, rushing in the dark toward their cars, apparently afraid of further gunfire or unable to think about the service after what they'd seen. Megan thought she saw a familiar face flash by and looked around for the Callons but couldn't see them in the crowd.

When the police and the ambulance arrived, Ruthie climbed in beside Ben's inert body, and they sped away to Columbia Hospital. By the time Tom got everyone else crammed into his van, the ambulance was out of sight, its siren screaming as it raced down Wisconsin Avenue. When they got to the hospital, Ruthie was leaning against the pale green wall outside the trauma room, her eyelids red and swollen, her attention focused not on the family but on the sounds coming from behind the curtain. Two D.C. police officers were seated on the edges of their green vinyl chairs, also staring at the curtain.

"Can I see Dad? Is he all right?" Caleb asked.

"Caleb, you're probably hungry again," Celia said. "I saw a candy machine down that corridor. Here, take this money and get whatever you want."

Finally a doctor emerged, his green gown spattered with dark blood. He had peeled off his rubber gloves and was removing his face mask. The police officers rose.

"Sorry," the doctor said. "We got a flicker of heartbeat a few times, but it was too late." He surveyed the group. "The cause of death was through perforation of the chest wall. The bullet went straight into his heart. Do I understand that one of you is an FBI agent? I'll let you fight with the Washington police for the slug."

Ruthie stared at his blank face. "You mean Ben's dead?"

He appeared to focus briefly on her face. "Yes. He was my third gunshot wound tonight. We tried." He stopped, blinked, and added, "There's a room down the hall where you can sit until arrangements are made. They'll want his liver and kidneys, of course." And with that he walked away. Megan stared after his back. *I wonder if, deep down, all doctors are as cold as this one.* She looked at her watch; it was a minute after twelve. Christmas.

Celia left to find Caleb while Tom stayed behind to talk with the police. Ruthie said, "His voice. I never even got to hear his voice again." She began to sob, and Iris took her in her arms, patting her as they walked along. When they found the small room, a records clerk wearing white pants and a pink-checked smock approached them and said cheerfully, "I'll come back in a few minutes to talk to you about your insurance and where you want the body sent."

"We don't have any insurance," Ruthie sobbed into Iris's bosom. "Or money for a funeral, much less this hospital."

Megan, glad to have something positive to inject into the situation, said, "Ben was decorated in the Gulf War, Ruthie, and an FBI agent. He can be buried at Arlington National Cemetery. With full honors. And don't worry about the hospital bill."

Celia appeared with Caleb, who told Ruthie, "You let him die. You let him die when you were with him in the ambulance. He was my dad, and you let him die!"

A nurse appeared and asked in a gentle voice if Ruthie wanted to see her husband.

"Yes, yes." Ruthie looked around the room. "Caleb, you come with me."

"No! He's dead. Why would I want to see him?"

"Come with me," Ruthie said with steel in her voice, and Caleb took her hand.

Celia wiped her eyes. Her shoulders drooped, and her face was almost gray. George patted his wheelchair arm.

"I know, dear. You want to say good-bye to Ben too, don't you?" Celia turned the wheelchair back toward the hall. "We'll go down and wait outside until Ruthie and Caleb are finished."

Megan and Iris were alone in the little room. Neither of them spoke; finally Megan said, "You could take a cab on back to the hotel if you want to, Iris. I think I better stay here."

"I'll stay." And the usually composed Iris began to weep. "I wonder how we can go on in such a horrible world," she sobbed. "There's nothing decent left anywhere. Not even a holiday."

Megan nodded. The pain of Ben's death throbbed in her own chest.

"What is it Christians have?" Iris asked, taking out a mirror and looking at her smeared mascara. "You grew up believing, didn't you? Why did you stop?"

"I realized one day it was more habit than belief. And after tonight, who could believe in God?"

"I think I want to," Iris said, mopping her eyes again. "I think I've got to find the answer."


Ruthie and Iris went ahead into the hotel lobby while Megan paid the cab. A woman and a ragged child of uncertain gender shuffled out of the bushes.

"Could you help us get something to eat?" the woman asked. Both mother and child were dressed in faded, threadbare garments; the woman was wearing knit gloves with the fingers cut out.

"Why don't you go to a shelter?" Megan asked.

The woman shook her head. "The shelters are full. We're on the waiting list. We slept back here by the wall last night," she said. She kept glancing around behind her. "They'll call the cops if they see me out here again, but it's warmer under this overhang."

*Why doesn't she get a job?* Megan wondered.

As if she had read Megan's mind, the woman said, "I've got a temp job, cleaning restrooms at Engraving, but there's no work today because it's Christmas. I only have work for four hours a day, that's eighteen dollars, and I had to buy my son's insulin."

*That's ridiculous. There must be scores of agencies who can help this woman, especially if she has a diabetic son.*

"I suppose you can't get welfare?" Celia asked.

"Not unless I get laid off at my job. If I do, I can get my boy on Medicaid so he can see a doctor. He ain't seen a doctor in seven months. But here in D.C. the welfare money is short, so I still might not get on; and, besides, it only lasts a few months, and then you're in the street again."

Megan wondered how much of the woman's story was true. She probably had a nice home and a fine new car and was making easy money panhandling. She started toward the door, but Celia opened her purse and gave the woman two twenty-dollar bills.

"Oh, Ceelie, don't! This woman can—"

The beggar burst into tears. "Oh, God bless you, ma'am. God bless you." She turned to her child saying, "See, honey? We can eat something good, and then we'll go to that hotel on Connecticut Avenue, to sleep indoors. Tomorrow we'll go to Goodwill and get you some sneakers without holes."

Involuntarily, Megan looked down at the child's shoes. His socks showed through the holes over his toes, and the tongues were gone. They were each tied with half a frayed shoelace.

"God bless you," the woman called again over her shoulder.

"I wish I'd had more," Celia said, watching after them. "I'll cash a traveler's check, and if we see her again, I'll help her more."

"Ceelie, she can surely get help. She could get a better job, for that matter."

Celia looked at her coolly. "I think our senator needs to do some research. And besides," she said, zipping up her purse, "the sixth chapter of the Gospel of Luke says to give to anyone who asks you."

"But what if they spend it on drugs or wine or something?"

"Jesus never asked anyone if they were worthy of his help,"

Celia said. Megan took her arm and they headed for the round settee in the lobby, where Ruthie and Iris were waiting.

*I wish I could just break down and cry. I haven't really wept since I was a little girl.* Megan had decided after she had sobbed for her parents for weeks, dreamed of them, lain awake at night aching for her mother's touch and her father's laughter, that she would let nothing ever hurt her so much again.

She had also known early that she wanted to be a lawyer like her father and had started toughening herself in high school, not letting her feelings be hurt easily, not reacting to teasing no matter how mean spirited it was, not giving in to grief or frustration, because someday she would be playing in the big-boys' court.

As they walked into the hotel lobby, Ruthie's head was against the high center of the round couch, and her eyes were closed. When Megan touched her hand, Ruthie opened her eyes slowly and looked around in confusion. She rose and leaned on Iris, dragging her feet, almost unable to walk. Celia pushed her husband's wheelchair, silent and with her head bowed.

"It's Christmas," Caleb said in the elevator, his moist eyes full of hot wrath. "Nobody is supposed to die on Christmas." As they walked down the gallery toward their room, the sound of the two indoor waterfalls, rushing down their black stone courses, mingled with voices of people talking happily over breakfast.

"I hate to admit it at a time like this," Megan said, "but the smell of bacon is almost irresistible."

"We'll have some breakfast sent up," Iris said. Somehow her dress was still crisp and unwrinkled, even though she'd held the weeping Ruthie in her arms at the hospital. In fact, not a lock of Iris's miraculous hair was out of place.

Megan, on the other hand, felt gritty and soiled. She wanted to stand under the shower, shampooing her hair and scrubbing her body until the picture of Ben Tolufson, bleeding to death on the floor of the National Cathedral, washed out of her head and down the drain.

Upstairs they found not one but two men guarding the gallery outside their doors, one sitting on the upholstered bench and one leaning against the wall, reading the *Washington Post* and glancing up every two or three minutes. Megan took the half-swooning Ruthie to her room and convinced her to swallow the sedatives the doctor had given her, but she couldn't coax her into her bed.

"I can't even look at the room where Ben and I slept," she said, and flopped down on the couch. Megan threw a blanket from the closet over her and sat in an easy chair. When Ruthie's breathing said she was sleeping, Megan found Celia in her suite, holding up a can of George's liquid food supplement so he could drink it through his straw. They struggled to hoist him into his bed in his shirt, socks, and underwear. Although they called Caleb for assistance, he didn't move.

"We'll get you fixed up better later, Grandpa," Megan said, kissing George's forehead.

Tears were still seeping down the creases in his face, and he sighed as he put his cheek against the clean white pillow.

She knew she couldn't ignore her hunger much longer, so she was glad when she opened the door to her own suite and saw bacon, scrambled eggs, mixed fruit, and soft, fluffy oatmeal. She ate a piece of bacon, then dished up a bowl of oatmeal and began spooning the porridge into her mouth as fast as she could.

"Thanks so much for getting some food up here," she said to Iris, who was sipping a cup of coffee. "I'm starved. Ceelie and Caleb, dig in. I have a feeling it's going to be a long day."

Caleb ate a bite of toast and put it down. "I want to talk to Mom."

"Oh, honey, let her sleep," Megan said. "Let's open a gift." She reached under the tree to pick up the package containing the gargoyle wind chime. "Here, take a look at this." She also dug out the electronic game and packages addressed to Caleb from Celia and Iris. She piled them at his feet; the presents from his parents she stacked under an end table. He stared down at the gifts but didn't move to open them.

The telephone rang, and she glanced at her watch as Iris

answered. It was nine-thirty. Probably the call was from Brenda, saying she and Rick were on their way, or maybe Tom, calling to bring them up to date on the investigation of Ben's murder.

Iris, her face unreadable, handed her the phone.

"Megan? Merry Christmas."

A thousand memories stirred inside her. "Mark?"

"Are you having a nice holiday?"

She wanted to say, "Yes, now that you've called." She wanted to say, "I love you." Instead, she said, "Mark, Ben Tolufson was murdered last night."

"Tolufson? You mean your grandparents' neighbor, the pastor?"

"He was shot last night at the National Cathedral. We were there for the Christmas service."

"But why on earth would—"

"Nobody has any idea. Maybe it was mistaken identity or just a random shooting."

"Good grief! What happened?"

"Ben took Grandpa out into the entry hall to get a drink of water, and that's when—" she glanced down at Caleb, whose cheeks were again covered with tears— "Mark, how are you?"

"Lonely." Mark's voice crackled. "I think we should talk."

"Go ahead." Her heart began leaping in her chest.

"Well, not when you've been up all night. Maybe I could come to Washington in a couple weeks."

"The swearing-in is on January 8. Maybe you'd like to be here for that," she said, wanting to add, *Please come, oh, please...*

"I'll try. I want to see you, Meg. I miss you, and I think we should reconsider our breakup."

Her knees were turning to jelly, and she sat down. "I'll be glad to talk to you, Mark."

"Me, too. I hope your New Year is happier than this. Give my best to your family, won't you? And say good-bye to Iris for me."

The phone clicked, and he was gone.

"It was Mark," she said as she hung up.

"Well, he took long enough," Celia said, picking at her tiny portion of eggs and toast. "I thought he'd turn up Thanksgiving weekend." She rinsed off her plate and set it in the sink.

"Really, Ceelie? Why didn't you say so?"

"Because whenever I mentioned his name you changed the subject. All right, Caleb, help me get this package unwrapped." She opened the blue-topaz pin. "How wonderful! My mother had a pin almost exactly like this." She kissed Megan and fastened the brooch to the front of her blouse. Megan gazed at the pin, but what she saw was Mark Combs's face, and she smiled for the first time since Ben's death. In fact, she was still smiling when she answered a knock at the door.

# SIXTEEN

She had expected Rick and Brenda. Instead, it was Tom, carrying a poinsettia in a foil-wrapped pot.

"I know you're not celebrating this morning," he said, "but I did want to drop in. I sent one of your two hall guards home for a couple of hours so he could play with his kids and their new toys." He glanced around the room. "Mrs. Tolufson. Is she—"

"Asleep in her own room. Grandpa's in his."

"I wanted to bring you up to date on everything. The coroner said—"

She inclined her head toward Caleb. Tom stopped.

Iris said, "Caleb, why don't you go lie on my bed and watch television? You can open your gifts later," she added, noticing the pile he'd abandoned.

Caleb stalked off to the bedroom. In a moment they heard the sound of the television.

"I still haven't seen my own kids yet," Tom said.

"You have children?"

"Two girls, six and eight. Both at my mother's in Alexandria. I'm going over there in a while, unless something new happens on this case."

Megan poured him a cup of coffee. "Sit down, Tom, and have breakfast."

He slid into a chair without waiting to be urged. "Okay," he said as he started to dish up some scrambled eggs, "here's what's happening. According to the coroner, Ben Tolufson was killed by a hollow-point bullet from a nine-millimeter automatic pistol. That's the same kind of gun and the same kind of bullet the local police carry. He was killed at medium range, which means the killer could have been standing in the shadows in the hall, or even outside. Someone who maybe cracked open the outer door and fired. There was nobody else in the entry area at the time of the shooting; all the ushers were standing inside the nave, in front of pillars near the doorways. And all facing the altar. So nobody but your husband, Mrs. Likely, saw anything before Tolufson went down." He took a deep breath and gulped some coffee.

Celia was nodding, her shadowed eyes fixed on his face. "Now all we need is a reason for the murder, Mr. Warburton," she said, sighing.

"I believe the two deaths, Linderman's and Tolufson's, are connected somehow. Ellen Linderman's suicide is probably not part of some plot, but the threatening note is. In fact, I believe that somehow, Megan, you may be at the center of this. Tomorrow, when some of the wheels of government are turning again, we'll have a round-the-clock guard on each of you. They'll be like the Secret Service, accompanying you wherever you go. My office will page me if there are any developments," Tom continued. "When Mills comes back, that's the guard who went home, I'm going to go see my kids and then grab some sleep." He looked at his watch. "It's ten-ten. He'll be back at eleven. And yes, I'd love another cup."

Iris gathered up the dishes and set the breakfast tray outside in the gallery. Celia started a new pot of coffee. Megan opened the door to her bedroom and peeped inside. Caleb was sound asleep on Iris's bed, the remote control in his hand. She realized her fists were doubled. Why was she so angry? *Because the FBI will solve this crime their own methodical way, and a friend of mine is dead. They'll take a year to figure this out. I've got to find the murderer myself.*

That thought made her too tired to stand up. She decided to just stretch out for a minute and listen to the television choir singing Christmas carols.

She woke almost two hours later. The television was giving a news break, and she watched a reporter who said no suspects had been identified in the National Cathedral murder. It hadn't been a dream, then. Ben Tolufson was dead, and she wouldn't have a minute's peace until she figured out who did it.

In the living room she found Ruthie sitting on the couch,

dazed and half awake. Tom had left, but Rick and Brenda were seated beside Ruthie. Celia was holding Ewok, who was growling steadily at Rick, now and then building to a real snarl.

"I didn't mean to fall asleep. I just thought I'd lie down for a second.... Rick, Brenda, hello."

She crossed the room to embrace them; Ewok snarled and then barked, and Celia said, "Shh! Ewok, stop that!"

Megan bent to put her hand on Ruthie's cheek. "Are you all right? How long have you been up?"

"I could only sleep about an hour. So then I called my mother and Ben's folks." Ruthie started to cry. "They were so hurt. They didn't understand why anyone would do this to Ben," she sobbed. "And neither do I."

*When I'm sworn into the Senate I'll demand hearings on this murder. After all, the Congress controls the District, doesn't it?* Megan moved the coffee cups and sat down on the leather-topped coffee table, taking Ruthie's face in her hands. "I promise you, I'll find out," she said. "No matter what happens, I'll get to the bottom of this."

Brenda's face was sadder than Megan had ever seen it. "So terrible," she murmured. "So terrible." She rose and said, "We need to go, honey, and let these people get some rest."

"Wait." Megan turned and dug among the Christmas gifts. "This is for you," she said, handing Brenda the festive package containing their new Bible. "You can open it when you get home. We don't feel too Christmasy here."

"And we put our gifts for you right under the tree," Rick said, putting on his topcoat. "If we'd only known! We didn't listen to the news this morning. We went to church and then came straight over here, where we found out about this." He shook his head, as if in disbelief, and patted Ruthie's shoulder. "I won't say Merry Christmas, Ruthie. I'll just tell you again how sorry I am."

Celia put the dog on the floor so she could say good-bye; he rushed forward, snarling, and sank his teeth into Rick's ankle.

"Ewok, no! Bad dog!" Megan rushed to extricate Rick's ankle

from the dog's jaws. The black sock was torn and bloody. After the dog had been banished to the dark bathroom for punishment, Megan shook her head ruefully.

"I've never seen him act this way before," she said. "Here, Rick, let me wash that wound. Dogs have awful germs in their mouths."

"I always heard that dog saliva was very antiseptic," he said, smiling. He took the soapy cloth from her hand and scrubbed at the bitten spot. Megan could clearly see Ewok's teeth marks and was horrified.

"He's always been a good dog, friendly to everyone." She peered at the bite again. "Rick, that needs more than cleaning up. You'd better run over to Columbia Hospital's emergency room."

As soon as the words were out of her mouth, she regretted them. Ruthie began to weep again, and Megan sat down beside her, pulling her into her arms.

"He'll be okay," Brenda said. "Rick, let's get out of here unless we can do some good."

Rick left, promising to let a doctor see his ankle. Iris busied herself with the coffee cups. As she dried them with a hand towel she said, "Celia, unless you canceled it, Christmas dinner will be here any minute."

"I think we need it." Celia plumped the couch pillows and straightened lampshades. "Ruthie, you're going to grieve for Ben the rest of your life. So will George and I. But you need to keep your strength up for Caleb's sake. Let's at least try to eat Christmas dinner."

They did try. The restaurant had sent ham and sweet potatoes with raisin sauce that didn't taste like Ceelie's, along with Waldorf salad, rolls, butter, and two kinds of pie, both of which tasted store bought. The four women were toying with their food when Caleb emerged, rubbing his eyes. He declined any food, and when they gathered up the dinner things, he turned on the big living-room television set.

Instantly they were back in the cathedral. The voice-over was saying, "Worshipers at the National Cathedral's Christmas Eve service were shocked last night when a visitor from Wisconsin was shot by an unknown gunman."

Somebody, perhaps a newsperson taking videos of the church service, or a tourist hoping to record Christmas, had shot a tape of the scene. Megan saw herself in the crowd, saw Tom and Ruthie pushing through, saw Ben Tolufson's bloody body on the stone floor. And then she looked into the crowd in the background. *No. You don't see who you think you see.* She brushed the sight from her mind as Iris and Celia went to take care of George.

Iris said as they left, "Tomorrow we'll get a strong male nurse up here."

Megan put one of the trays with almost untouched dinner dishes outside the door.

"Ruthie, what will you do now?"

"Oh, Megan, I've been thinking about that all day. I guess we'll go home. To my home, I mean. My parents live in Iowa. Mama said when I called this morning she wanted us to come. So did Ben's mother, Irene, but I don't know them as well. She made me promise, Irene did, that I'd bring Caleb to see her. So far he's her only grandson, although she has a daughter who just got married last year."

"How long were you married?"

Ruthie looked down at her plain gold wedding ring. "Ten years," she said, with a catch in her voice. "We had Caleb right off the bat, but somehow I never got pregnant again."

Megan straightened the room again and glanced at the Christmas tree. She'd be glad when it was out of here so she and Iris had more room to live. In fact, she never wanted to see another Christmas decoration. *Why do we get excited over Christmas? It's just another day when someone can get shot.* "We'll go over to Arlington tomorrow," she said. "So we can find out about burial for Ben."

"Oh, Megan, it feels like Ben is close enough to touch, but when I turn, he's not there."

"He'll always be with you, Ruthie." *As if I knew anything about what happens after death.*

"No, he's in heaven with Jesus. At least I'm sure of that."

*I wish I were that sure.* Megan touched Ruthie's wrist, then switched off the television.

Someone knocked on the door. Megan opened it to let Celia push George through in his wheelchair, with Iris and Caleb following. Caleb threw himself on the couch beside Ruthie and eyed the Christmas tree.

"Would Dad be mad if I opened my presents?"

"Of course not, honey." Ruthie gave him a squeeze.

As he unwrapped the gargoyle wind chime, Megan held her breath. Would he like the ornament, or would it simply remind him of the place where his father was murdered?

He smiled his first smile of the day. "Cool," he said, and held up the wind chimes to let it jingle. The fierce gargoyle glared at all of them. Even Ruthie smiled.

"I've asked George what he saw," Celia said. "He just keeps shaking his head and pointing at the door."

*Oh, please, spare my grandfather, whoever you are. He saw you, but he can't tell anyone.*

By the time they all went back to their own rooms that night, Megan was exhausted again. Thank heaven she'd planned to take tomorrow off! She thought she'd be sightseeing with her family and friends; instead, she'd take the sad journey over to Arlington.

"I wish I could sleep for a week," she said as Iris removed her makeup and smoothed on alpha-hydroxy cream. Megan splashed water on her own face in the adjacent washbowl, then blotted it on a towel.

"Today was at least a week long," Iris said. "If you'd slept through it, you'd have had your wish. She leaned forward to inspect her face. Without makeup, a spatter of orangy freckles decorated her nose and cheeks. "I look a thousand years old tonight."

"So do I." Megan hung up her towel and trudged into her

bedroom, where she changed into pajamas and crawled into her bed. Every muscle was throbbing with fatigue. A spot behind her right shoulder was tender; so were the calves of her legs.

"I don't think I was meant for high stress," she said as Iris came back into the room. "It makes me ache all over."

"Just wait until you get into the Senate, kid. You'll probably have to have a live-in chiropractor." She sat down on her bed and removed her hose. "I can't believe I've had these on for twenty-four hours." Her face was pinched with sorrow. "What a rotten world we live in," she added, turning off the light.

The next day they left George with Iris and a young man sent from the nursing registry and took a cab across the Potomac to Arlington National Cemetery. The day was cold and overcast. As the cemetery tour bus wound through lane after lane of endless gray crosses and grave markers, Megan found herself becoming depressed.

"Maybe this would be better in the summertime," Ruthie said. "When the flowers are blossoming and the trees are leafed out."

"I hate this place," Caleb said, moving into the seat across from them. "I don't want my dad to be here. I want him to be buried in a place I can go to."

"We'll take him home," Ruthie said, and Celia nodded.

Megan looked out the window. *Everything to do with Ben's death is wrong. I can't just give in to grief like the rest of them, I've got to find the murderer.*

Megan and Joseph Ferguson, her constant daytime bodyguard, accompanied the sad little party to the airport. Megan had persuaded Caleb to open the electronic game she'd bought him for Christmas, hoping he'd play it on the plane. But at Dulles he drooped against his mother, not speaking or even looking around.

They all wept as they said good-bye. Megan's tears were angry as she kissed her family and friends. Without Ben, the group was not a full circle, and she silently vowed again to find Ben's murderer. Was Tom Warburton right in his theory that Linderman had been cut down by the same killer?

"Thank you for helping with Ben," Ruthie said. Megan had made all the phone calls that made it possible to take his casket home to Wisconsin. It hadn't been easy; the FBI lab had wanted to do a complete autopsy. Tom intervened, saying the cause of death had been determined already. Then there were the District police, who insisted George stay in town so they could question him further. Megan made a trip downtown, taking her grandfather with her, to speak to the police commissioner. It was soon obvious that he could tell them nothing. And the cost had been far greater than Ruthie knew. Megan bought Ben a bronze coffin and paid the extra air freight out of her savings.

"I'll probably never come back to Washington. I'm sorry, Megan," Ruthie added. "I just couldn't."

"Of course you couldn't," Megan said, holding her in a fierce hug. "And I haven't forgotten my promise, Ruthie. We'll put the fiend who murdered Ben in prison forever."

Celia and George both looked withered and fading. "I pray God surrounds you with angels, Megan, dear. I'll call you tonight." Celia kissed her granddaughter, and then Megan squatted down beside George's wheelchair.

"Good-bye, Grandpa," she said, kissing his fingers and then touching his cheek. "I love you." George nodded, but he didn't smile. His eyes were dull, and she wondered if he even heard her. She would never really know what he knew or felt or thought. Ceelie did, or was she just imagining things, putting words into his mouth, crediting him with wisdom and understanding he didn't really have?

# SEVENTEEN

Megan walked outside the airport to the line of people waiting for taxis, Agent Ferguson hastening after her. They took their place in line under a narrow canopy that let the wind smack against their faces and sear their lips.

"The Capitol," she told the taxi caller, and in a few minutes they were sharing a cab with a woman going to Pentagon City. When Megan got to her office, Iris was already there, supervising the installation of her draperies and directing Bryan in the reorganization of their electrical system. Iris had been right: the old rose carpet Megan hadn't been sure about looked wonderful. In fact, it gave the room balance.

"I took the Christmas tree down before I left the hotel," Iris said without any other greeting. "Mr. Ferguson, could you hold this stack of folders for a minute? Megan, you need to be in the majority leader's office by eleven-thirty. That gives you ten minutes to powder your nose or whatever."

"Why does he want to see me?" Megan asked as she looked through the stacks of government brochures and leaflets that had been delivered to her office. Or maybe dumped was a better word; the reception desk was piled high.

"I have no idea. His aide called and asked that you be in Dirksen 211, that's all." Iris turned to the two men installing the pale gray linen curtains that matched the walls. "Oh, no, wait. Hang that rod farther out. I want the draperies to clear the windows when they're open." The woodwork and wainscoting had been painted ivory, and Iris inspected it carefully, looking for runs or splotching.

"Hi, Boss," Bryan called. He was on his hands and knees, taping electrical wire to the carpet around the edge of the room. "The electrical outlets in here must have been installed about three hundred years ago."

"I thought we gave you the week off," Megan said.

"Yeah, well, Iris called me this morning and asked if I'd like to help out."

"And Iris, I thought you felt blah and were going back to bed."

"I did. For about ten minutes, and then I decided the only cure for the doldrums was work."

"Where's your bodyguard?"

Iris grinned. "In your inner office, putting books on the shelves. When I work, nobody sits."

"In that case I'm leaving. Did you by any chance bring my briefcase over here?"

"I did. It's on your desk. No, you can't come through here. Let me get it."

While Iris was in the inner office, Megan murmured to Ferguson, "Please keep your eye out for listening devices. I've already been bugged once." She glanced across the room at Bryan, or rather at Bryan's legs and feet, sticking out from under the reception desk. "And don't tell anyone," she added in a whisper.

Ferguson nodded. "Warburton already told us about this office," he said softly. "We'll go over it with a fine-tooth comb when everyone's out." In a normal voice he added, "I'm ready to accompany you to the majority leader's office, Senator."

She hesitated. "Maybe I should go over there alone. It may be a private meeting."

"Sorry. My instructions were to go everywhere with you. I'm sure Senator Hutchins will have a place where you can talk out of earshot."

The majority leader's suite of offices in the Dirksen Building was carpeted in a rich mulberry, and his furniture, like him, was massive. She gave her name to one of the people in reception, and in a moment the senator lumbered out, wearing a rumpled black suit and a wide green holiday tie.

"Well, here's one of our new members!" he wheezed.

"Welcome to Washington, Senator Likely. And come on into my den of iniquity."

Ferguson put his hand out to stop the inner office door before Hutchins closed it, and he thrust his head in to survey the room. Nodding, he withdrew, saying, "I'll be out here, Senator Likely."

Senator Hutchins raised his bushy gray brows. "What was that all about?"

"My life was threatened, and then a friend of mine was gunned down in the National Cathedral on Christmas Eve. The FBI thinks I need a keeper. And maybe I do."

"Well!" The majority leader puffed over to his desk chair and dropped into it. "Seems like there's more to you than meets the eye. Sorry about your friend; I read about it. All right," he added, suddenly serious, "let's get to work for a few minutes. Are you familiar with SB7738? The—"

"The poverty alleviation bill. If you're trying to sell it too, forget it. I'm going to vote against it."

The heavy eyebrows rose again. "What do you mean, 'too'? Who's tryin' to sell it to you?"

"Sen—" Megan stopped. Maybe Luke Callon didn't want to publicize his involvement with the bill. "I'd prefer not to state the name," she said.

"You don't have to. You're talkin' about our colleague Luke Callon and his proposed amendment he thinks will make the bill acceptable to us conservatives." He coughed into the side of his fist and finally reached into his breast pocket for an asthma inhaler. He took two puffs and held his breath for a moment, then said, "I think Luke's off the mark on this one. In fact, he may be off his rocker. So, you're going to vote against it no matter what happens on the floor?"

"Politics is always said to be the art of compromise," Megan said, sitting down in a red leather wing chair. "However, I haven't heard or seen anything yet that would change my decision."

"All right, great, so much for 7738. Which will have a new number when we go into session. Same for 9832. Have you studied it?" He passed a heavy, bound report across the desk. Within a few moments, she saw the majority leader's famed intellect at work.

"Now," he continued. "Addressing section 6, clause 54..."

For a whole hour, Megan forgot about Ben Tolufson and all the events of the past two weeks as she focused on the intricacies of a bill that would let dairy farmers, not the government, set the minimum price of milk. At last! This was the reason she had wanted to come to Washington: to explore ways to make the country and her own home state a better place to live. And though the price levels of milk and cheese and butter sounded unimportant next to nuclear treaties or constitutional amendments, they directly affected a huge percentage of Wisconsin's population.

"You've got one fine mind, young woman," Hutchins finally said. "You grasp things quick, don't you? I'll be expectin' you to speak for about five minutes on this bill when we go back into session. After you're sworn in, of course."

"You'll want me to speak in favor of the bill on the Senate floor?" She felt her heart quicken.

"I certainly do. And now—" He looked at his watch—"we're almost late. Let's go."

"Go where?"

"To lunch, of course. In the Senate dining room." He took her elbow and guided her back into the anteroom. Ferguson put down his magazine and stood.

"All right, guard dog, you can come too," Hutchins panted, grinning. "Lois, phone down and tell them I'm bringing two for lunch, not one." He clumped into the hall and toward the elevator, moving Megan along by the elbow so she was slightly ahead of him. Instead of being annoyed, as she usually would have been in the presence of a controlling man, she was amused by his bumbling Southern manners.

"Wait." Ferguson stepped forward. "I need to walk next to Senator Likely," he said.

"Why? You afraid you're goin' to lose track of her?"

Ferguson gazed at the majority leader and finally said with firm lips, "So if someone shoots at her, I can shield her body with mine."

The joy of the morning's work fled. Her heart again turned into a thick lump in her chest. Ben Tolufson was dead. So were the Lindermans. And maybe she would be dead soon, before she could even take her oath of office.

"I-I don't know if I can go for lunch today, Senator Hutchins," she said.

He smiled and his eyes squeezed nearly shut. "Too late," he said. "I got me a whole passel of dignitaries, waitin' to meet you. So if your friend here wants to walk front or back, I don't care. But I'm awful hungry, so let's go."

She was silent as they took the elevator down to the crypt. She followed Hutchins down the maze of hallways because he was too wide for anyone to squeeze in beside him. As they boarded the subway tram, he put his hand on his chest and gasped.

"Too much exercise for these old lungs," he said over his shoulder to Megan and Ferguson, who sat behind him. "All right, horsies. Take me to the Capitol."

The Senate dining room looked from the outside like another office, but when they opened the double doors, the otherwise plain chamber was filled with red-covered round tables, each with six chairs and each bearing a holiday bouquet. Most of the chairs were full, but when the majority leader entered the room, everyone stood until he was seated. Senator Callon was there, along with Ruthwell and other men and women she recognized only from newspapers and television. She was about to eat lunch with thirty United States senators.

Ferguson didn't sit; he stood unsmiling against the wall behind her and watched the room, but Megan slipped into the empty chair beside Luke Callon.

Luke stood to say, "Shall we bless our food?" Most heads went down, and some people shut their eyes. Megan stared straight ahead, trying desperately to feel something about prayer. But if she had ever believed in God, the brutal murder of her grandparents' dearest friend had ended the possibility.

She waited for "amen," then picked up her spoon and started on her black-bean soup.

"How was your morning? I went by your office, but your manager was there, rearranging the world," Luke said.

"I went to the airport to send my grandparents home, and I—"

"Do you prefer the whitefish with a baked potato, or the chef's salad?" A waiter was hovering near her, bent at the waist. She ordered the salad and turned back to Luke. But now he was absorbed in conversation with Mary Minton, the senator from Florida.

"I've got Mary on my side about the amendment," he said, turning back to Megan. "Now we only need to convince three more, and I've got good feelings about the junior senator from California."

Megan put her spoon down. "Don't count me in," she said. "I don't think I can vote for the poverty bill."

"But, Megan, doesn't your Christianity say we have to feed the poor? You know, in Luke, my namesake Gospel, it says—"

"Don't count me in on that yet either, Luke," she said, trying to keep her voice gentle. "I'm not exactly a believer. And my last experience in church wasn't too helpful." She felt anger rising in her breast. Why was she flaring up at Luke this way? "I'm sorry," she added. "I guess I'm still a little upset about Ben's death."

"I should think you'd be a whole lot upset. Do the authorities have any suspects, or even a motive for the murder?" Luke's face was so kind, so genuinely distressed for her, that she forgot about Celia's warning about angels of light. Instead, she told him about the cream-colored envelope on her bed, told him Tom Warburton leaned toward the belief that Ben's and Robert Linderman's deaths were somehow connected, almost told him about the slip of paper in her pocket, until she realized she was talking to the husband of a woman she completely distrusted! To change the subject she said, "My former fiancé, Mark Combs, may come for the swearing-in."

"Combs? The district attorney in, where is it? Green Bay?"

"Fond du Lac. You know him, then?"

"I met him when I was governor, but I didn't realize you were engaged to him. He's a good prosecutor."

"I said *former* fiancé. He didn't want me to run for the Senate."

"But he's coming for your swearing-in? Does that mean it's on again?"

"Maybe." She looked up to see Iris standing beside her.

"I'm sorry, Meg, but Mark Combs's lawyer just called. Mark's been arrested for the murder of Robert Linderman."

# EIGHTEEN

**M**egan felt the floor falling from under her. She gripped the edge of the table to keep from whirling downward into the vortex, and after a few moments she recovered her wits.

"Mark was arrested? For murder? Iris, could this have been a crank call?"

"The call was from someone named—" Iris looked down at the memo pad in her hand—"let's see. A lawyer named Andrew Foss."

Megan sighed. "I know him."

Luke Callon put his arm around her, so Ferguson moved closer, his eyes fixed on Luke. Iris's bodyguard was also lurking nearby.

"You'll have to excuse me," Megan told Luke as she rose and picked up her briefcase. Mary Minton was looking at her with a question on her face. "I'll explain later," she added, nodding also to the senator on her right, a man from Ohio to whom she hadn't yet spoken.

When they got to her office, Iris picked up a sheet of pale gray memo paper with "From the Desk of Senator Megan Likely" printed at the top. "Here's the number, Meg."

"Where's Bryan?" Megan asked absently as she punched in the Milwaukee number.

"Searching the building for the paint crew. They did a wretched job on the woodwork in your office."

In a moment, a female voice said, "Lucas, Williams, and Foss. How can I direct your call?"

"This is Senator Megan Likely. Can I speak to Andy Foss, please?"

Andy's voice was a high, nasal tenor, almost a whine. He usually dressed in jeans and a ratty flannel shirt. He chain-smoked, and his fingers were stained. But he was one of the best criminal lawyers in the Midwest. Maybe in the country.

"Megan! We've missed you in Wisconsin. Here's what's happening. Someone in Washington sent word to the authorities that Mark and Robert Linderman had some kind of altercation or something just before Linderman was killed. So they questioned him at his office and then took him in handcuffs across the street to the police station. He asked me to let you know he probably won't make it down there for the swearing-in. But I'm working on bail right now." He sounded as if he were about to hang up.

"Andy, wait. When did they get the call from Washington?"

"It wasn't a call. It was a letter, sent some days ago. It got into a pile at the Oshkosh police station. The prosecutor and I each received a copy from the police chief this morning." She could hear him shuffling papers. "Let's see. The letter came from...Ah, here it is. The letter came from an FBI agent named Thomas Warburton. Okay, Megan, I've got to get to the bail hearing. Mark can call you when he gets out of jail." He clicked off, and she laid the phone in its cradle.

*Tom did this. Tom did this to Mark!* She dialed Tom's pager, then punched in her office number. He called back in a few moments.

"Tom, why have you attacked Mark this way?"

"Who?"

"Mark Combs. The district attorney in—Tom, you know who I mean."

"Who is he? What do you mean? Why did I do what to him?"

"He was arrested for Linderman's murder, as you well know."

"Hey, I just got to the office. I've been tracking another dead end on the Tolufson case. I don't even know what you're talking about."

Megan drew herself up to her full five feet, one inch. "Don't lie to me, Agent Warburton. Do you think I'm a fool? Mark's lawyer said the tip came from you."

"Megan, I swear I don't know anything about this. Look, give me an hour to see what I can find out. Did you say you know this—what is his name?"

"Mark Combs. We were engaged once," she snapped, and hung up.

"It was Tom," she told Iris. "Tom Warburton sent the Oshkosh police some crazy information about Mark. Something about a threat or a blackmail note or something." She walked through Iris's unfinished office, then into her own, where she sat down at the elegant Queen Anne desk and looked around the room. She hadn't been inside it since it was painted light gray with ivory woodwork and carpeted in the same dusty rose as the outer office. Her office was finished, light, airy and serene, but she was having a hard time centering herself in it. She finally began making a list of factors in Ben's murder, jotting down, "Who in Washington knew Ben?"

She wrote, Me, his family, Ceelie, Grandpa, Iris. After thinking a moment, she added Rick and Brenda. Well, that was ridiculous. None of those people would hurt Ben or anyone else. Well, what about Priscilla? She hadn't met Ben yet. But wait: Bryan had. Bryan had turned up everywhere she went on Christmas Eve except the Cathedral, when he'd said he had to work.

But why would Bryan have killed Ben? Was it part of a plot to hurt her somehow? Or even ruin her Senate career? She scribbled, "Check on Bryan's alibi," and folded the sheet, slipping it into her pocket.

She felt relieved when Iris bustled in with several "while you were out" messages.

"That last call was Fern. She's leaving from Chicago even as we speak. I'll pick her up at Washington National at four."

Megan had called Fern on Christmas afternoon, asking her to delay her arrival for a few days while the family dealt with Ben's death. "I'll go," Megan said. "You're working too hard. By the way, we never did talk about your salary. I'm not paying you enough for all you're doing."

"We can do that tonight." Iris's voice was brisk, almost impersonal. "Right now you might want to take care of these." She laid the memo sheets down on the empty desktop, then was silent for a moment before she said, "Meg, I only saw Mark two or three times when you were going together, but I can't imagine him committing a murder."

~ ~ ~ ~ ~

"It was twelve years ago. I was in my last few months of law school," Mark told Andy Foss. He sat across the interrogation table from the lawyer in a room with dirty gray walls and no windows. "I took the weekend off to visit with my older sister Gail. She had been trapped, or thought she was trapped, for three years in a violent marriage. Living in Seattle."

"You wanted her to leave her husband?"

"We'd never been close. In fact, we really got on each other's nerves. She was eight years older, and we always fought. But, yeah, I wanted her out of there. I called her and said she could come live in my apartment until she got on her feet. Our parents were all for it. Gail's husband was in law enforcement, but he was an abuser and an adulterer. Gail thought he also might be involved in some kind of underworld dealings because he had too much money to spend. I never met the man. He wanted nothing to do with the family."

"Cut to the chase, Mark. How does this have anything to do with the murder?"

"Just wait a minute; I'm getting there." He was used to sitting on the other side of the table with an assistant as they questioned a man or woman accused of a crime. Usually the arraigned person had a lawyer present. Now he and his attorney were waiting for the state prosecutor.

"Gail always said she felt unable to make a break. But finally after her husband had really knocked her around one time, we decided on impulse to go to Lake Superior for the Memorial Day weekend. We thought we could fish while we talked about her options. She flew in to Milwaukee, and I drove us up to the lake. On Sunday afternoon, Gail was having no luck fishing and got tired of sitting on the dock. She said she was going for a walk."

"And?"

"She never came back. I looked for her for four hours before calling the police. On Monday morning, they found her shoe in the woods. They searched the area and even dragged the lake for two days, but no trace of my sister was ever found."

"Did the cops question you?"

"Oh, boy, did they. They finally gave up, but for a couple years I had a cloud of suspicion over me. Even my father gave me a funny look a few times."

"What about her husband?"

"He had an airtight alibi. He was an FBI agent, at a seminar in Minneapolis. The police questioned him and decided he couldn't have killed her and hidden her body or dumped it in the water and gotten back to Minneapolis, all in the time when nobody could vouch for him. Actually, when I read the report, it sounded to me like he had plenty of time. I don't think they ever decided I was innocent. They finally announced that Gail had been lost in the woods and probably killed by a person or persons unknown and closed the case. Unless they find her body, which may be at the bottom of the lake, we'll never know. I decided I had to get out of Milwaukee or I'd never have any future as a lawyer in this state." He sighed. "Gail owned three dairy farms she bought before she was married. I was shocked to find out she had left them to me. I live on one of them."

"And this is what Linderman was threatening you about?"

"I guess." He showed Foss the "fishing" postcard Linderman had sent him, and Foss told him about the evidence the FBI agent had found in Linderman's house, with the Paul Bunyan ax circled and the question, "Is this how you did it?"

"Were you paying him any money?"

"You mean blackmail money? Of course not."

"Well, did he try to extort money from you?"

Mark paused. "Not money," he said finally. "Linderman wanted something else." The sound of a guard jingling keys in the door told him the state prosecutor was coming into the room.

"Say nothing," Foss advised. "Let me do the talking."

But Mark had to answer the prosecutor's first question, which was, "Okay, Mark. Can you tell us where you were on Christmas Eve?"

Megan looked back at the Capitol as she and Ferguson were whisked away by the taxi. The white building was tinted almost pink in the winter sunset. This time their cab was driven by a black man who spoke only broken English. His accent was French; maybe he was from Martinique. He understood "Washington National Airport," though, and they drove through the fading daylight.

Fern appeared at the gate wearing a heavy coat and gingerly carrying several sacks and bundles. As she embraced Megan, she whispered. "I know Mark. It's a horrible mistake." Fern had worked in the prosecutor's office in Madison when both Mark and Megan were there, and then she had gone with Megan to Ripon. She'd been a witness to the whole romance.

"I feel like I'm going crazy," Megan said. She hadn't dared say that to Iris, but Fern was like family.

"You probably do. Well, I'm here now, and maybe I can carry part of the load. And speaking of load, I brought three huge suitcases."

At the luggage terminal Ferguson helped lift Fern's heavy, oversized suitcases off the conveyer and onto a luggage carrier. While he looked for a cab, Megan explained to Fern about his presence. "They'll probably give you a bodyguard, too," she said. She and Iris had decided that Fern would share their suite until they moved on Thursday, with Iris sleeping on the folding couch in the living room. They'd argued about it for a while, but Iris had won by saying that Megan was the target of some nut, and she would be safer in the bedroom. But when she told Fern about the plan, the secretary shook her head. And when Megan told the taxi driver, this time a young Pakistani, to head for Embassy Suites, she said, "No, Driver. I have a furnished apartment waiting for me."

"A what? Aren't you going to live with Iris and me in my flat?"

"Well, I'll be about ten streets away, in Washington Circle. I rented a place through an agent," she said.

"An agent?"

The secretary blushed. "If you have to know, I did it on the World Wide Web. They have a service called RentNet." Megan started to protest, but Fern's smile had always assured Megan that the world was all right, and it did so now.

"Not Embassy Suites. Washington Circle," Fern told the driver, and handed him a slip of paper with the address, 2250 Halloran, written in her neat, small hand.

The paper reminded Megan of the one Iris had found in her pocket. Fern was chattering about the weather in Wisconsin and the comical male flight attendant. Finally, Megan asked, "Fern, did you ever give me an address for Robert Linderman?"

Fern frowned. "Let's see. I don't think I ever...oh, no, Megan, remember? When we wanted to arrange the Kaukauna debate, we did it through campaign headquarters in Madison. We didn't have his home phone number or his address."

"That's right! Then—" She stopped, not wanting to say someone had to have stuck the slip of paper in her pocket the day she flew out of Appleton, Wisconsin. She could think of only one person who had been with her after she dressed in the black suit, and that was Iris. And Iris certainly wouldn't want to implicate her in Linderman's murder, would she?

She pushed the thought out of her mind. "What did you think of Linderman?"

Fern laughed. "As little as possible. I only met him once in the flesh, and I wanted to wash my hand after he shook it. I don't know what it was about him." She dug through her purse and pulled out a set of keys. "I'd better be ready," she said. When they crossed twenty-third street, Megan realized how close Washington Circle was to the hotel.

"You'll eat with us tonight at the hotel after you drop off your things, won't you?" she asked. "It's just around the corner."

Fern laughed again and held up one of her plastic shopping bags. "Megan, dear, it's already six o'clock, and I need a whole evening alone to recover from the trip. I have a frozen, cooked chicken breast and a plastic bag of tossed salad in this sack, and my sheets and towels are in the blue suitcase." Fern had always been a model of efficiency. So was Iris, but the fifty-two-year-old Fern usually looked relaxed and always spoke in soft, slow tones. She was a widow who'd worn her dark blond hair the same way for the eight years Megan had known her; she usually dressed in tailored suits and most of her blouses were pastel, many with bows in the front.

She wasn't really overweight; she just had a short, soft body.

The apartment house was red brick, about sixty-five years old, and the stairs to the second floor made Megan glad Ferguson was there to help with the baggage. Inside, the apartment was clean and the beige furniture unsoiled. Fern opened a suitcase, took out a framed watercolor painting of a lake in northern Wisconsin, and hung it in place of the Currier and Ives print over the sofa.

"My daughter did that watercolor," she said proudly, hiding the other print behind her couch. Then she stuck several scribbled sheets of paper on the refrigerator with decorative magnets from her purse, explaining that these were her grandchildren's latest master-pieces. She hung peach-colored towels in her bathroom, set her travel cosmetic case on the counter, and put paper plates and cups in the kitchen cupboard. Within a few minutes, the apartment looked very much like the one Fern had lived in in Ripon. She opened one of the big shopping bags and took out a philodendron plant that she set on the dinette table. Finally she unpacked her Bible and several new magazines to arrange on the coffee table. Megan helped her make her bed with sheets, blankets, and a rose-printed bedspread, all from the blue suitcase.

"I don't need any more help now," Fern said as Ferguson hefted the other two bags onto her bed. "I just have to hang up my clothes, and I have thirty hangers in the black suitcase. You go home and eat. I'll come to your room in the morning, and we can all ride downtown together."

"This is amazing," Megan said. She had never seen anyone create an ambience so fast and so easily. ""We've been here less than an hour, and you've turned the place into a home. Do you have more things coming by freight?"

"Oh, no, I gave away everything to my girls except my computer and printer. Those should arrive tomorrow. If they don't, I'll have to wait until after New Year's.

"You gave your things away? But we may not be here forever, Fern."

"I figure I'll be here at least six years. If you're reelected, I'll stay another term, but if you're not, I'll retire then and go live with my sister in Florida. I do need to buy some dishes and pans tomorrow." She placed a clock radio on the bedside table and switched on soft music.

Ferguson was standing in the entryway, waiting for orders. Megan kissed Fern good-bye and put on her coat. "Let's walk," she told her bodyguard. "It's only four blocks." She missed the daily walk to and from her Ripon law office. Her run the other night had told her she was out of shape after too many months of campaigning.

When she and Ferguson arrived at the hotel suite, their cheeks pink from the cold, she sank onto the couch in her red coat and picked up the tourist magazine the maids had left on the coffee table. In the back was a map of the city that included the Metro routes and the points of interest. She hadn't done much to explore her city, what with one crisis after another invading her life.

"What I wouldn't give for one peaceful day, to go to the Air and Space Museum or something," she said to Iris, who had come home just before Megan and was hanging up her coat. Their bodyguards were outside in the gallery, waiting for the shift change. In a moment two other agents would come and accompany them to dinner.

"I know." Iris sat down on the edge of a dark blue chair. "Meg, what do you have planned for tonight?"

"Intense sleep. How about you?"

"Brenda called. She wants us to come to their Bible study. At Willie's restaurant at eight o'clock." She straightened the stack of file folders on the table. "I think I'll go, whether you do or not."

The thought of Rick's wholesome smile and Brenda's hospitality were irresistible. "I'll go," she said. "Let me change into a pair of slacks, and we'll eat downstairs." She stepped out of her gray skirt and hung it up, then slipped on black slacks. The black blouse she was wearing would be fine, she decided. Actually, so would the gray suit jacket. "Are you ready?"

"Yes, and hungry." Iris had somehow already changed into her navy blue dress and navy shoes. She never wore slacks except on picnics. "Meg, did you ever get lunch today? You were just starting on your soup when I got there."

"You're right! No wonder I feel so light-headed." They stepped outside the door and found Mills and Markov, the evening agents, waiting for them.

"To dinner," Iris said. Mills accompanied them while the other man stayed to watch the suite. They walked through the atrium, where hotel guests were drinking soft drinks and cocktails or filling wooden bowls with popcorn and pretzels. As they entered the restaurant, Megan felt too tired to eat, but she forced herself to consume spinach and pasta. Mills sat ramrod straight and spoke only when spoken to. When they went back to their suite, the guards stayed in the hall.

"Okay, where did you say the Bible study is?"

"At Willie's, in Georgetown. We could walk if you like. But it's cold."

Refreshed by the thought of another walk, Megan slipped into her down jacket and gloves. "All right," she said. "Let's go see if God can fix our lives."

They left too early to hear the phone ring.

# NINETEEN

T
om held the phone with his shoulder and chin while he dug a business card out of his wallet. Why hadn't the Oshkosh police let him know they'd made another arrest? They were still holding Henry Arlow here in Washington, for crying out loud, waiting for the extradition papers to arrive.

"Oshkosh Police Department," said a female voice. Tom checked the card in his left hand, then asked to speak to the detective who had worked on the Linderman murder and interviewed Mindora Arlow.

"He isn't in," said the woman at the other end. "However I can connect you with—"

"Let me speak to the chief, then, please. Tell him it's Tom Warburton."

"He isn't in, either. Would you like to leave a—"

"This is the FBI in Washington, D.C.," Tom said. "Please patch me through to wherever he is immediately. This is urgent." She apparently put him on hold, because the next sound he heard was the voice of Jimmy Buffet singing "Margaritaville."

*We've got to straighten this out. Somebody's throwing my name around and now Megan won't even speak to me. And what do they have on this Combs guy that's better than the evidence pointing to Arlow?*

As she entered the banquet room of the restaurant, Iris kept her eyes on Rick. He was standing at the front of the room near a small table, nodding and smiling at the men and women who were filling the chairs. People who knew each other were chatting, some standing in small clusters at the back of the room. When the vice president arrived in a cloud of Secret Service agents, Rick reached out to shake hands, but he didn't move to talk to anyone. Brenda was seated at the table, making notes in the margins of her Bible.

Iris sat down in the far corner of the back row, with Megan and Agent Mills following. Iris didn't want to talk to people around her or join in any activity; she was there for one thing only: She wanted to see if the Bible story had any truth to it. Or at least any truth she could capture for her own life.

When most of the seats were filled, Rick said a brief prayer, then picked up the Bible Megan had given them for Christmas, and stepped forward.

"Our study tonight continues where we left off in the Epistle of Jude. Move to verses 5 and 6. Let's take a look at the fifth verse, which says, 'But I want to remind you, though you once knew this, that the Lord, having saved the people out of the land of Egypt, afterward destroyed those who did not believe.'"

Brenda rose and secured a map of northern Africa to the wall with picture clay as Rick continued to read, "'And the angels who did not keep their proper domain, but left their own abode, He has reserved in everlasting chains under darkness for the judgment of the great day.' We don't know much about fallen angels," Rick continued, glancing at Megan with a brief grin.

*Get to it,* Iris thought. *Come to the part about God and me.*

"But we are cognizant of what's happening on the Egyptian borders at this very moment. Libyan and Sudanese troops are massing, ready to be deployed. Libya alone has enough ordnance to destroy Egypt, especially if she makes preemptive air strikes over the Nile Delta. But the God who delivered the people of Israel into the Sinai will save a people out of the land of Egypt again, and it's my belief that he desires our help in doing that."

Iris shuffled through the Gideon Bible she'd brought from the hotel, but she couldn't find Jude. It probably didn't matter; Rick was already out of her range of interest.

"Egypt, Libya, and Sudan may hold the keys to the world's future," Rick said, pointing loosely to the area on the map. "And I am constrained to say that our country's participation is absolutely required. I've never been one for eschatological speculation, but I'm now aware that the sooner the United states gets onto Libyan soil, the sooner Christ's work can be done. Libya has now declared war on Egypt, just as Revelation 11 tells us she will."

He flipped the pages in his Bible, and as he began to read again, Iris shut him off. She could see he wasn't going to tell her how to know God. She glanced over at Megan, who was staring at Rick with apparent alarm.

"What's the matter?" Iris whispered. "You look upset."

"I am. Do you get what he's saying? He's telling us we should declare war on Libya. And the room is full of members of Congress. Iris, if this is what—"

The woman in front of them turned slightly and put her finger to her lips, and they settled back in their chairs. Iris began mentally planning the next day's office activities; she would get Bryan to move the wooden file cabinets into her office area, and then she'd start in on those files.

At the end of the study time, waiters carried in tea and coffee urns and Styrofoam cups, along with platters of cookies and Christmas fruit cake. Iris took a cup of hot tea and dropped a dollar bill into the basket labeled Coffee Donations. She stayed close to Megan, who waved at Luke and Priscilla, weaving through the crowd to greet them.

"How did you like it?" Priscilla asked in her bright voice.

Megan looked at Luke and raised her eyebrows slightly. "I'd like to hear what Luke thinks." She looked down at her teacup.

"No comment now," he said quietly.

Iris poured a cup of decaf for Megan. Priscilla opened her mouth to speak when Brenda joined them.

"I'm so glad to see you two!" she said, embracing Megan and Iris at the same time.

"And you Callons, too. Megan, did your grandparents and Ruthie get home all right? And did you like our little study?"

Nearby, the vice president, flanked by Secret Service agents, was talking to two congressmen.

"Little study?" Iris said. "This looks to me like a pretty influential group of people. Well, we've got to go," she added, squeezing Megan's arm slightly. "We're both snowed under with work, aren't we?" She nodded at Agent Mills, who was lurking a foot or so away, looking morose. "And we've got to let our bodyguard call in his report." She had been carrying her coat; now she put it on and pulled her gloves out of her pocket. "Put on your mittens, Megan," she said. "I'm sure you haven't forgotten how cold it is walking outside."

"Oh, no, you don't," Priscilla said. "Luke and I are leaving now, too. We'll drive you back to your hotel." She kissed Brenda goodbye, then took Megan's arm and headed her toward the door. Mills strode forward and retrieved Megan's arm, pushing her almost roughly behind him.

Rick interrupted his good-byes and rushed to intervene. He put his arms around Megan from behind and drew her backward against his chest as she struggled and yelled, "Stop it!"

"Stay away from this woman, whoever you are!" Rick shouted.

"Freeze! FBI!" Mills yelled, drawing his .45 and pointing it at Rick. Four people hit the floor. Five more squatted behind chairs, and the others tried to get behind one another. Secret Service agents surrounded the vice president and pushed him out the door; two remained and drew their guns.

Megan managed to push Rick's arms away, saying, "Oh, for crying out loud, Rick, he's the FBI. Let go of me!"

Rick sighed, released her, and raised his hands, shamefaced. "All right, folks," he said. "You can all get up now. I'm through being a hero for a while."

For a moment, the tension in the room was heavy enough to make the floor sag. Then Mills holstered his gun. So did the Secret Service agents, but the vice president didn't return. Luke Callon, who had dropped to his hands and knees, began to laugh. So did Iris, who was leaning against the soft-drink vending machine near the refreshment table. Eventually, they were all laughing, brushing themselves off, grabbing the edges of chairs to pull themselves up.

Priscilla, who had frozen against the wall, reached out to help her graying husband get up. She shook her head sadly.

"Wow! I only wanted to give my friends a ride home," she said. "I didn't realize the law was going to object."

"Can we still get that ride?" Iris asked.

The trip home was quiet until Priscilla said, "Well, outside of the scene with poor Agent Mills here, how did you folks like the study?"

Iris waited, wondering if she had missed something. Mills was looking out the window.

Finally, Megan spoke. "I thought it was dangerous," she said. "Rick surely knew how strong his influence was on some of those who have to vote this week on sending troops into Sudan."

"It wasn't like him," Luke said. "Last week, when he started the book of Jude, he was talking about the gift of salvation and the verse that says, 'Mercy, peace, and love be multiplied to you.' I don't know what got into him tonight, but he was treading on dangerous ground."

Iris was relieved. Rick just had an off night. She would give him one more chance. She said so when they were out of the Callons' car, but Megan didn't hear her. She was wondering when she had left the torn white handkerchief in her jacket pocket. When had she worn the down coat? Last winter. Probably when she went sledding with Mark. It was a man's handkerchief with a blackened hole in the middle. Like a bullet hole.


Mark looked at the dark blue bruise on his left wrist where a handcuff had pinched his skin for more than an hour. He felt completely disoriented: One day he was the respected district attorney of a county in Wisconsin; the next, he was sitting in a jail cell with an open toilet, charged with the murder of Robert Linderman. Now he was out on bail, but temporarily suspended from the Wisconsin Department of Justice until the grand jury could be convened on January 7.

"My client did not know Robert Linderman," Andrew Foss had told the police over and over. "Furthermore, on the critical dates, he was in Milwaukee, attending a seminar on Miranda exclusions. Have you checked with the hotel?"

"You could have driven up here, killed Linderman, and gone back for the evening session," they answered, ignoring Foss and the fact that Mark hadn't driven his car to Milwaukee.

Today the police chief had "dropped by" his house to chat with him again.

"I rode to Milwaukee with Angela Purvis, one of the assistant DAs," Mark said for the fourth time. "Ask her."

"As you well know, Ms. Purvis has left the country."

Mark smiled. Angela had gone to her brother's place in Montreal for Christmas and would be back the day after New Year's. "Well, until you question her, I can't tell you more. Furthermore, I'm not going to answer anything unless Andy Foss is here with me." Mark knew his rights. He also knew that once he was indicted, one of his own assistants, maybe even baby-faced Angela Purvis, would have to conduct the prosecution. Unless Andy got him a change of venue, which was unlikely. The case against him was flimsy. All they had was a postcard, maybe two, with cryptic messages on them, and he wasn't going to volunteer any information about Gail. And what about Henry Arlow? If the police were going on circumstantial evidence, they had a stronger case against Arlow. He was in the area, his whereabouts were unaccounted for, and he had reason to want Linderman dead.

Well, they couldn't hold two people for murder. Why was Arlow still in Washington? Had they given up extradition?

He was desperate to speak to Megan. But would she talk to a man accused of murder? He imagined her eyes and her smile and the beguiling way she had of standing absolutely motionless when someone was talking to her. Well, unless something happened fast, he wouldn't be there for her swearing-in. And if the grand jury indicted him, the prosecutor was sure to ask for the death penalty.

~~~~~

"What do you think?" Priscilla asked Luke as they drove away from Megan's hotel. "About Rick, I mean."

Luke repeated his earlier assessment of the study. "I don't know what got into him tonight. He usually just talks about the unconditional love of God and our responsibility to proclaim the gospel."

"Apparently the action in Egypt got him off track. Luke, you won't vote to send troops in, will you?"

"Do I look suicidal? That place is a hotbed. Every international crazy or ex-spy is hiding out in Libya, and the country has a mercenary army ready to strike. Both Egypt and Libya may have the bomb. The Sudan could end up as a nuclear wasteland."

Priscilla leaned back against the headrest. "I'm glad I just stick to lawyering, not international relations. I had hoped when the cold war was over with Russia and the Eastern bloc countries, we could relax."

"Now we're in danger of not a cold war but a hot one. We have to watch everywhere these days," Luke said as he stopped at the red light on Twenty-fourth Street.

Priscilla recited, "'The devil walks about like a roaring lion, seeking whom he may devour.'"

"Well, he may be ready to devour peacemakers. I just hope he doesn't show up as the majority leader." He turned onto their street. He wasn't smiling. "We'll see what happens on the Senate floor this week."

"And I've got an argument to write for the Supreme Court." She reached up to flick the button on the garage-door opener. "I hope I can be as persuasive as Rick is."


Amelia Hutchins was twenty years younger than her corpulent husband, the majority leader of the Senate. When they married, he was forty-six, and she was a Ph.D. candidate in political science, working part-time in his office. She wasn't in love with her husband, had never been in love with him, and he knew it; but she had a built-in social position and, what with Hutchins's inheritance and investment, and his perks as majority leader, she now had enough money to live well without being employed. In return for her status, she was unfailingly affectionate, an efficient and creative homemaker who managed the help well, and a brutal campaigner for her husband. In the twelve years since they had been married, she had effectively destroyed his opposition. She became his campaign manager, arranging debates, setting up caucuses, and writing policy speeches. She created television ads that convinced the people of Tennessee that Senator Roland Wickham Hutchins was their only hope in the confused and broken world.

Amelia was also a perfect hostess. She knew whom to invite to what party, she dressed impeccably, she never forgot a name. Now she was in charge of a Senate reception in the East Room of the White house, and she was going over the guest list one last time. Newly elected Senator Allworthy would be alone; his wife was still in Arizona, selling their house. Senator Auburg, yes, with his wife and mother; Senator Bigelow, down with pneumonia, not coming. Senator Brujegski, yes, with wife and her parents; Senator Callon, yes, with wife and son. When she got to Senator Megan Likely, she noted that the family guests had been crossed off, due to what? She racked her brain for a moment, not wanting to make a faux pas at the party. Ah, that's right. Senator Likely's friend had been shot in the cathedral, and the family had gone home. She would be coming alone.

Amelia wrote a reminder to herself to ask Senator Likely about her grandparents and the man's widow; she'd have her friend in Fairfax get her a news printout about the National Cathedral murder. And one about the daughter of the senator from Maine; the girl had won some kind of scholarship, and Amelia wanted to be sure to congratulate her.

She checked her notes. Guest list, complete. Flowers, to be delivered at 11:00 A.M. tomorrow. Orchestra, engaged. The president would appear at exactly 9:45. And the food...

She ran over the gourmet menu one more time. The food would be brought in by Table D'hote, the best caterer in town. She wasn't trusting the White House chefs with her beef Wellington and the holiday brioches.

Now. What should she do about Senator Arlow? He had been arrested, but reliable sources were saying he'd be released before they could extradite him. The Wisconsin police had another suspect. What if he and his wife showed up at the reception? Their invitations had gone out just like everyone else's, and before Arlow was arrested, Mindora had sent an acceptance. Should Amelia have White House security stop them at the door?

She decided that since Henry Arlow would still be a United States senator until the following Tuesday, she would have to admit him, albeit with misgivings.

CNN said the situation at the Sudan border was tense and an Egyptian soldier had been killed by a sniper. When the world news was over and *Showbiz Today* started, Megan turned off the TV and headed for the bedroom, stopping at the closet to check her long red crepe dress, the one she hadn't worn to church on Christmas. She wanted it for the reception the next evening. Apparently Iris, who was now curled up in her bed, had pressed the dress, because it was wrinkle free.

Ewok was standing on her bed with his head cocked in a question, so she shut the closet door and got under the covers, gave the dog his nightly biscuit, then picked up her three-week-old copy of *Wisconsin Law Review*. As she turned the pages, with Ewok as usual snuggled against her knees, she thought about the fiasco at Rick's Bible study. The others had laughed, but she'd been mortified by the event.

She turned off the lights and tried to sleep, but something kept niggling at her brain. Finally she got up and tiptoed back to the living room. She sat down at the round table and thumbed through the publicity file Iris had brought home to update. Yes, here was a clipping from the day after the election, a photograph of herself with sparkling lights spattering around her hair. She held the clipping under the hanging table lamp to see if she could identify the person standing in the background, as Tom Warburton had asked her to do. He was right: she'd have to use a magnifying glass. For an instant the television broadcast of Ben Tolufson's murder scene flashed into her mind, but she turned off the light and the thought and tiptoed back to bed.

# TWENTY

Amelia Hutchins stood beside the majority leader, just to the right of the double doors in the White House East Room. She wore a gray, ankle-length chiffon dress with a wide sash of pink satin; her long blond hair was tucked into a modest French roll. At thirty-eight, she was more beautiful than she had been at twenty, and the gossip mills ground constantly, always hoping for news that she had strayed from her marriage with a younger, more attractive man. They were always disappointed, but one rumor constantly floated to the surface: the one that said she was involved with a Virginia businessman.

Roland Hutchins, known to his friends and congressional colleagues as Rollie, was trying his best to breathe. He had begun to wheeze, probably because of the perfume worn by a number of the women who shook hands with him. He was sensitive to all scents, but especially to a popular fragrance called Firethorn. He had detected it several times, and now his right hand was plunged into his tuxedo jacket pocket, where he kept his albuterol inhaler. But first, he had to stop and shake hands with Senator Megan Likely, who was gowned in red, her hair piled in curls on top her head. Not only was she the youngest and probably best-looking member of the Senate; she had a legal mind like a steel trap. He was glad she'd be sitting on his side of the aisle.

"Senator-elect Megan Likely," Amelia murmured, and he smiled, thrusting out his hand, despite the fact that he couldn't exhale. As soon as Megan walked off without introducing her escort, he took a deep breath of the medicine, holding it until he could feel his bronchial tubes start to relax.

"Are you all right, dearest?" Amelia asked solicitously. She was always concerned with her husband's health, always compassionate and caring. She was a perfect wife, beautiful, bright, kind, and loving. Nobody in the whole world, including Rollie Hutchins, could prove that for the past six years she'd been having an affair.

"I'm okay, thanks, Amelia," he said as he welcomed the senator from Connecticut. He needed to get outside in the damp evening air; that would fix him up. Most of their guests had arrived, and it was a half hour before the president put in his appearance. The orchestra was playing a suite from *Cats,* and one elderly couple was dancing.

"I'll be right back," he wheezed. He slipped out the glass doors and stood looking up at the south portico of the White House. He could see only a few of the brightest stars; electric lighting in the District of Columbia had dimmed the heavens. If he were at home on the family estate in Tennessee, he'd be able to see lightning bugs flitting through the trees, and millions of stars. He'd also be able to breathe.

His present term would be over in four years. His physician kept telling him he'd die if he didn't lose sixty pounds and get out of the Beltway, so if he lived that long, he wouldn't file again for election. But in the meantime, he had to stay in Washington to run the government and keep an eye on his beautiful wife. Which was becoming harder and harder, so now he was putting a pair of detectives to work.

He would never divorce Amelia, but he needed solid proof of her infidelity, discreet though it be. Then he could make her sign a postnuptial agreement and cut her off from the rolling Tennessee farmland and woods, the great house with its white columns, the old drugstore he owned in the village, and the eighteen million dollars he had inherited and which was now tripling itself.

Megan sat on a gilt chair and looked up at the delicate plaster decoration on the ceiling and then at the three cut-glass chandeliers. She had planned to schedule a White House tour for Celia and Ruthie, but when Ben Tolufson was murdered, their vacation stopped. She hoped her grandparents were all right; they'd looked old and weary yesterday when they flew out. Celia had called late that evening to say they arrived all right and that a local funeral director had met the plane to whisk Ben away, but she didn't quite sound like herself.

The East Room chandeliers were as big as the Steinway grand piano whose gilt legs were carved to look like eagles, a gift, Priscilla Callon had said, to the White House from the piano manufacturer. On the long wall hung the famous full-length portrait of George Washington by Gilbert Stuart.

"They say Theodore Roosevelt's children used this room as a skating rink," Priscilla said. She did, as Brenda had told Megan, wear her clothes over and over: she was clad in the same high-necked burgundy princess dress she'd had on at her dinner party.

Megan imagined children on skates, hurtling across the polished parquet floor, jamming into the gold draperies and the fluted paneling, tumbling over gilt chairs, and shrieking at one another. The scene was a huge contrast to the present one, where beautifully dressed women and men in black tie were sipping beverages and talking in soft voices.

"Would you like to dance?" said a voice in her ear, and she looked up to see Tom Warburton.

"I came to relieve Agent Mills," he said. "Go home, Pete, and play with your kids."

"They're in bed," Mills said, rising. "But my wife will be glad to see me." His tuxedo fit badly; it was either rented or borrowed. Tom, on the other hand, wore his dinner clothes easily. He pulled Megan to her feet and began to dance right there beside the table. Luke and Priscilla looked surprised, but they nodded approvingly.

"You look wonderful," Tom said as he moved her toward the middle of the room. The top of her head came exactly to his shoulder.

"You don't look too shabby either. But, Tom, I can't forgive you for trying to pin Linderman's murder on Mark Combs."

"Why do you think I came here tonight? I finally got a fax copy of the letter I was supposed to have written. I have it with me if you want to see it. Megan, it was on paper the FBI hasn't used for five years, and the signature is nothing like mine."

He looked sincere, but…

"And why would I lie to you? I don't know anything about this Combs guy. In fact, I had never heard his name till you told me I was supposed to have tipped off the police about him."

She was silent a moment, finally saying, "Well, you're not a bad dancer. However, since I haven't danced since my high-school prom, I'm hardly one to judge."

"Have you ever been married?"

She looked up, surprised.

"I'm sorry," he said. "It's none of my business. I usually don't get into the private lives of the people in my cases." The music turned into a waltz, and as he guided her to the center of the floor, they swung in one giant circle after another.

"Where did you learn to dance?" she panted. They were at the center of the room, now; she could feel the hem of her dress whirling as they turned.

"My mother taught me. And if I didn't know you had to be at least thirty to be a senator, I'd swear your high school prom was last year."

The waltz ended, and several people applauded. Megan didn't get a chance to answer Tom's compliment because the orchestra started "Hail to the Chief." The president and his wife were in the doorway, flanked by Secret Service. And the vice-presidential couple were right behind them, also surrounded. The four arranged themselves near the Washington portrait and shook hands with the majority leader and his wife, the minority leader and her husband, and then began greeting the senators and their families. When Megan's turn came, Tom stood back discreetly; the President said, "I saw part of that waltz, Senator. It's just as I feared. You're going to dance circles around all of us."

Tan Luyin kissed Megan's cheek and murmured, "I'm so sorry about your grandparents' friend. You and they are in my prayers."

*She spoke to me as if we were friends, but everyone has heard about the murder; that's why the First Lady remembers. Her secretary probably reminded her.*

She shook hands with Vice President Barnes, who nodded and said, "Welcome to the Senate." His wife wore a designer gown but still managed to look frumpy, and her flyaway hair was already slipping out of its bun. She made a poor foil for the president's dazzling little wife.

General Martinez, of the Joint Chiefs, suddenly appeared. He was dressed in a black polo shirt and slacks, and he stood out among all the dinner clothes. Martinez strode to the president and whispered something in his ear. President Jackson looked shocked; he leaned across his wife and beckoned to the vice president, and the two of them, accompanied by the general, disappeared. Silence hung over the room like a mist for a few moments, and then the orchestra began to play again.

Megan accompanied the Callons back to their table, with Tom following. "What do you think?" she asked Luke.

"Well, it must be a military matter. I just hope it doesn't mean an all-out war in Egypt."

Luke's hopes were in vain. In less than a half hour, the president returned and held his hands up for silence.

"I need to inform you that Libya has invaded Sudan, and Egypt has declared war," he said. His famous smile was absent; in fact, he looked like a man just informed of the death of a close friend. Megan wondered what presidency did to a person.

As he began to describe what this might mean to the United States, Megan bit her lip.

She had hoped to be part of a government that stabilized the domestic economy, found a way to keep the streets safe, and made a real effort to solve the drug problem that was consuming the country's youth. Instead, when she took the oath of office in four days, she might be looking at the possibility of war.

"And so," President Jackson continued, "I'm going to ask the majority and minority leaders and members of the Senate Armed

Services Committee to join me up in the Oval Office. I apologize for ruining your beautiful party, Amelia," he added, nodding toward Mrs. Hutchins. "And I hope the rest of you still have enough Christmas left in your hearts to keep dancing." He turned and left the room, stopping to gather up his wife and take her up the stairs.

Luke Callon was not one of those who hurried after him, even though he was on the Armed Services Committee.

"I'm afraid the world may be in for another expensive real-estate war," Luke said. He looked tired. "Pris, come with me and let's shake some hands, and then I'll put you in a cab."

"Would you introduce me to whomever you think I ought to know?" Megan said. "And then I'll leave, too." The shining party spirit was gone. Ben Tolufson was dead. Mark was accused of murder. And Megan had to go home to think and to do some reading about the strife along the Nile. She followed the Callons around the room, shaking hands with the men and women who would share the Senate chamber with her, and their spouses, women in exquisite gowns and men who had perfect manners. Finally, she turned to say good-bye to her hostess, but she couldn't see Amelia Hutchins anywhere in the room; so she nodded to Tom, and they headed for the coat room. As he helped her into her coat, she said, "No."

"No? No what?"

"No, I've never been married," she said.


Andrew Foss was trying to quit smoking, and his disposition had turned sour. The nicotine patch he had on his left shoulder was itching fiercely, and his mouth felt like the inside of an old sneaker. But he hadn't lost his legal acumen; it was now almost murderous in its sharpness as he leaned across the desk of the Oshkosh chief of police.

"I understand my client gave you the name of a witness who could vouch for his presence in Milwaukee but you failed to follow that lead," he said, reaching inside the neck of his blue plaid flannel shirt to loosen the itchy nicotine patch.

"As you well know, the party in question is out of the country," the chief said.

"And as *you* well know, she left a telephone number. Did you even bother to call her up?" Foss squinted over the tops of his reading glasses. "And did you, for that matter, check with any other participants in the seminar my client was attending?"

"How am I supposed to track down any of those people? They all went home long before we arrested Combs."

"Ah!" Foss exclaimed in his hoarse semiwhisper. "Ah! But lo, I have discovered something called the conference roster. Everybody at the seminar got one." He waved a sheet of paper at the chief's face. "And if you take the trouble to actually read this list, you'll notice that two people have their names and addresses circled. That's because they also rode in Angela Purvis's car. And one of them lives—be still my heart!—lives right here in Oshkosh, Chief Busch." His yellow-stained teeth clenched in a grim smile as he passed the sheet of paper across the desk.

Busch sighed. "I still feel pretty sure I can make the case against Combs stick," he said without conviction. "The grand jury convenes on Monday. I presume you've subpoenaed these folks?"

"Subpoenaed, and even offered rides to the courthouse," Foss said. He thought about strangling the chief, setting fire to the building, and possibly throwing himself off a cliff. Instead, he reached inside his pocket and took out a stick of nicotine gum. As the juice ran under his tongue and a jolt of nicotine shot into his bloodstream, he relaxed. He had the chief by the short hairs. He went in for the kill. "Now. I understand you've gone and dropped the charges against Henry Arlow," he said with another unpleasant smile.


Arlow was asleep in his airline seat, clutching his ticket to Chicago in his right hand; every few moments he would jump, paw the air with his left, open his eyes to glance at his ticket, and fall back to sleep. Since the flight was direct from Washington to Chicago, and since he had brought a carry-on but checked no luggage, he no longer needed the ticket. He'd purchase a shuttle ticket to Madison when they got to O'Hare.

He kept dreaming of the Capitol rotunda. He was looking up at the dome, where a circle of dark painted figures were standing around a fire; somehow he knew they were from Sudan. One of the androgynous figures suddenly moved and turned his way. "Tickets," it said, and Arlow held up his ticket. "This won't do," the creature said. "Now we will have to go to war." The painted fire in the dome flared downward and began to lick at his face, and the senator jumped and rumbled.

Finally he sat up straight, his eyes open wide. His chest felt tight; in fact, he had told his friend on the way to the airport that his chest felt…full. Almost ready to explode. His friend, who had driven him to the airport, had suggested he loosen his tie a little, and offered him a packet of Tums.

"You'll be fine," the friend had said as he pulled up to the curb in front of Northwest Airlines, but now Arlow wondered if maybe the flight attendants had some more antacid tablets or something. He felt terrible. He reached for the call bell and then fell back against the seat, panting madly, pulling at his shirt collar with his index finger. When the flight attendant arrived a moment later, he was in the grip of a major coronary, and he tumbled over the arm of his seat.

Two attendants lugged him to the back of the plane and started CPR while the other one picked up her phone to speak to the plane's captain, saying she wasn't sure they'd be able to revive the passenger.

# TWENTY-ONE

Megan stood in the center of her living room and sighed. The movers had brought all the furniture and had set the larger pieces in place, but now there were forty-four boxes of papers, books, and household goods to unpack. As she unwrapped the last piece of her mother's china, her stomach was growling.

"I've got to eat something," she said, looking at her watch. "My gosh, it's five o' clock, and we never ate lunch. Or even much breakfast, just a muffin. Let's go down to that little café on Nineteenth."

"Oh, no," Iris said. "Tonight we're eating in." She smiled and opened the refrigerator door. She took out two large baking potatoes, a raw sirloin steak, garlic, and a plastic bag of mixed greens.

"Iris! When did you do this?"

"While you were shelving books. Fern gave me the idea, and there's a small market just two blocks from here." She took a fork from the silverware drawer and poked holes in the potatoes, then thrust them into the microwave. "And the electric frying pan is here." She opened a cupboard and took the pan out. "Okay, go relax, and I'll have dinner in fifteen minutes."

"Oh, sure. I'll just go stretch out and watch television while you slave over a hot skillet." She emptied the greens into a large saucepan because the bowl wasn't unpacked. "Do we have any salad dressing?"

"Three kinds. Ranch, Italian, and raspberry vinaigrette." Iris turned on the skillet and began rubbing the steak with a garlic clove.

In twenty minutes they were sharing the vinyl-upholstered breakfast nook with boxes of papers that Megan had not unpacked. They had rented a three-bedroom apartment so they could have an office; the movers had brought Megan's father's big oak desk from the office at Likely and Twiss, and Iris's French Provincial one from her real-estate office in Madison.

They had decided to use Megan's furniture, but Iris had brought her own bedroom suite; like her desk, it was French Provincial and in mint condition. They had the movers set Megan's black walnut table and chairs in the dining area, but they knew they'd eat most of their meals in the dark blue vinyl breakfast nook.

Slicing into her steak, Megan said, "Why did you go into real estate when you can cook like this?"

"The pay was better." Iris took a second helping of salad. "I feel guilty, eating when poor Mr. Mills is sitting outside the door."

"His relief should be here soon," Megan said. It wouldn't be Tom; he was in Wisconsin again, at the grand jury inquiry where Mark was the accused. Thinking about the event made her mind wander until she realized Iris was asking her—what?

"I said, are you going to be okay for tomorrow? Do you need anything pressed?"

"I'm going to wear my black suit again. I assume you're going to be there tomorrow?" Ewok, who had been lying by her feet, barked a short, questioning woof.

"No, you can't go." Megan said, looking down at the dog's bright eyes. "And you're not getting any of my steak. But we'll take you for a walk after dinner. Iris, you will be there for **my** swearing-in, won't you?"

"Try to keep me away." She looked thoughtful. "Mark won't be able to come, will he?"

"I guess not. He's going before the grand jury." She looked down at her plate and rearranged her salad. "I wish he'd never called me. I was better off not hoping for anything. But I do know he couldn't have murdered Linderman; in fact, I doubt they ever even met."

Much of the snow on Mark's farm had melted. The day was almost springlike, but since this was only the first week in January, he knew the worst weather might be yet to come. Besides that, he was cold inside.

His freezer was full of food, his cleaning service had left the place spotless, and a pair of new movies lay on his VCR, ready for viewing; but the day felt empty. Finally, he reached for the telephone and called Embassy Suites in Washington, D.C.

"I'm sorry," the clerk at the desk said. "Senator Likely and Ms. Millman checked out this morning."

"This is the district attorney of Fond du Lac, Wisconsin. It's a matter of great urgency that I know Senator Likely's whereabouts."

"I'm sorry, sir. The only address we have is the Russell Senate Building. Maybe you could try there."

He didn't respond but dropped the phone into its cradle. He stared out the window at the northwest pasture. Protected by thick rows of trees as a windbreak, it still had wide white patches of snow lying on the dark brown soil. Next summer the field would be thick with dark green cornstalks, but now it looked as cold and empty as Mark felt.

Tomorrow, Megan would take her oath of office as a United States senator. He hadn't been sure when he talked to her if she really wanted him there. Well, he wouldn't be there in any event, because tomorrow he would testify before the grand jury.

He sank into his brown plaid chair and picked up the remote control. In a moment, scenes of battle in the streets of Khartoum, Sudan, flashed onto the screen. All American embassy personnel were being flown out of Sudan this morning, and Egyptian President Alkabarih would address the United Nations in an hour. He began surfing the channels. As he passed a religious station, he saw a vaguely familiar man named Samuelson in dialogue with the program's host.

"Well, although no man may know the exact hour, I suspect

that Christ is at the very verge of returning," Samuelson was saying to the host. "Even those who have been dubious about a pretribulation rapture are now interested in the world situation. And if the United States lays the groundwork for battle, it's my opinion that Jesus Christ will achieve the victory."

Mark turned to the next channel and watched a PBS special on crocodiles.


Mills's relief was a quiet man wearing a camel hair coat.

"Mason," he said.

"Okay. Are you in the mood for a walk?" Megan asked, holding Ewok under her arm. "We've got to take the dog out."

They decided to take the stairs instead of the elevator; after all, they were just one floor up, and they wanted some exercise. Megan set Ewok on the sidewalk and fastened his leash onto his red collar. He strained forward, spying a calico cat that crept between the bushes; then he coughed to let Megan know how uncomfortable the leash was.

"I thought when we left Wisconsin, the winter would be easier," Megan said. "This is practically down south, and I haven't seen a magnolia blossom yet." The skies were black, but the street lights made the whole Dupont Circle area bright. They walked as far as Hadley's, the coffee shop that faced the circle park; while Mason and Megan stood outside with the dog, Iris dashed in for two cups of espresso, Mason having declined one. Walking around the block, they sipped the brew through plastic lids, chatting about the next day's events.

"I'll be a real senator tomorrow."

"I hope you get a good committee assignment." Iris took the lid off her cup and put it in her pocket.

"Being an absolute newcomer with no political clout, I'll probably get on some obscure subcommittee or something. I wish I could be in a position to make decisions against getting involved with the Sudan war."

"What would you do at this point?"

"I still think we need to show restraint. I hate to admit it, but this time, the president's policy is right."

Ewok suddenly froze in his tracks. He looked over his shoulder and began to snarl, baring his lower teeth.

"Good evening," a voice said from behind them. Mason grabbed both women's arms. Megan managed to turn and saw Rick Samuelson, in a tan trench coat. Like them, he was drinking coffee from a Hadley's cup.

"Rick! What are you—" She stopped to pick up the growling dog. Why did Ewok hate the sight of Rick?

"I had to come into town on business, so Brenda sent over a casserole and some pastry. When you didn't answer your door, I got some coffee to bolster me up. Can I walk you home? I left the goodies in one of the cardboard boxes in the hall by your door, with a note."

"Come on, Ewok," she said, setting him on the sidewalk. "You've explored enough lampposts and fire hydrants for one night." The dog turned and raced toward Rick, yipping and growling. Iris snatched him up before he could bite another ankle.

"Rick, I'm sorry." Megan's cheeks had turned hot. "I've had Ewok since he was six weeks old, and I've never seen him act this way." Well, almost never. He hated Robert Linderman, too. "You must remind him of someone else."

"Or maybe he's catching the scent of my dogs. I have three Doberman pinschers."

"Three!" Iris said, petting Ewok's head. "Here, Meg, take your beast."

They began to walk toward the apartment complex, Ewok growling with every step, Mason beside Megan. As Iris unlocked their door, Mason sat down in the chair, and Rick leaned over one of the boxes they'd left in the hall. He lifted out a stack of foil-wrapped packages he'd parked there earlier. Megan pulled his note off the door; it said simply, "Look in the cardboard boxes," in Rick's thin, right-slanted handwriting.

"Whoa! This is beautiful!" Rick exclaimed, walking in and looking around the room.

"If you ignore the boxes and the crumpled newspaper." Megan put Ewok in the bathroom and told him in stern tones to behave himself, while Iris put Brenda's food offerings in the refrigerator.

"Casserole?" Iris exclaimed as she peeked under the foil. "This is no casserole. It's a plate of roast turkey and dressing. And a carton of gravy. And cinnamon rolls and cupcakes." Rick was wandering through the living and dining areas, looking at framed pictures that were on the floor and leaning against chairs.

"We'll eventually get settled," Megan said, coming from the hall. She reached down to pick up a small afghan that had slithered off the top of a box and down to the floor.

"I can see the whole apartment will be a delight. I hope you'll invite us over soon."

"Very soon."

Rick said he had to dash. Megan stood in the doorway and watched him saunter down the hall. He was whistling the hymn "Morning Has Broken."

"What a sweetheart," Iris said. "I could become a Christian with a guy like him around."

"Back to work," Megan said, lifting a box onto the table. She stopped at ten o'clock to get ready for bed and make a few notes on her yellow legal pad.


The intravenous monitor began to beep, and the ICU nurse stepped from the desk to put on a new bag. He watched the monitor for a moment, added fifty milligrams of lidocaine to the IV, then straightened the sheet over Henry Arlow's chest. The man was only semiconscious. If they could keep him alive for another day or two, the cardiologist would probably perform at least an angioplasty, or possibly even bypass surgery.

Arlow opened his eyes and said, "Mindora. Want Mindora."

"Sir?" These were the first words the nurse had heard the patient say.

"Wife."

"Your wife will be here in the morning, sir. Do you know where you are?"

Arlow's eyes roved wildly around the room; then he shook his head.

The nurse eyed the monitor again. He couldn't keep the man stabilized.

"You're in Chicago," he said. "You had a heart attack on the plane. Your wife will be here tomorrow." Arlow tried to speak but only made a choking sound. The heart rhythm shot up to a hundred and ninety, then flat-lined.

"Code blue!" the nurse yelled as he climbed up on the bed. Kneeling over his patient's body, he began CPR while three other nurses came running, one pushing the crash cart. "Lidocaine, epinephrine," he recited. His efforts weren't making any headway, but he kept the rhythmic pressure on Arlow's chest until the paddles were ready. When the other nurse shouted "Clear," he jumped down from the bed.

They shocked Arlow twice; the second time they got a jerky rhythm and began pumping medicine into him. When it was safe to leave him for a moment, the nurse called the cardiologist.

"Your airplane patient is going sour over here, Dr. Swaboda. He coded seven minutes ago, and we've got him going again, but it's not going to last."

The cardiologist said to prep Arlow for emergency bypass. "Is the wife here yet?"

"Tomorrow morning. She was with her children in Oshkosh. Do you want me to call her?"

"What time is it? Almost ten? She may not be able to get out tonight because of the storm. Go ahead and call her, but tell her she can't see him till morning anyway. I'll be there in twenty."

~ ~ ~ ~ ~

At 1:00 A.M., Wisconsin time, Police Chief Busch was leaning back in his desk chair with his eyes closed. He hoped the detective who had arrested Mark Combs would do well at the grand jury hearing; the evidence against Combs wasn't as weighty as Busch would like, but his gut feeling told him the man was guilty. There was some kind of connection with Senator-elect Likely; if the case went to trial, as he prayed it would, she would probably have to come testify. After all, Linderman had been her opponent's campaign manager. There had to be a link. Besides all that, Combs had been a thorn in police flesh for years, and Chief Busch wanted to get rid of him.

His phone rang, and he picked it up quickly so it wouldn't wake his wife.

"Busch," he said, and then he sat up straight. "What do you mean, he can't testify? He was on his way this afternoon. A what? A heart attack? Oh, swell." He slammed the phone down. Now the DA would have to present the case without the senator.

# TWENTY-TWO

D r. William Swaboda had performed about five hundred bypass surgeries in his career and had looked at a lot of hearts. This was one of the worst he'd ever seen.

"You say this was the guy's first heart attack?" he asked as he switched his patient onto the bypass machine. He watched the blood circulate up through a transparent tube, and then turned his attention back to Henry Arlow's heart. "Well, he may only *know* about one coronary, but look at this." He pointed with his scalpel at the lower part of the heart. "Some of this tissue has been dead for years." He pulled down his transparent plastic mask. "All right. Let's see what we can do."

An hour and forty minutes later, he had two sections of a vein from Arlow's leg attached to replace plugged arteries. He was just finishing the replacement of the third, the coronary artery at the top of the heart, when the alarm sounded. Drat! The fool was having a stroke!

Dr. Swaboda did not know Henry Arlow or anything about him. He didn't realize his patient was a senator or that he was needed to testify to the grand jury. But Swaboda was determined to save Arlow's life. He would, in fact, take it as an affront if any patient died while under his knife.

Eventually he got Arlow stabilized, but by now he'd been on the bypass machine long enough so that the anesthesiologist was warning him.

"All right, ready to close," he said, sighing with fatigue. "But we'll have to watch him for another stroke. I want someone by his bed at all times."

An hour after Arlow left the recovery room, his friend from Washington, D.C., arrived at O'Hare. He took a green Checker cab to the hospital and after making inquiries at the main desk, he rode the elevator up to the cardiac unit on the sixth floor.

Arlow was in a curtained cubicle a few feet from the nurses' station and the central monitor.

"You can stay for five minutes," Arlow's nurse said, glad of a few moments to run to the bathroom. Sometimes in ICU she didn't go for ten hours. "Less if he gets too excited. His wife will be back soon, and she has first privileges. If he shows any sign of a problem, yell for someone. He's never supposed to be alone."

"Fine," the man said, pushing the curtain back and standing beside the bed. Arlow was breathing through a ventilator. Tubes protruded from under the bandage on his chest; his bare left thigh was also bandaged.

The man smiled. He wouldn't even need five minutes.


Because of the time difference, Megan stood to take the oath of office at the same time Henry Arlow's friend arrived in ICU. The chief justice of the Supreme Court, the vice president, and the president pro tempore of the Senate all rose to face the group. Megan raised her right hand and repeated the vow read by Justice Minor, remembering her campaign promise to light up dark places. Now, at last, she'd have a chance to do something for her country and her state. And the first thing she was going to do was figure out who killed Ben Tolufson. A murderer was loose, and she wasn't going to stand for it.

When the oath of office was over, she waved up at Iris in the gallery, wishing she could see Mark there, too. Someone else was also waving at her: Brenda. She must have dashed over to the Senate right after the House convened.

Luke Callon embraced Megan and murmured, "You're going to be a wonderful senator."

The majority leader wheezed up to Megan's row of desks to plant a kiss on her cheek and said, "I'm happy you're here, Senator Likely."

Senator Likely! She'd been addressed that way for two months, but the title had been courtesy. Now she was really part of the lawmaking body of the government. So why didn't she feel teary and excited? Probably because she had murder hanging over her.

After a half hour of greetings and celebration, the vice president pounded his gavel on his desk, and sixty people sat down; the others rushed off to hearings and committee meetings. After his welcoming speech to the Senate, the vice president left and Martha Byrd, the president pro tempore, picked up the gavel.

"The clerk will read the names of the committee appointees," she said. "And if you don't like your appointments, kindly refrain from telling me." Her black face was wrinkled, but her eyes shone with intelligence and wit.

The clerk's voice singsonged the assignments: Senator Gordon Allworthy, to Ethics; Senator Frances Auburg, continuing in Ways and Means; Senator Yvonne Brujegski, Ethics; Senator Luke Callon, continuing in Armed Services. When the clerk said, "Senator Megan Likely, Armed Services," Megan was stunned. She knew they were required to put at least one freshman on each committee, but she hadn't thought she had enough clout to get in Luke Callon's group. It must have been Luke's influence. Or Senator Hutchins's. The majority leader liked her, she could tell.

"For what purpose does the majority leader rise?" Martha asked.

"I rise to ask for a reading of SB15, formerly SB9832, Madam President." Hutchins took his seat in the first row as the clerk began to read the bill and the pages handed out thick copies to each senator. Nobody really listened, except for some of the brand-new people. Senators wandered in and out of the chamber as the clerk read clause after clause of the bill that Megan and Hutchins had worked on. Megan found herself looking around the chamber, wondering how Ewok was doing in the office with Iris. He had accepted Iris easily, often sleeping with his small, fluffy head on her foot. She'd been glad to hear about Rick's Dobermans; perhaps it was the scent of Rick's dogs that made Ewok go crazy.

Suddenly she felt a light tap on her shoulder. It was Senator Hutchins, wheezing into her ear. "Will you be ready to speak for this bill the first thing tomorrow morning?"

Speak? She'd just been sworn in! She couldn't possibly!

"Of course," she said with a smile, and opened the first page of the document.

Mark sat in a chair outside the grand-jury room. They did not use a regular courtroom for the grand jury; instead, the eight men and women sat in writing-desk chairs in two short rows. Mark had been at scores of grand-jury hearings, but always in his capacity as district attorney. The police were testifying now, and his lawyer was inside. Mark trusted Andrew Foss, but he found himself fidgeting. What if he really was indicted?

Foss appeared in the doorway. He was dressed up for court, which meant he wore a stained blue necktie, a red plaid shirt, and black suspenders.

"C'mon, Mark. Go show 'em what fools they are."

"How long since you've smoked, now, Andy?"

The lawyer bared his teeth in one of his grim smiles. "Nineteen days," he said. "And I own a gun."

Mark chuckled and went into the grand-jury room.

The bailiff ushered him to a chair at the end of two long golden oak tables. The jurors included six women and two men; one man was possibly Hispanic, but maybe Italian.

After her first questions about his name, occupation, and history, the assistant DA stood. She was twenty-four years old; she'd been out of law school eighteen months, and she had never before prosecuted a murder, or even presented one to a grand jury.

"Mr. Combs, will you please tell us where you were on Sunday, December 15?"

"I was at a seminar on Miranda exclusions in Milwaukee. I believe I saw you there, Ms. Munsen."

Lisa Munsen's Norwegian ancestors had bequeathed her a

head of pale blond hair and thin, alabaster skin. She now flushed dark red and had to shuffle her papers several times to continue. Clearing her throat, she asked, "And do you have any proof that you didn't leave the conference at any time?"

"Yeah, I do." He nodded at the bailiff, who produced the affidavits Andy had given him from Mark's two roommates at the conference. As the man handed the documents to the clerk, Mark said, "These are sworn statements from my two roommates, who spent both days with me, stating I was never out of their sight. Furthermore, Angela Purvis is sitting right outside. She drove the car that took me to and from the conference."

Ms. Munsen, now bright scarlet, turned to stare at the police chief; he hung his head and twiddled with his key chain.

"I see no reason to continue," she said. "Do the jury members have questions?"

They all shrugged and shook their heads, No.

Lisa Munsen glared at the chief again and said, "The state withdraws." She left the room with her blue silk print dress whirling around her slender frame.

The jurors got up. The two men, both in baseball caps, stood for a moment talking about silage; all the women left.

"Well, you're sprung, Mark," Foss said, coming in from outside.

"I don't understand why we had this hearing. I had an airtight alibi."

"Ssssomebody thought they had a case," Foss hissed, glancing toward the chief, who now had his elbows on his knees, his hands clasped in front of him, and was staring at the space between his feet. He was just about to write a confession about his part in laundering the money Robert Linderman had embezzled from campaign funds.


Megan ate lunch in her office with Iris and Fern. Iris had brought her microwave to the office and they warmed up Brenda's turkey and dressing. They plunged in, moaning with pleasure.

"Ceelie got that ham dinner for Christmas, and I don't think I ate four bites of it," Megan said. "Maybe we ought to put the tree back up and start Christmas all over."

"Never again," Iris said. "All that tree brought us was bad luck."

"Well, I saved the angel decorations. Iris, you don't really believe in fate or luck, do you?"

"I'd like to believe in something," Iris said. "Shall we try Rick's Bible study again tonight? How about it, Fern? Want to go with us?"

"Oh, no, I've still got work to do at home. And I've found a lovely church at the end of my street. You two don't have to include me in everything you do."

Megan said, "I'll have to go straight home after the study because I have a little speech to write. In fact, if Rick gets off on the Middle East again, I may leave early." *And I want to write down some more thoughts about the murder. It has to be Bryan. And maybe his mother. But why?*

"I don't see how he'd think he could, with the House getting ready to vote on military appropriations for Egypt," Iris said.

Megan nodded. "The Senate Armed Services Committee wants to override the president's refusal to send in advisors. If they do, we'll have a joint session with the House."

After she finished her lunch, Megan took Ewok out for a stroll on his leash and was immediately approached by a man wearing a tarnished black coat over his frayed, dirty black jogging suit.

"Do you have any spare change?" he asked. He looked able bodied, but he was also carrying on a murmured conversation with someone she could not see.

She pulled a dollar out of her purse and handed it to him without looking in his face. She left wondering if the man was really poor. She took a deep breath of the wintry air and walked the entire length of Constitution Avenue, past the back of the Smithsonian castle, all the way to the Lincoln Memorial. The reflecting pool was frozen over, and children were skating on it despite the fact they were breaking a law and could have used the free rink only two blocks away. Ewok barked and sat down when Megan began climbing the stairs to see Abraham Lincoln. She picked him up and carried him up to the sculpture of the first Republican president.

"Ewok," she murmured into the dog's ear as she walked, "did you know the Republican party was born right in Ripon, Wisconsin, just a few blocks from my old office?" The dog cocked his head and she kept climbing.

She wanted to feel a surge of emotion when she looked at his statue, just as she'd hoped to feel more when she took the oath of office. Instead, she only felt admiration for the sculptor. But when she turned to the inscriptions on the walls, the Gettysburg Address, the Emancipation Proclamation, the Second Inaugural, she was moved. She especially loved the words "new birth of freedom," and she said them to herself again and again.

How had that rebirth of freedom manifested itself in the last hundred and thirty years? Pornographers were claiming immunity by the first amendment; criminals and madmen carried concealed weapons by the second. Schoolchildren were imbibing alcohol and dangerous drugs. She went back to the figure of Lincoln in his massive chair.

"I promise," she whispered. "I promise to do what I can to change things. I won't forget."

And then at last the rush of emotion came. She felt tears spring to her eyes. *This was my real oath of office,* she thought. Standing in the memory of Abraham Lincoln and swearing to change the world. She had also sworn to Ruthie that she'd find Ben Tolufson's murderer. The strength of that renewed resolve and her longing to make the world better gave her all the energy she needed to walk the mile and a half back to the Capitol.

When she got back, she dropped Ewok at the office, where he lapped up about a cup of water from his stainless-steel bowl and then flopped down under Iris's desk. Bryan had come straight from the university and was struggling to unjam the copy machine.

"Brenda was here," Iris said as she handed Bryan a stack of sheets to be copied.

"I'm sorry I missed her. Well, now it's almost two. I'm going back to work," Megan said. "I've got to read that whole bill before I'm absolutely certain about it."

A pair of teenage Senate pages flung open the double glass doors as she approached the chamber.

"Good afternoon, Senator Likely," one of them said, and she nodded and smiled, savoring the words. "This came for you," the girl whispered, handing her a red-and-white cardboard courier packet. "A delivery service brought it."

She sat down, holding the letter for a moment, and bookmarked the tenth page in the cheese bill. When she opened the packet, she found a piece of blue-bordered white memo paper. The message, printed in the same childish letters as the last note, perhaps written with the left hand, read,

SO NOW YOU'RE A REAL SENATOR! BUT NOT FOR LONG.

YOU'LL NEVER LIVE TO THE END OF THE TERM.

# TWENTY-THREE

Henry Arlow opened his eyes for a moment. Through the white fog he saw someone he knew, smiling down at him. He couldn't speak with the respirator tube in his mouth; actually, since he'd had a stroke, he couldn't speak at all, but he slowly raised his left hand a few inches in greeting, then let it drop to the bed. How did he get here, wherever here was? He tried to remember, but the effort was too great. He recognized the man beside his bedside, however, even though he couldn't think of the man's name.

"I brought you a wonderful surprise," the man said. "Close your eyes."

That was no problem; his eyes easily closed by themselves. He let his eyelids shut and was starting to drift off when he felt something tighten around his arm. As the hypodermic needle plunged into his vein, he tried to raise his head, but something was holding him. His eyes flew open at the last moment; but by then the hypo had done its work, and he remained forever staring at the white ceiling.

"Help!" the friend shouted. "Help! Something's wrong with Senator Arlow!"

The nurses had already started for Arlow's bedside because they'd seen on their monitor that his brain wave and heart had both flat-lined. His friend backed out of the room quickly, to get out of their way, and headed for the elevator. This time the nursing staff were unable to get a response. When his wife came back twenty minutes later, they had declared him dead.

Tom shouldered his pigskin carry-on and headed for the taxi line. The ride into town from Dulles when he finally got a cab, if ever, would take about forty minutes.

He'd flown out of Washington at dawn, taken the shuttle from Chicago to Oshkosh, rushed to the hearing, and then sat dumbfounded as the state failed to present a case. And the cell phone Tom carried on his hip had rung while he was back at the Chicago airport. Kinkaid, his supervisor, had given him the news that Henry Arlow had died after open-heart surgery. Well, if Arlow killed Linderman, they'd never know for sure.

And in Tom's mind a nagging little bell kept ringing. Somehow, the murders of Robert Linderman and the innocent young pastor from Wisconsin had to be related. The two men hadn't known each other, but they'd both known Megan. Kinkaid also said Megan had received another oblique death threat, this one right on the Senate floor.

Ten after five. He decided to go straight to Megan's.

The taxi manager yelled, "Downtown D.C. Anyone want to share a cab?"

He climbed into a taxi with the one of the consulate assistants from Chad.


Brenda Samuelson had been sitting too long; it was now four-thirty, and not only did her back ache, but her mind was beginning to wander. The undersecretary of defense was on the hot seat, and the congresswoman from South Carolina had been questioning him for twenty-eight minutes. Before she started her interrogation, the committee chairman had probed interference in Egypt for nearly an hour. Brenda thought the subject had been exhausted; now the questioners were becoming repetitive and quarrelsome.

She had called Rick's pager twice, wanting to check some Bible verses with him. Now, sitting in the committee hearing, her own pager, turned on "silent," began to vibrate against the waistband of her dark suit skirt. She checked the number; the call was from a 212 exchange in New York, which meant it was Rick, calling back. Good. Now she had his number. And if the congresswoman from South Carolina would just ease off...

When the chairman called for a fifteen-minute break, Brenda dashed into the hall to call Rick on her cell phone.

"I got the program," he told her. "They signed a three-year contract, and not only will that mean a nice piece of change for us, but it will help put the station on the map. Bren, I'm thinking of going to a hundred thousand watts."

She had to hurry, so she switched to her questions about the Bible study. "I can't mention the prophecies about war with Libya while these hearings are going on. In fact, my congressional seat might be in danger if I do so." She waited for his answer, twirling a lock of her hair.

Rick was expansive. "Sweetheart, just tell them how much the Lord loves them," he said, and she began to relax. By the time she got to the hearing room, she was ready to question the secretary about the threat of chemical weapons. But as soon as she was seated again, the buzzer rang for a vote in the House. They were ready to pass their version of poverty alleviation legislation; if it passed, it would go to the Senate, then to a conference committee.

Brenda knew how she was going to vote. If Rick asked her, she'd have to tell him the first lie of their brief marriage. With luck, the House would accept the voice vote, and hers wouldn't have to be recorded.

"Tom Warburton will be home tonight. I'll let him take charge of this note," Special Agent Joe Ferguson told Megan. She watched as he reread the words, then handed the message back. "It's too late to get transportation home for you now, but from tomorrow on, no Metro. You ride in a car."

It was nearly six when she and Ferguson got off the Metro and rode the escalator up to Connecticut Avenue. She was lugging her briefcase, where she'd stashed the cheese pricing bill, but Ferguson was carrying the entire printout of the poverty alleviation bill. The house had passed their version of the legislation just before the end of their session, so sometime in the next few weeks she'd have to be ready to vote. She still opposed it, although not only Luke Callon but Senator Lewis of Idaho had lobbied her about changing her stand. They were probably the two most conservative men in the chamber, and in light of their urging she was willing to reread the bill once more.

"Ma'am?" A shabby black man, whose thin brown sweater was full of moth holes, was standing at the top of the escalator, holding a paper cup containing a dollar bill and a few coins. "Could I ask you for your spare change?"

Ferguson started to step between them, but she shook her head: The beggar's eyes were full of such pain that she almost cried out. *I've got to remember not to look these people in the face....*

"All right," she sighed. She took her wallet out of her pocket and peered inside. She had no singles; the smallest bill she had was a ten. She started to drop a quarter into the paper cup, but she was blinded by a flash of light; car headlights no doubt, but the sparkle lingered on the back of her wrist. Almost involuntarily she gave the panhandler a ten-dollar bill.

He stared at it, then looked up at her with sad, liquid eyes.

"Ma'am, did you mean to give me a dollar? This is a ten."

This was her chance. She heard Ferguson mutter something. She could say, Yes, it had been a mistake, she was sorry; she could take back the money and give him a handful of change. But headlights blinded her again, and she found herself saying, "I want you to have it." *He'll probably buy wine with it. Why am I doing this?*

She looked over her shoulder at the man she'd given the money to. He was carrying the bill like a calling card, in front of him, as he went into Hadley's Coffee.

"Wait," she told Ferguson. Finally the man came out. He was drinking coffee from a paper cup and carrying two large cookies in a square of waxed paper. She could hear him shouting, "Thank you, Jesus!" all the way across the circle.

*Jesus didn't give you money. I did,* she thought as she and Ferguson walked toward the apartment. It was starting to snow, and the wind was fierce. She ducked her head and walked fast, trying not to wonder where the man would sleep in the fresh snowstorm.

"Please, Senator, be more careful about letting people approach you," Ferguson said. "That man could have been carrying a weapon, or even a bomb. Say, look at the way the light's reflecting on your hair."

She didn't really hear him. She was trying to ignore the struggle inside her as she looked back at the beggar, huddled on a park bench, eating his cookies.

Mindora Arlow's almost-black eyes were snapping. "I want an autopsy and I want it tonight."

Dr. Swaboda also wanted an autopsy. But the strident insistence of the dark-haired woman in the black turtleneck made him hold back.

"If you don't consent to do an autopsy, I'll ask for a congressional order. My husband was a United States senator." She didn't mention that his term had expired. "And there's something fishy," she added. "A visitor comes in, someone not identified, and while he's there, Henry dies." She leaned forward and looked Swaboda in the eye.

"Is there some reason you don't want an autopsy, Dr. Swaboda?"

"All right," he said. "I'll sign the order."

"Are you going to do the autopsy yourself?"

"No. But I will ask them to look for specifics."

"So will I."

203

"Well, now, are you a nurse, Mrs. Arlow? Or a nurse's aide?"

She smiled. "I'm a doctor," she said. "Now, shall we get going on this?"

When Megan saw Tom standing inside the entrance hall of her apartment building, she almost cried with relief. Sure, Ferguson did his job; so did the other men and women the FBI sent to protect her. But Tom had been in on the case since the beginning, and he obviously cared a great deal about it. And about her.

After Tom dismissed Ferguson, saying he'd stay with her, Megan allowed him to take the plastic bag containing the seven-hundred-plus pages of SB7738, or SB615, as it was now called, and carry it up the stairs.

"Hey, I saw a perfectly good elevator back there," he complained. "How come we're walking?"

"I need the exercise," she said.

"Well, here's all the news," Tom said when they were inside. He set the stack of congressional documents on the Queen Anne chair and stretched. "Your friend Mark Combs was not indicted, and the state has dropped the case. Henry Arlow died after heart surgery and a stroke in Chicago. And Green Bay is going to the Super Bowl."

"Mark's free? They're not going to prosecute?"

"Apparently the state depended on something the police chief thought Arlow was going to say. When Arlow didn't appear in court, they were doomed. You should have seen the assistant DA. She looked about fourteen and embarrassed as all get-out." He waited a moment, then said, "I guess your news isn't so good. Let me see the note you got this afternoon."

She sighed. For a minute, thinking about Mark, she had forgotten about the threat. She reached inside her briefcase and took out the stiff courier envelope.

"Windhill," Tom murmured as she handed it to him.

"What?"

"Windhill Delivery Service. I recognize the packet." He slid his gloved hand inside the cardboard and pulled out the memo paper. "I suppose you handled this thoroughly, destroying any chance of fingerprints?"

"Sure. I had no idea it was going to be something so important." She paused a moment and then asked, "Is Mark free to leave Wisconsin?"

"What?" He looked up, trying to make sense of her question. "Oh, Combs. Yes," he said.

"Tom, do you believe Henry Arlow killed Bob Linderman?" she asked.

"If he did, then Ben Tolufson's murderer was someone else, because Arlow was in custody."

"That's what I was thinking. How long does it take to get from here to Oshkosh? I can't remember the flight out here very well." *In those days, my biggest concern was a phony fraud charge, not murder.*

Tom pulled the back page of his airline tickets out of his pocket. "Let's see. I got to Chicago in two hours. Of course, I made a perfect connection in Chicago for the twenty-minute shuttle to Oshkosh."

"If a person left here at noon, they could be in Oshkosh at three. Right? And they could return early the next morning?" When he nodded, Megan looked thoughtful. *I only know one person who was in Wisconsin when Linderman was murdered and who was also at the National Cathedral on Christmas Eve. Priscilla.* But what about that video of Christmas Eve? And the clipping? It wasn't Priscilla she'd seen. "Next time you come over, bring your magnifying glass, will you? So I can look at that clipping."

"Oh, I will. With all that has happened, I forgot about it."

"And do you have a copy of the news clip at the National Cathedral, the night Ben was shot? The one that showed the crowd out in the entry?"

"No, but I can get one. Why?"

"There's something I need to see. If what I think is there shows up, I'll tell you. Now, didn't you say you had to call your supervisor?" She picked up the two Senate bills and moved them to the table, throwing the plastic sack in the recycle bag while Tom dialed his cell phone.

"Kinkaid just left," he said. "I'll leave a message on his home phone about the threatening note." He dialed him and left a message for Kinkaid to call his pager as soon as possible. He sat down in a dining-room chair and loosened his tie. "Well we're stuck with each other for a few hours," he said, smiling. "Do you want to go eat?"

"Iris will be here in a few minutes, and we're going to a Bible study; so I think I'll just make sandwiches and chips. Tom, am I really in danger? Or is this some kind of harmless crank thing?"

"No crank is harmless," Tom told her, jumping up to look out the window. "Hmmph. I thought I saw someone looking up at your window with binoculars, but nobody's there now."

Megan came to his side and surveyed the street outside. Then she made sure the window was locked, and she pulled the draperies shut. "I have one more question," she said, looking toward the door as Iris turned her key and came in.

Iris was also carrying a stack of paper. After her FBI escort looked into the apartment and nodded at Tom, he stepped outside. Iris collapsed on the sofa, still holding her armful of file folders and information sheets.

"I'm going to buy a little red wagon to pull all this paper around," she said. She worked the strap to her handbag off her shoulder and shoved the purse across the sofa. "We never got a seat on the Metro. However, I have to admit you were right about one thing, Meg. The office runs like clockwork with Fern there." She put her head back and turned it from side to side. "I just wish she were twenty-six and a size five so she'd be more decorative."

"She wouldn't be so quiet and efficient if she were a five," Megan said. She stepped into the kitchen and took out a loaf of bread. "Do you want avocado on your BLT, Iris? Tom, can you eat with us?" She slapped bacon into a skillet. Iris trudged into the bathroom and then to her bedroom to change clothes. Megan turned her frying pan down. She stood in the doorway and said to Tom, "As I told you, I have one more question. Do you think all this activity is generated by one person, or do you think it's a conspiracy?"

Tom didn't get to answer because Iris flew out of the bedroom.

"Libya has bombed Cairo," she said. "The UN has ordered troops into Egypt, and President Jackson will ask Congress for a declaration of war."

# TWENTY-FOUR

Megan wasn't really listening to Brenda's lesson on the Gospel of John. She was thinking about the bombing in Egypt and wondering whether she'd get a chance to make her speech about milk prices or if the Senate would instead have to be in a joint session with the House to debate sending troops into northern Africa.

It might take a day or two for the president to make his own decision and call upon the Congress. In fact, she might have to go into active Armed Services Committee meetings tomorrow. But she'd still better be ready with her brief speech to gain votes for what was being called the cheese bill. Before she spoke, she'd have to read the last fifty pages to see if there was also a price ceiling.

Brenda's voice penetrated her thoughts. "And Jesus says, in verse nine, 'As the Father loved me, I also have loved you; abide in my love.'"

Megan glanced up, then over at her chief of staff. Iris's eyes were shining and her lips parted. She looked—Megan searched for a word. Iris was consistently well groomed, with every apricot hair in place, her makeup unsmudged, and her posture perfect. She was a slender forty-three and always attractive in her tasteful clothes. But at the moment she was transformed.

*I wish I could respond to the Bible that way,* Megan thought. Then her mind strayed again to the business of the Senate. If the president wanted war, and there was a rumor that he was beginning to lean in that direction, the Senate might invoke the War Powers Act, which had been designed after Vietnam to prevent a president from keeping troops for an unspecified time in a foreign country. The Act could be used either to prevent or to authorize the president to declare war on Libya; it had been used once before, to commence the active Gulf War.

If the threat of war died down, Luke Callon's amendment to the poverty alleviation bill would come up for a vote. Then the bill itself would rear its head. And she had so far found nothing in Luke's amendment that would convince her to allocate a billion dollars to hoboes and freeloaders. Americans were already taxed too much. Megan believed that if someone made a million dollars, they should not have it spent by a big, bleeding-heart government.

At the end of the study, Iris rose and headed toward Brenda. She didn't look back at Megan, who was still sitting in her folding chair with Tom standing behind her. What was Iris doing?

She heard Iris say hesitantly, "I want to know. What do I have to do to be—" she gestured toward Brenda's Bible, lying on the small table—"to be a Christian?"

They were quiet on the two-block walk from the Metro stop to their apartment. White flakes were falling, but the wind had stopped. Their steps were almost noiseless because the snow had turned the streets to velvet. Tom hummed tunelessly until they got to the apartment building.

"Your night guards should be here any second," he said. When Megan turned her key in the lock, she glanced up at Iris, whose face was still radiant.

"You look happy, Iris," Megan said as they waited outside the door for Tom to check out the apartment.

"Maybe for the first time ever," Iris said, and when they were inside, she went straight to her room, gently shutting the door.

Megan turned to look at Tom, but he was already on his cell phone. Momentarily at a loss for something to do or say, she sat down at the dining-room table, where her speech notes and her copy of the cheese bill were stacked. She ploughed into the bill, finally finding the safeguards on maximum price levels she had been concerned about, and began jotting notes for her speech on a yellow legal pad.

She was so absorbed in her work, she didn't notice that Tom had finished his call and was now just sitting on the couch. She finally glanced up: He was watching her.

"Hello?" she said, her eyebrows raised.

"I'm sorry. I was enjoying looking at you. I forgot it isn't polite to stare."

"Tom, are you a Christian?"

He looked surprised. "Yeah. Have been most of my life. Why?"

"I guess Iris is now, too," she said almost wistfully. "Well, maybe someday I'll have time to think about it." She turned back to her notes and continued to write until the doorbell rang.

Tom opened the door to Mills and Markov, their night guards, and Tom gathered up his things. "Now I get to lug home my duffel bag," he said. "I came here straight from the airport. Tonight and tomorrow I'll be in Alexandria with my kids and my mother, but I'll have my pager. Call me the minute anything happens. I mean *anything*. Do you have my card?"

"In my wallet."

Tom started to leave. At the door he hesitated. "You know, I don't believe you can think your way to God," he said. "Good night, Megan. Say good night to Iris for me."


President Jerry Jackson sat at the polished mahogany table, staring at his Salisbury steak.

"Jerry?"

He looked up, startled.

"I was waiting for you to say grace, Jerry."

He prayed quickly and they started to eat. Or at least Luyin did. The president was now gazing at the finial on the lid of their coffee server. "This is awful," he said finally. "No matter what decision I ask the Congress for, a lot of people will get hurt by it."

Luyin smiled. "Well, the way you're shouting, dear, the whole world knows what you're thinking."

He smiled back and lowered his voice. "I would have made a great sportscaster," he said. "And it would have been an easier life.

Luyin, if we declare war on Libya, we're sure to have American men and women killed. If we don't, thousands of Egyptians may be slaughtered. Egyptian and Sudanese troops are only semi-trained, which is our fault. In countries like Egypt, we discourage having a powerful army. We didn't want our soldiers to get caught in a Sudanese military coup while trying to fight Libya."

Luyin cut her marinated tomato slices with the side of her fork. "And are you getting close to a decision?"

"The Joint Chiefs keep hammering at me. I'm meeting with them at nine tonight. I'm afraid what it may come down to is the degree of attrition. How many would be killed in each situation. Martinez says one American life is worth ten Egyptian ones, but I see things differently."

"How do you see them, dear?"

He shook his head slowly. "It's hard to define. I just wish God would talk louder."

Luyin closed her eyes for a moment and prayed silently for her husband and the country. She would be speaking the next day at a Sierra Club event, and she had planned to bring up the subject of war as an environmental hazard. But she would wait now until she heard an answer from God.

The president finished eating his dinner. The candles flickered as the waiter removed their plates. "It's the lobbying that's driving me crazy," Jackson said when they were starting on their peach pie. "In fact, there's one guy, he's the husband of one of our congresswomen, who has his lobbyists relentlessly grinding away in favor of war. And from what my sources tell me, nobody can figure exactly why he is so gung ho to get the country into battle."

"Ah," Luyin said. She was not naturally a silent woman, but she didn't want to break his train of thought. His cheeks were starting to flush, always a sign he was upset or felt passionate about something.

"And to top everything else off, my poverty alleviation bill was supposed to go to a vote in the Senate this week. Now that bill may

211

be put on hold while the streets are full of homeless people."

"You've fought very hard to help the poor, Jerry. I don't know what more you can do."

"I think I almost have the votes in the Senate. I just need three more, and two fellows are already teetering. But I don't have time to push for more votes when the country is on the brink of war. If I ask for a declaration of war against Libya, I'll both gain and lose votes on the poverty bill. It's a dicey situation."

"Have you ever thought of calling Mr. Samuelson here, to discuss his lobbying efforts?"

Jackson was startled. "Samuelson?"

"He's the husband of Congresswoman Penning, isn't he?"

"You're amazing, Luyin. How did you figure it out?"

Luyin's smile was gentle and exotic. Never did she look so Oriental as when she smiled that smile. "I have my sources, too, Jerome. I even read the newspapers. And I do think you need to talk to Mr. Samuelson. Or ask your chief of staff to deal with him."

The president nodded. "I'll invite him to come see me," he said.


At nine o'clock Megan yawned, watching her printer churn out her "cheese" speech. She was preoccupied with the videotape of Ben's murder. She'd have to have more than that to go on if she were really going to present a case to Tom. Meanwhile, she had to act normal around the person she suspected, and that wasn't going to be easy.

She made herself a cup of instant hot chocolate and was wiping the counter when Iris came out of her room. They had spent almost no time together since they returned from Bible study: Megan had gone into the office to put her speech on the computer while Iris had puttered in the kitchen, preparing her lunch for the next day. They hadn't really talked. And she didn't want to while she was trying to sort out the murder.

"Want some chocolate?" she asked. "The water's still hot."

"I guess. I wonder if the boys want some," Iris added, referring to their FBI guards, both stationed outside the door. She thrust her head outside and then shut it, shaking her head. "They have a six-pack of cola out there in their little ice chest. Brrr! How can they drink cold things on a night like this?"

The wind was whipping wet snowflakes against their living-room window. Iris pulled the draperies and turned on the gas fireplace. Yellow flames leapt up and pretended to consume the log.

"A cozy scene," Megan said, carrying the tray of hot chocolate to the living room.

Iris settled into a wing-backed chair and sipped her cocoa. "Megan, the words, *Abide in my love,* sounded like the best invitation I'd ever have. When I went up to Brenda, I didn't know any prayers, but she said just to tell God what I wanted in my own words."

Iris looked to Megan as if she were five hundred feet away. And speaking another language. The woman who had been her best friend was now a stranger, thanks to God.

Roland Hutchins sat on the edge of the sofa in the Oval Office, his arms dangling between his legs. He was breathing noisily as he listened to Rudy Martinez, chairman of the Joint Chiefs, discuss the situation on the Egyptian-Sudanese border. Hutchins was also thinking back to the days when he played with toy soldiers. He'd been half sick with asthma and colds and chronic bronchitis for most of his childhood, but after his mother read him Robert Louis Stevenson's "Land of Counterpane," he'd learned to play war in his bed. He would line up two armies, then decide who would win. He'd hide snipers behind the hills of his knees and put others into the mud bog designated on the bedspread between his ankles. As a consequence he was, although physically unfit for any branch of the service, one of the best military strategists in the world. He was jolted back to the present when Martinez said, "Mr. President, the countries of the world are waiting. We must send in troops or take a chance Libya will occupy all of northern Africa."

Hutchins had been through three presidents, and he was learning to read their faces. The president's cheeks were growing pink. Hutchins glanced to his left, at Rita Mulligan, the Speaker of the House. She looked calm, as she always did, sitting back against the sofa, her hands clasped in her lap, but he noticed her right foot was swinging nervously.

Obviously, Hutchins was going to have to say what he really thought. He sighed, stood, pulled his trousers up by the belt, and said, "If you send troops into Egypt, Mr. President, I will be constrained to ask the Congress to invoke the War Powers Act. The Hala'ib is a hotbed of guerrilla groups and scraps of little armies, and I think it would be a rash act to enter a Mideastern border conflict."

Speaker Mulligan glared at him, then sat forward and said, "The majority leader is wrong, Mr. President. We can't shilly-shally. We've got to go in. And if Senator Hutchins does ask us to invoke the War Powers Act, he may have a shock coming. I think we'll get the declaration of war."

Hutchins gritted his teeth. Speaker Mulligan usually took his side; in fact, they'd been known for the past two years as the Terrible Two. But tonight she was impossible. He asked, "How many troops are you talking about, Mr. President?"

The president nodded as he spoke. "A million, massed, to begin with, on the Egyptian side of the borders of Libya and Sudan."

"A million?" Hutchins wheezed. "Come now." For a second, his mind strayed to his wife. Was she really visiting her sister in Pennsylvania? He hoped wherever she was, the detective he'd hired was close on her heels.

Megan pushed her feet under the crisp, clean sheets on her bed and burrowed into her pillow. She felt oddly disoriented by Iris's sudden conversion. Or was it so sudden? She'd been asking questions for awhile.... Megan was also trying to remember the frame of the Christmas Eve videotape. She tried to make her mind print it out before her eyes, but the memory was brief and fading. Well, she'd just have to get some other evidence or forget what she'd seen. She didn't want to believe it. There had to be a reasonable explanation.


Tom pulled the pad of requisition forms from his drawer and wrote in "Videotape of Murder Scene: National Cathedral, December 24." He stuck it into the fax machine on his desk and sent it to the D.C. police. He put his magnifying glass in his briefcase and snapped it shut. Then he left the Hoover Building, climbed into his van, and headed for Alexandria. He had hardly seen his children all week.

He was heading over the bridge when his car phone rang. He flipped on the speaker and said, "Warburton."

"This is Kinkaid. Where are you?"

"On the Arlington Bridge. Why?"

"Keep going to Fairfax. Congresswoman Samuelson's car was just blown up."

# TWENTY-FIVE

Megan was sailing on Green Lake. She and Mark were laughing together in the sunshine when something woke her. She sat up in her bed and caught a glimpse of hundreds of tiny gold lights rising up and then falling toward her, like a fountain of golden sparks. She reached out but couldn't touch the sparks; when she shook her head to clear it, the glowing display was gone. A dream, probably. She was about to lie back down when her telephone rang. The voice on the other end was sobbing hysterically.

"Brenda? Is that you?"

"Oh, Megan…" Her voice trailed away into crying.

"What? Brenda, what is it?"

"Someone tried to kill me," Brenda sobbed. "And Rick is still out of town and…that FBI agent you know is here. He said he'd bring me to your place."

"Someone tried to—Brenda, did you say Tom was there? Could I speak to him?" She heard the phone clank against a table or counter, and she waited a long time. She was about to hang up and call Tom's pager when he came on the line.

"Megan?"

"Tom, thank heaven it's you. What is going on?"

"Someone put a bomb in Congresswoman Samuelson's car. She had just entered her kitchen from the garage when it blew up. It destroyed the garage and most of her kitchen and knocked out some windows. She's got some nasty glass cuts, but she'll be all right."

"You said a bomb? Was it—"

"Megan, Mrs. Samuelson's husband is out of town, as you know from their Bible study tonight. Can I bring her over there? She doesn't really have any place to go, and the house is in no shape for anyone to live in. I've got three men plus a team from

EU-BDC here, so I can leave for a while and let them work."

"EU—"

"Explosives Unit. Bomb Data Center. Can I bring her?"

"Of course." She hung up and opened the linen closet in the hall, being quiet so she wouldn't wake Iris. She removed a set of sheets and two blankets, then unfolded the sofa bed in her living room. She made up the bed and was getting out cups for another batch of hot chocolate when Ewok gave a short bark and began dancing about in expectation. Iris had emerged from her room, her dark blue robe tied tightly at the waist.

"Megan?" Iris glanced around at the made-up bed, the sofa cushions stacked on a chair.

"Brenda's coming," Megan said. "She's—she's got a problem."

Iris said, "Maybe I should sleep out here and let Brenda have the bedroom. She may need the quiet and the privacy. I'm fine anywhere. Just let me put clean sheets on my bed for her." She rose and started toward her room.

"Iris, wait." Megan took a deep breath. "She may not want privacy at all. She may want us to sit out here with her. Her car was blown up. A bomb."

"A car bomb? Is she—oh, Meg, is Brenda okay?"

"She was already in her kitchen. Apparently whoever did this misgauged the timing or something, so she wasn't killed. We can find out more when Tom comes." She poured boiling water into their insulated cocoa pot, then measured in several tablespoons of hot chocolate, glad for something to do.

When Brenda arrived, her face was cut, and her left wrist was bandaged.

"We tried to get her to go to a hospital, but she refused," Tom said, setting Brenda's suitcase down. Brenda walked straight into Megan's arms and held on tightly, clinging like a child even though she was much taller and broader shouldered. She was trembling all over.

Tom said, "I've got to get right back. I'll talk to you tomorrow, Mrs. Samuelson." He was out the door before Megan could even speak to him. She heard him say good night to Mills, who was stationed outside the door.

"Six years in the House, and nobody ever did anything like this to me before," Brenda said in a shaky voice. "Maybe it was today's vote."

"Don't try to talk now, Bren," Megan said, patting her shoulder. "Sit down and drink some cocoa."

"The paramedics gave me a couple of tranquilizers. I guess I can take them now." She reached into her coat pocket and brought out a small while envelope. Megan gave her a cup of hot chocolate, and Brenda swallowed her pills.

"Where did you say Rick was?" Iris asked, pouring two more cups of cocoa.

"He's in New York."

"New York? Business?"

Brenda took a deep breath and exhaled slowly. "Yes," she said, sitting down in the breakfast nook. "He just signed on a really big syndicated program." She named a news commentator they'd all heard of. "That should do a lot for the station. Oh, Megan, I'll never feel safe again. And I can't get hold of Rick. The hotel said he didn't answer, although I don't know where he'd be at this hour." Her eyes looked glazed.

"Why don't you stretch out on the couch?" Megan took Brenda's cup and carried it to the end table beside the sofa. "Come on, Bren. Lie down for a while."

Brenda handed her coat to Iris, who hung it in the closet. "I won't sleep," Brenda said. "There's no point in my undressing."

"Okay. Just take off your shoes and lie down."

Brenda collapsed on the couch and burst into fresh tears. "You can't know how terrifying it is to find out someone wants to kill me."

Megan looked up and caught Iris's eye. *Oh, yes, I do know how it feels. Someone, maybe the same person, wants to kill me, too.* And she felt certain she knew who it was. She just needed a little more evidence.

~ ~ ~ ~ ~

Mark Combs had been dozing in his brown plaid recliner since seven-thirty. Now it was twelve-fifteen, and he sat up, stretched, and started taking off his tie, when the television, still on CNN, as it had been when he first sat down, flashed a "Breaking News" banner. The screen showed the scene of a bombed-out car, still burning. Mark heard the reporter say that the bomb was apparently intended for Wisconsin District 4 representative Brenda Penning Samuelson. He walked to the refrigerator without taking his eyes off the television and poured himself a glass of cold milk; then he sat back down, this time on an ottoman he pulled close to the television. He had met Brenda Samuelson once: a bright, efficient woman with a real instinct for good government. And she was his congressional representative to boot.

When the news shifted to a story about Siamese twins being separated in Sacramento, he turned off the set and headed into his bedroom. He was now reinstated in his job and had to work the next day. But the first thing he planned to do when he got there was to call that FBI agent who'd spoken to him at the grand-jury hearing.

Brenda fell asleep almost immediately. Shock, fatigue, and the tranquilizers had done their work. Megan and Iris covered her with blankets.

"I can't believe this," Iris said quietly. "Why would anyone want to hurt a fine woman like Brenda?"

Megan shrugged. "I just wish things would quit happening in the middle of the night," she said. "I'm getting so I always feel knocked-out during the day." She felt wide awake; but tomorrow was a working day, and she had to be on the Senate floor at eleven o'clock, ready to speak. She went back to her own bed but left her door open in case Brenda woke before morning and needed calming down again.

Megan had told Ruthie on Christmas day, *No matter what happens, I'll get to the bottom of this.* Well, she was down toward the bottom, and what she thought made her miserable.

When the clock radio started the NPR news at seven the next morning, Megan longed to stay in bed for the rest of the day. Instead she got up, splashed water on her face, gathered up Ewok's newspaper, and poured herself a cup of coffee. *Thank heaven for the timer plug that starts this coffee. I'd expire without it.*

The telephone rang. It was a secretary at the FBI. They were calling off the daytime guard so they could send more agents to the bomb scene. Mills would be there tonight.

*I'll take a cab to work,* Megan decided. She sipped her coffee as she pulled on jeans and a sweater, tied her sneakers, and tiptoed with Ewok past Brenda, down the stairs, and out the front door. She missed hearing the news on the radio that *Washington Window* editor Ladonna Thurmond, better known as Donnie, was in critical condition at Georgetown Medical Center after an apparent overdose of sleeping pills.

The dog bolted forward on his leash to resume his vendetta with the calico cat, lurking between potted bushes. Megan held tightly to the leash and let the cat escape; Ewok looked at her with reproach, then busied himself with the fire hydrant and the bus-stop signpost. They were heading back toward her building when she heard someone softly calling her name. It was Tom, coming from his parked car across the street.

"We always meet at odd hours," she said as he approached.

"Odd's fine with me, so long as we meet." Tom's smile was incongruous in his exhausted, soot-smeared face. "I came in the wild hope you were up. I just drove in from Fairfax. We've got the house secured, and the fires are all out; but several windows, some plaster, a lot of the kitchen, and the front door are all gone."

"The house is just sitting there, blown open?"

"Nope, we've got the blasted-out parts covered in black plastic,

220

and the whole place is under guard. We're hoping the perp may show up."

"The who?"

"Perp. Perpetrator. Law-enforcement jargon. How is Mrs. Samuelson?"

"When Ewok and I left the house, she was still asleep. The paramedics gave her some tranquilizers, so she'll probably be groggy today. Unless there's a vote in the House this morning, she should probably stay down. Are you coming up?"

Tom hesitated. "I stood my daughters up last night. I think I better have breakfast with them and then swing by my office. I put in a requisition for that video you wanted. Do you want to see it here or at the Hoover?"

"Not here," Megan said. "I'll meet you down there."

For a moment Tom reached out, as if to embrace her; then he changed the gesture to a wave and got in his car. Megan watched him drive away until Ewok barked and tugged her toward their door.

Brenda was sitting up on the couch. Iris was dressed, handing Brenda coffee and a muffin.

"There you are," Iris said. "Megan, Rick just called. He heard what happened on the news. He sounded pretty frantic, poor guy."

Brenda said, "I've got to get to Fairfax and see what's happening to my house."

"Not yet," Megan said, peeling the paper liner off her muffin. "Tom drove by, and he said your house is sealed and under guard. When is Rick coming back?"

"He just got off the shuttle. He's on his way here right now. I told him to go check the house first, but he wanted to pick me up." Brenda's voice was still furry and slow. She sipped at her coffee, then drew the cup away quickly. "Boy, this is hot." She took her overnight bag and headed into the bathroom.

Iris said, "I've got to get to work. Fern is going to beat me to the office as it is."

"Wait, Iris." Megan took another muffin and poured fresh coffee for both of them. "Fern can manage for a while. Let's wait here with Brenda."

Iris raised her eyebrows for a second, her face questioning Megan's. When no answer came, she took Brenda's sheets to the laundry hamper in the hall. They heard the shower running.

"All right," Iris said softly. "What did you want to tell me?"

Megan motioned for Iris to follow her into the kitchen. She sank down in the breakfast nook and said in a hoarse whisper, "I think I know who killed—"

The doorbell rang and someone called, "Megan? Brenda?" It was Rick. Iris let him in, and Megan knocked on the bathroom door.

"Rick," Brenda said when she got to the living room, her blond hair damp and curly, fresh Band-Aids on her cheeks and forehead.

"Brenda! Oh, look at your face." He enfolded her in his arms. "My poor sweetheart," he said. "Thank God you weren't hurt worse!"

"I'm all right," Brenda said, her voice muffled by Rick's overcoat. She slowly withdrew from him and said, "Rick? How did you know where to call me?"

"You left a message at my hotel desk, remember? I was dressing for the early A.M. shuttle from JFK when I saw the light on my phone."

"But where were you when I called last night?"

"Asleep. I didn't even hear the phone ring. Are you ready to go home?"

Megan tried to shake off her impatience and said, "You may have to stay somewhere else for a day or so. Part of your house is blown out."

Rick's homely face was horrified. "Our house? I thought the bomb was under the car seat."

Brenda finally spoke. "The front windows and most of the kitchen are gone. And the garage. It was a pretty powerful bomb, Rick."

"You can't possibly go home, then," Rick said. "Why don't you ride over to the Capitol with Megan while I go take a look at things at home? Megan, let me give you my pager number in case you or Brenda need me." He reached into his breast pocket and pulled out a leather memo pad, scribbled on one of the sheets, and tore it off, handing it to Megan. Without looking at it she stuck it into the pocket of her briefcase, which was sitting on the table. She wouldn't need it. Brenda was upset, yes, but not out of her head. She could call Rick herself. But before Megan did anything else, she made another note on the legal pad in her brief case.

Brenda said, "But I want to see—"

Rick put his arm around her. "I know you want to look at the damage, sweetheart, but the bomb squad probably has the place taped off. Let me talk to them." He accepted a cup of coffee from Iris but remained standing. Megan looked at her watch: It was nine-fifteen. She needed to call Tom and find out when she could go to the Hoover to view the video, then get to the Senate to make her speech. Somehow the price of cheese wasn't as important as it was yesterday.

## TWENTY-SIX

B ryan Callon tapped on the study door.
"Mom?"
Priscilla looked up at him over the tops of her rectangular reading glasses. Her slender neck was bent over a heavy law book.

"I'm probably as prepared for the court as I'm ever going to be," she said. "Okay, what do you have to report to me about Megan and Brenda? Besides the bomb?"

"Brenda has made four visits to the Bureau of Vital Statistics in the last week."

"Four? Have you found out why?"

Bryan shook his head. "And yesterday afternoon, I snuck over to the House chamber—"

"No, you sneaked over."

"Okay. When Iris was in conference with two lobbyists, I sneaked over to the House chamber and watched the vote on their version of poverty alleviation. It was a voice vote, but I could see Brenda. She voted for the measure."

"Rick will be upset."

He nodded again. "If she tells him."

"Vital Statistics, huh? Maybe Brenda's researching genealogy or something over there. I think you'd better check on it. What about Megan?"

"The FBI has stayed pretty close to her. I haven't had a chance to get between her and her guard. And she was suspicious on Christmas Eve when she found me working at Blackie's."

"Well, so long as she doesn't know you took the job so you could see her coming and going at the hotel."

"Yeah, and I think she's getting close to the truth." He shut the door and edged closer to his mother. "I overheard her telling Iris they needed to talk about the murders. Not murder, murders."

Priscilla's gaze wandered to the door Bryan had closed. "Bry, why did you shut that door? Nobody's in the house except us."

"What about those appliance guys? Their truck was in the driveway when I came home. I figured they were working on the dryer or something."

"Appliance guys?" Priscilla jumped up, and the law book fell to the floor, narrowly missing her foot. "I didn't call anyone. Who—" She rushed to the front door and flung it open. A white van was parked in the short, uphill driveway, but as soon as she stepped out on the porch, the driver backed out and sped away.


Mindora Arlow was asleep in her room at the Ambassador West Hotel in Chicago when her telephone rang. As she picked up the phone, she craned her neck to see the clock, but it was turned the wrong way and slightly out of her reach.

"It's back," said a tenor voice.

"What? Who is this?" Mindora managed to turn on the lamp.

"Sorry," the voice said. "This is Dr. Bill Swaboda. The autopsy report is back."

"What time is it?"

"Five-forty. Did I wake you up? I had to come over and do an emergency mitral valve replacement, and when I saw the report in my in basket, I thought I'd better call you. You were right."

"Right? About what?" Mindora's throat was dry.

"He was full of DTC. D-tubocurarine chloride."

"Curare," Mindora said. Curare was used by natives in South America to poison their blow-gun darts; DTC was the purified medicinal form of curare, used to temporarily paralyze the muscles of patients undergoing surgery.

"Right. Curare. Plus another paralyzer, a quicker-acting depolarizing one. Succinylcholine."

"Murder," Mindora said. "Henry was murdered." She could almost see Swaboda squirming at the other end of the phone. "You know perfectly well that none of the nurses gave him curare after surgery. Have you called the police or the medical examiner?"

"Well, I—"

"Dr. Swaboda, my husband was injected with enough DTC to kill him. Are you going to call the police, or shall I?"

She heard Swaboda sigh. "I just hated to say the word *murder* yet. I hoped it was just a terrible mistake."

"Whatever happened wasn't 'just' anything, Dr. Swaboda. You call the cops, and I'll meet you in the hospital lobby in forty minutes." She hung up the phone and lay back on her bed for a moment, absently fingering the bedspread. Henry was murdered, probably by the same madman who had slashed Robert Linderman to death. Someone wanted to wipe out everyone connected to Henry's years in the Senate. She wondered about his replacement, Megan Likely. Could she have anything to do with Henry's murder? Mindora thrust her feet out from under the covers and onto the floor, then stood up. She never wore slippers; she liked to go barefoot. Henry had been kidding her about it for years. *Henry!*

She sat back down on the edge of the bed. The reality of her husband's death seized her, and she began to cry. She needed to call their children about the autopsy, but she decided to wait until she had talked to the police. Still weeping, she took off her blue nightgown and stepped into the shower.

Megan pulled on her all-weather boots, tucking her blue pumps into her briefcase. The weather outside was cold, slushy, and windy. Brenda had changed into a suit and was sitting on the living-room sofa, half watching the morning news. Megan stepped into the room with the back of her blue wool dress open.

"Would you do me up, Brenda?"

Brenda had just pulled the zipper up to the neckline and was fastening the button when the phone rang. It was Iris, now at the office.

"Rollie Hutchins just called here," she said. "The president will ask tonight for a declaration of war against Libya. You need to be in the Armed Forces Committee hearings room in thirty minutes to interrogate the Joint Chiefs. And tonight at five-thirty you'll go into session with the House."

"Oh, boy. And all I'd been thinking about was my speech about the price of cheese."

"Which will have to wait," Iris said in her crisp voice. "You'd probably better tell Brenda to ring her office."

"She'll actually be there in just a few minutes," Megan said. "We'll skip the Metro and take a cab." She hung up and reached into the closet for her coat, explaining the situation to Brenda. In four minutes, Ewok had been stationed in his basket in the kitchen, and they were out the door.

"That which I feared most is come upon me," Brenda said. Megan responded with a blank look. "It's from the book of Job, in the Bible," Brenda said. "I've been terrified that war would break out."

"But I thought you and Rick were all for it," Megan said, waving her arm at a passing cab. The taxi stopped and they climbed in.

"Rick is all for it," Brenda said.

"But you're not? Then why don't you say so, when Rick talks about it?"

"At the Bible study? I don't think it's good to contradict him when he's leading the group."

Megan nodded. "Okay. But you talk to him when you're alone, don't you?"

Brenda bit her lip. "Well, Rick believes a wife should reverence her husband."

*Reverence? Reverence is Ceelie with Grandpa!*

"Did you hear about Donnie Thurmond? It was on the news," Brenda said when they were inside the cab and on their way to the Capitol. "She's in a coma. A possible suicide attempt."

"Good grief!" Megan shook her head in confusion. "Will someone tell me what's going on in the world? Everyone I know is getting killed. Or almost killed," she added, touching Brenda's hand.

The cab pulled up in front of the Capitol. As they marched up the steps with the wind biting at the backs of their legs, Rita

Mulligan, Speaker of the House, raced by them. She looked back over her shoulder and stopped.

"Brenda! Are you all right? I heard on this morning's news about the car bomb." She ran back down the steps to embrace Brenda.

"I'm all right," Brenda said with a thin smile. "My husband is over there now, surveying the damage. I was just going to a meeting of—"

"Wherever you were going, change your course and head to the House chamber, pronto. We've got to hold a general debate before we go into joint session tonight for the president's speech." She went on past them, her slender legs carrying her up the steps and in the House door.

"Brenda, let's meet for lunch at about one-thirty if we can," Megan said. "Come to the Senate dining room."

Brenda hesitated. "I'll try," she said. "Ring my pager about one." She scribbled her pager number on a slip of paper and handed it to Megan.

"I guess I'll have to break down and get a pager, too," Megan said.

"Rick likes for me to use one. That way he can always get hold of me."

They hugged quickly, and Megan said, "Everything will be all right, Bren," tucking the pager number into her briefcase pocket. She strode into the Senate Armed Services Committee room, where other senators, including committee chair Luke Callon, were taking their places behind a long desk with microphones placed in front of each chair. She sat down behind her nameplate.

On the other side of the room, Rudy Martinez and Admiral Ron Beatty were seated, their hands over their microphones as they murmured together. Martinez nodded at Megan, then turned back to his discussion.

Within ten minutes, all nine senators were in place, the audience and witnesses for the hearing were seated, and the entire Joint Chiefs faced the committee in rapt attention. Photographers sat on the floor with their legs folded, most of their cameras aimed at the military personnel.

After fifteen minutes Luke Callon stood. "We're met here today on the grave matter of whether the United States of America should enter into a state of war with the country of Libya. We'll start the questioning today with Senator Linda Chasen of New Mexico."

"Thank you, Mr. Chairman," Senator Chasen said. "General Martinez, are all members of the Joint Chiefs in agreement that war should be declared, or do we have another battle here on the home front?"

Everyone chuckled; Luke tapped his gavel a time or two, and Martinez began to explain the position of Egypt and Sudan. Megan leaned forward, her mind on fire with interest.

By one-fifteen, three senators had questioned the Joint Chiefs, mostly about troop placements and predictions of outcome. Finally Luke tapped his gavel again and declared the committee in recess until three.

Megan reached into her briefcase for her cell phone, then pulled out the memo sheet. As she read it, she realized she was looking at Rick's pager number, not Brenda's. She rubbed her thumb absently over Rick's logo at the top of the page, then stuck it back. After she found Brenda's number and called her pager, she began walking toward the House chamber, listening to the *tap-tap-tap* of her own heels on the floor. As she was about to mount the stairs to the gallery, pages opened the doors, and the representatives began to drift out.

"Brenda?" she called. Brenda's usually erect back was slumped, and her face was downcast.

"I just got your call," she said. "You got here before I could call back."

"Brenda, come with me," Megan said firmly. She took Brenda's arm, and they moved through the crowd toward the elevator.

"I thought you wanted to eat in the Senate dining room," Brenda said as the elevator lurched downward.

"Let's go to my office. We can send Bryan out for some food, and you can stretch out on my couch if you like." They climbed onto the subway and rode with three other senators, who nodded at Megan. They were beginning to recognize her when they saw her now.

She held Brenda's hand as they whisked along the tracks, and then guided her to the front door of her office. She didn't want to go through the private door because she wanted to see who was here.

Fern Loftis took one look at Brenda and rose from her chair at the front desk. "I'm Fern, Megan's secretary," she said, smiling as she put her arm around Brenda and began moving her toward the inner offices. "Why don't you come in here and relax?" She escorted Brenda through Iris's office and into Megan's. "Just kick off your shoes for a while, why don't you? I'll hang up your coat."

When she returned, Fern whispered, "That woman belongs at home in bed. Iris told me about the bomb. Have you heard from her husband?"

"I'm going to call him," Megan said.

"Bryan phoned to say he's on his way, and Iris has gone to a church service. She'll be back shortly. Isn't it wonderful that Iris has found the Lord?"

"She went to church? At noon on Tuesday?"

"There's one with a midday service a few blocks from here." Fern had relieved Megan of her red coat and was hanging it up. "You're probably starved," she continued. "Why don't I call Hofbrau? A nice German deli not far from here, and they deliver. I explored this area the first day I worked and found several places where we can order."

"You're incredible, Fern."

"No, no, I just have more time than you do." She ignored Megan's snort of laughter and added, "I left your card in each restaurant so they'd recognize your name." She picked up the phone and began punching in numbers. Megan walked into Iris's office and then peeked into her own. Brenda was lying on the couch, her arm over her eyes. Megan thought at first her friend was asleep, but then she realized that Brenda was crying.

"Oh, Bren," she said, moving toward the couch. "It will be all right."

"No, it won't," Brenda said. "Nothing will ever be all right again. Congress will declare war on Libya, people have been murdered, and Rick—"

Megan waited, but Brenda didn't go on. Finally she asked gently, "Are you having problems with Rick, Bren?"

"Forget it. I shouldn't have said anything. Let's go to lunch. We have to be back at three." She wiped her eyes and blew her nose on a tissue.

"Fern called to have food delivered. You can rest here for a while; you're probably still groggy from those tranquilizers. And didn't you want to call Rick, to see what's going on with your house? Maybe the FBI has some information about the bomber."

Brenda looked at her watch. "I'll wait for Rick to page me," she said and closed her eyes. Megan heard the phone ring in the outer office and tiptoed to the door.

"I didn't want to buzz your phone if Brenda was asleep," Fern said. "Tom Warburton is on the telephone. He says it's important."

"I'll take it out here so Brenda can lie back down."

When she answered, Tom said, "Two things: One, the car bomb was a sophisticated device made with plastique. The second thing is, I just got a call from your friend Mark Combs in Fond du Lac. He had received a report from the doctor in Chicago that Henry Arlow didn't die of a heart attack."

"He didn't? You mean he's still alive?"

"I mean he was killed with a massive dose of muscle paralyzer. There was an autopsy. Probably murder, because no anesthesiologist would have made a mistake like that."

"Murder! Tom, that makes three, plus the attempt on Brenda. Unless that was meant for Rick."

"People who plant bombs know their victims' habits. Samuelson never drives Brenda's car. When they go out together, they take the Taurus. She drives to work and shops in her Saab.

**231**

Someone has been watching her for a while."

Megan was almost unable to answer. "I'm a little over-whelmed, Tom," she finally said. "And on top of everything else, the president has switched gears and wants to go to war."

"So they said on the news. Do you know why?"

She'd listened to the Joint Chiefs for two and a half hours, but she had no real grasp on a threat to the United States. "Not yet," she said.

A young man, wearing a white apron reaching from his chest to below his knees, came to the door, bearing a stack of foil-wrapped packages. "Hofbrau," he announced. Iris was right behind him, smiling as if she'd found a cure for cancer or the way to world peace.

"My lunch is here," Megan told Tom, and they said good-bye; then she said, "Wait! Tom, where in the car was the bomb planted?"

"I'm not sure," he said, and they hung up.

To Iris, she said, "You're just in time. We're about to eat. How was church?"

"Church was great. The minister did a healing service. They do it every day at noon. Oh, this food looks wonderful!"

It was now two-fifteen, and Megan woke Brenda. Fern set everything up on the conference table in Megan's office. She spread out roast beef, potato salad, pickles, condiments, and fresh pumpernickel bread.

"There's cheesecake for dessert," she said. "I'm glad they remembered I said no Styrofoam. We can recycle foil."

Iris brought soft drinks from the pint-sized refrigerator in her office. As they sat at the conference table, faint classical music from Fern's radio drifted in.

"You'd never know there was any trouble anywhere," Brenda said. "It's so peaceful here."

"Iris's beautiful decorating and Fern's office management." Megan let her own eyes sweep around the attractive room.

"And all of you," Brenda said. "You work so well together."

"How long have you been married, now?" Fern asked Brenda, handing her the pickles.

"A month. It seems—" She broke off.

"Time is funny," Fern said. "I was married to my husband, Don, for thirty years, and now it seems like only a minute. But the five years since he died feel like a lifetime."

Megan suddenly remembered something she had seen. She went back to the front office and pulled a memo sheet out of her briefcase pocket. And then she knew that what she'd suspected was true. She knew, and the knowing filled her not with satisfaction but with terror.

# TWENTY-SEVEN

Megan tried to concentrate on the words General Martinez was saying, but her mind kept wandering back to Brenda and the car bomb, Donnie Thurmond's overdose, Henry Arlow's murder in the Chicago hospital, and the terrifying truth that lay two inches away, in her briefcase.

"Therefore, I want to urge the senators to consider the threat to the peoples of Egypt and the Sudan, and also to our oil interests along the Sudanese border. My sources tell me—" Martinez held a sheet of paper out and tilted his head back so he could see through the bottom of his glasses—"tell me the Libyans are bombing Cairo even as we speak."

*Egypt, Libya and Sudan may hold the keys to the world's future,* Rick's voice said in Megan's head. General Martinez was now sitting back, cleaning his glasses, showing his noble Mayan profile as he turned to listen to Senator Wendell of Vermont question Admiral Anna Mason about the proposed use of naval support.

As Admiral Mason answered in her smooth voice, Megan was reminded of Ruthie Tolufson and her sweet singing in the National Cathedral on Christmas Eve. How happy they'd all felt that night until the fateful moment when her grandfather had needed a drink of water and Ben had taken him to the foyer. Well, now she knew the answer! But proving it would be—Luke Callon's voice cut into her thoughts.

"When we return from our break, we will begin with Senator Megan Likely of Wisconsin."

Now she'd have to pull herself together and think about the possibility of war, not letting her mind wander to the person who'd murdered Ben and probably Linderman and maybe Henry Arlow. She walked to the ladies' room to splash a little water on her face. She was startled when, in the mirror, she saw Priscilla Callon come through the door behind her.

"Good. You're here," Priscilla said. Her eyes were twinkling. "Luke said you'd probably start your questioning at about four."

"Luke called you?"

"No, he was talking at breakfast about the hearings, and I asked him when you'd start."

"But why do you want to hear me?" Her natural suspicion of Priscilla and, for that matter, suspicion of her aide, Bryan, boiled up inside her.

"I want to hear anyone who's against the war ask some cogent questions."

*I don't know if I can even think up any questions, cogent or otherwise.*

"I'd better get back," she said, moving past Priscilla, who was looking in the mirror, pushing a lock of her blond pageboy into place. Megan slid back into her seat in the hearings room and looked down at the yellow legal pad lying between her and her microphone. She had written, "What changed the president's mind? What information am I not receiving?" By the time Luke tapped his gavel again, she knew she was as ready as she'd ever be.

"General Martinez," she began, "a week ago our president was still opposed to war. Yesterday he wasn't sure. Now he's asking us to declare. I realize he will speak for himself this evening, but I want to know what you told him that changed his mind."

Martinez stared at her a moment, looking disconcerted, so she added, "What does the president know that I don't know?"

Martinez and Admiral Beatty looked at each other. Finally the general said, "Senator Likely, for one thing, we reminded the president that United States corporations own extensive oil fields along the Nile Delta, the highlands, and especially in the Hala'ib, that strip along the Sudanese border now annexed or at least occupied by Libya. That is some of the highest-grade crude in the world. We feel that our very way of life in America might be threatened if we lose this resource."

A murmur swept the hearings room. Photographers crawled up to get a good shot of Megan as she continued to speak.

"Then am I to understand, Senators and Mr. Chairman, that you're not really so concerned with Sudanese peasants who might be killed by our bombing raids on the Libyan border, but that you're really making sure we have access to our own oil. Is that oil also what the Libyans want?"

The murmur grew louder, and Luke hammered his gavel on the podium.

"Let's please have order," he said mildly. "Senator Likely?"

"Don't get me wrong, ladies and gentlemen," Megan said, feeling the swell of passion in her chest. "I sit on the conservative side of the Senate aisle, and I'm all for benefiting the corporations in this country because they create employment and bring vast sums of money into our commerce. In fact, I'm all for making and keeping money. But I'm constrained by my need to give the truth to the people I represent before we send—" she glanced down at the sheet in her hand and drew in her breath—"the million men and women President Jackson wants to send to war. Now is this about justice or about oil?"

Martinez appealed wordlessly to his fellow military officers. Admiral Anna Mason said, "You've asked questions I'm not sure we've asked ourselves, Senator. We are, of course, committed through the Suez Treaty to protecting Egypt and the Sudan and their citizens, but we must also consider those interests that affect life here."

"Then perhaps one of you can tell me just how much American life will be changed if we do not enter the war?"

Generals and admirals covered their microphones with their hands, and the room buzzed softly. Finally Rudy Martinez said, "Without Egyptian and Sudanese oil, in which some American companies are heavily invested, we could have a gasoline shortage, to start with."

"What percentage of our American gasoline is dependent on those sources?" Megan wanted him to blurt out his truth. And she suspected he didn't know for certain what it was. She was right.

"I would have to study that further in order to give a definitive answer," he said finally.

"Perhaps that means you don't know," Megan said with a smile, the one her opponents in courtrooms had come to fear. "Then the question is whether American transportation or manufacturing will be affected or whether the investors alone will be in danger." Luke began to pound his gavel over and over as the murmur in the room became something close to a roar.

Auto-wind motors on cameras sounded like a hundred rattlesnakes. Finally Luke stood and said, "We'll take a break and resume in fifteen minutes. At that time, if there's any disturbance, I'll have the chamber cleared of everyone except the committee, staff, and witnesses."


"Thanks, Dr. Swaboda." Tom Warburton clicked off his phone and gripped it close to his chest as he mulled over his conversation. Swaboda said Mindora Arlow had insisted he call to tell him Senator Arlow was dead, apparently by way of foul play. Tom explained that Mark Combs had also called him. Now all the links were in place, and he still couldn't see the end of the chain.

He began to read back through his notebook, turning the pages and sighing when he could hardly decipher his own handwriting. There had to be something there that would give him a hint. *Hello? What's this?*

The line read, "Megan says ask about a former FBI agent named…" Named what? Something beginning with a *D*. Durban? Doberman? He turned his desk chair around so he faced the computer, and he began to pull up lists, looking for a name that resembled the scribble on his notebook page. When he found a possibility, he clicked on it and then scanned the page that came up. He was halfway through the D files when he tried another name. What appeared on his screen made his mouth drop open.

$\sim \sim \sim \sim \sim$

Brenda tiptoed out of the House chamber and stood in the ante-room, looking down at her pager, which was vibrating wildly against her waist. She checked the readout; Rick was calling, all right, from his office at the Fairfax station. She hesitated a moment, wondering if there were any way she could postpone calling back. Among other things, she wanted to hear what the representative from North Dakota was saying about the country's need for a strong military presence in north Africa; that speaker would be followed by Gutierrez from Texas, who was noted for his antimilitary sentiments. And besides…

She took a deep breath and punched Rick's phone number into her cell phone. Her battery was getting low, and she wasn't sure her call would be completed.

"Samuelson," Rick's voice said in her ear.

"It's me. You called?"

"The house is a shambles, and the window people can't get in until morning because crime labs are searching the house and yard. So let's stay in town tonight. You want me to call a hotel?"

"Okay," Brenda said. She had started to tremble again. She felt tears pushing over her eyelashes. "I was so scared."

"I know, sweetheart. That's why we're going to stay in town. I don't want you to live through all that again. And besides, you'll be working late, won't you?"

"Probably. We'll get a break after the president's speech and then go back into joint session."

"How about I meet you and Megan for dinner? Seven-thirty at La Fontaine? It should be quiet there."

"Okay. Oh, I need my nightie and clothes for tomorrow."

"I'll pick out something special."

*Oh, no! Rick always picks out something red, which makes me look like I'm in the last stages of a long illness.* "Thanks," she said. "Rick? Remember the other night when you were telling me about the history of your name? What was that old name you said it was derived from?"

She jotted the word in the margin of her daybook, said good-bye, and started back toward the House chamber. Suddenly she stopped, turned around, and headed through the outside entrance, toward the Library of Congress. She didn't like to miss the debate on the floor of the House, but she didn't have much time left to find what she needed.

Richard "Wolf" Robinson had been a *Washington Post* photographer for ten years, and nobody, not even the publisher, was allowed to bother him in the darkroom. Now, with only a half hour before deadline, he had funny light-leaks in every shot he'd made of Senator Likely as she stood the Joint Chiefs on their ears. Man! What a powerhouse she turned out to be, and all the while, looking so calm. But either something was wrong with his camera or the light in the hearing room was crazy, because every picture of her had light circling her.

He picked up the phone and called Fritz Wampler, over at the *Washington Window*.

"Hey, man," he said, "all my shots of Senator Likely have funny arcs in them. You had any problems with light in that room?"

Wampler chuckled. "Why didn't you just look at her? Those lights spattered all around her even when we weren't shooting. That's why they call her the Angel."

"What you talkin', man? What angel?"

"Senator Likely. They say she has a halo."

Wolf muttered a long, complicated oath under his breath. "She got a halo, right?" he sneered. "Ever' picture in the world of her got a halo."

"Not every one. But they do today."

"You all got arcs of light round her head?"

"That's right. They say she gets a halo every time she jumps on government sleaze or something. Now if you're through grilling me, I've got to get my disk into the computer."

Wolf hung up, muttering a long description of Fritz Wampler and his ancestors under his breath. He picked a three-quarter shot of Senator Megan Likely, leaning toward the microphone, a partial arc of light splashed around her. He clipped the picture onto his drying line, turned off even the red light, and started coursing his batch roll of film onto its roller.

Admiral Beatty's face was growing more florid by the moment.

"Then, Admiral," Megan said, "you're saying that we should have three carriers in the Mediterranean, possibly within range of Libyan ordnance? I presume you'd want guided missile frigates to protect the carriers, and AWACS bombers stationed in Turkey? And nuclear-powered Los Angeles flak-attack submarines on the perimeter?"

Beatty harrumphed and mumbled as she looked directly into his eyes. Those in the gallery were whispering to one another despite Luke's warning.

"We have to have proper support," Beatty said.

"Israel, Lebanon, and Iraq might have opinions about this much sea power on their shores. What feedback have we received from them about our plans?"

Beatty began to slap the table in rhythm to his words. "This-is-a-matter-of-national-security," he said, biting the words off one by one. He coughed, pounding his chest with his fist. "It would be very foolish for me to inform anyone, allies or enemies, of our armament power."

"Indeed," Megan said. "But the American people are entitled to know as much as possible before we, their representatives, vote to involve them in war." Turning back to General Martinez, she asked how the United States would deal with the fact that even before Libya got involved, Egypt and Sudan themselves had a history of discords about their southeastern border.

"The Sudanese were occupying the Hala'ib administrative area before Libya invaded, but the land is actually owned by Egypt. Now Libya has occupied that corridor. What are our oil holdings in Hala'ib?" she asked.

"This ends our time in the hearing room," Luke said before Martinez could respond.

"The president will address us in less than an hour. I urge you to be prompt in getting over to the House chamber."

That meant she could no longer lose herself in the hearings. She had to face what she knew.

Brenda was waiting for her. "Rick wants us to have dinner with him after the president's speech. Is that okay?"

"Sure." Megan tried to make eye contact, but Brenda was staring at her feet. "Brenda, what's wrong?"

Brenda looked up suddenly, tears spilling onto her cheeks. "Let it alone, Megan. I don't think there's anything you can do. Not you or anybody else." By now she was starting to sob, and two senators looked over their shoulders as they passed. Megan put an arm around her and moved her toward the ladies' room.

"The joint session won't start for a while," she said as their heels clicked over the white octagonal tile. "Do you want to find a quiet place to talk?"

Brenda closed her eyes and shook her head. "We'll be going into the joint session soon" she said. Megan went into one of the stalls, then washed her hands. "Well, at least, how about a cold drink?" she asked.

They found a vending machine on the first floor and dropped in their coins. As she popped the top of her cola can, she glanced at her watch. "Five-fifteen," she said. Brenda was silent, almost trancelike in her motions. "Brenda, talk to me."

"Here, take this." Brenda dug in the pocket of her coat and pulled out paper from a legal pad. Megan started to read aloud, but Brenda said, "Oh, no, don't let anyone hear!"

Silently, then, she read, *His name is from Sammael.* What? She looked up at Brenda. "I don't understand."

"You will. I've got to go, Megan, just put that away. If anything should happen to me, remember it."

"Something *did* happen to you," Megan said, lowering her voice as a small group of office workers passed. "Your car was bombed."

"Something else. If I should die."

"You won't die. I won't let you die," Megan said. But she shivered.

# TWENTY-EIGHT

La Fontaine was on North Massachusetts, two blocks from the National Cathedral. Its white Provençal-style building was set back in a small grove of bare-branched elm trees that gave its exterior a bleak look; inside, heavy carpeting and pleated wall coverings in pale green and mauve made Megan feel as if she were inside a coffin.

It was a Monday night, so the restaurant was not crowded. Megan asked if they could be seated in a banquette, where they could watch for Rick, and she ordered a cup of espresso.

Brenda said suddenly, "Megan, I meant what was in my Christmas note."

"Christmas note?"

"The one I left on your bed. Remember?"

Megan drew in her breath and said, "I remember."

"Even though we haven't known each other long, you're a really good friend. And that wasn't just Christmas sentiment."

"That's what you said in your note."

"I meant it. Rick was so sweet that day. I was out of envelopes and he put the note in one of his for me. That's why the paper was blue but the envelope didn't match. No matter what happens, Megan, I'm glad you're here."

Rick arrived at the restaurant before Megan could answer, his cheeks flushed with the cold. After they were seated, his slow, reassuring grin stretched over his face. "I'll just sit here and feast my eyes on you two beauties," he said. "How was the Congress today?"

"Tiring," Megan said.

~ ~ ~ ~ ~

President Jackson's speech had been predictable. He urged the Congress to have compassion for her allies in Egypt, ignoring the fact that a huge contingent of fundamentalist Muslims in Egypt, some of them holding high government office, still referred to the United States as "the source of all evil." He brushed over the oil fields, saying only that "we have multiple vested interests in Egypt and the Sudan." He also ignored the Hala'ib border dissent, speaking instead in glossy tones about the two countries' ancient traditions and heritage.

Megan had grown more impatient by the moment as his speech went on. Her memory of Jerry Jackson's charm at their White House meeting vanished and was replaced by the image of a purely political figure who cared only about exercising power, about winning the Congress over to his point of view.

*Or is what I discovered today making me angry about everything? I wish I could get hold of Tom so I could tell him what I know. And prove it with that news clip.*

After the president left and the joint meeting had adjourned for a half hour so senators and representatives could talk to the press, they poured back into the House chamber, with senators in desks moved in by the Capitol janitorial gnomes who pushed equipment from room to room, discussing their opinions of bureaucracy as they worked. The other guests who had entered the house for Jackson's speech, the Supreme Court justices, the Joint Chiefs, and the honored guests had all been removed, and the galleries were off limits for the session. Megan wondered why they didn't just meet to vote in their own chambers, since it was obvious they'd have to do that eventually, unless the Speaker and the vice president somehow judged that the voice vote was conclusive.

It was not. Weary and irritable, the Speaker said that they would break for the night, then go back to their own chambers at eight in the morning and vote electronically. The vice president looked discomfited, and Megan wondered where he stood on the issue. As she and Brenda were working their way through the corridor, Luke Callon had waved her over to a doorway.

"I want to thank you for what you did today," he said. "Nobody in the hearings room was unaffected by what you said to the Joint Chiefs."

"Congress was tiring," Megan told Rick again. She glanced at Brenda. "I don't think it's been very easy for Brenda today."

Rick nodded and reached across the table for his wife's hand. "I got us a nice suite at the Sheraton," he said. "After that bomb, you could use a couple of days of luxury. Sleep in and call for room service."

Brenda began to twirl the carnation that was in the vase at the center of the table. "I have to be in the House at eight tomorrow for the electronic vote," she said.

"Well, we'll see how you feel in the morning," he said. "You may have to miss the vote this time. Now, let's order some dinner."

As the waiter took their orders, Megan wondered if Rick remembered that the last time they'd eaten together was with her grandparents and the Tolufsons. She'd had crab cakes, she remembered, and Ben had ordered barbecued short ribs. The thought of eating crab now made her stomach turn.

Rick asked for a Caesar salad and pork medallions and mentioned looking forward to dessert. He was expansive and enthusiastic, praising the crispness of his salad, nodding and smiling at the waiter. Finally Megan could stand no more.

"Rick, Brenda has been terribly upset all day."

"About having to vote for war? Now, Bren, just remember everything I told you. This isn't just an ordinary little border skirmish; it's—" Megan rarely interrupted anyone, ever, but she put her fork down and said, "Someone tried to kill Brenda, Rick, and she can't get that out of her mind."

Rick looked surprised, but he continued to smile. "I think perhaps you're exaggerating a little, Megan. Brenda's a strong woman."

Brenda looked at Megan with alarm and murmured, "It's all right, Meg. Rick's right." She looked down at the salad she'd been pushing around with her fork.

"It's not all right," Megan said. "Rick, how did you know the bomb was under the car seat?"

"It was on the news."

It was not. She stared at Rick and finally turned to Brenda, saying, "Rick knows who put the bomb in your car."

Rick was looking at her with an odd light in his pale blue eyes, and he reached across the table to grasp her wrist. "I'm sure you're kidding," he said through his teeth.

"Rick, don't hurt Megan!" Brenda's face was anguished.

Megan managed to wrench her wrist away, and she rose quickly, knocking over her coffee cup but not looking back. She hurried out of the restaurant and began to run. The street was dark, but she could see the floodlighted towers of the cathedral, gleaming on their hill.

Tom opened the office door. Fern Loftis and Bryan Callon were putting on their coats and mufflers.

"I'm looking for Megan," he said without preface.

Bryan nodded. "So are we. We're hoping she went to dinner, but my mother lost track of her in the crowd after the president spoke."

"Your mother?"

"You'd better tell him, Bryan." Fern nudged him from behind.

Bryan sighed. "Mother and I have been trying to follow Megan everywhere, especially today, with no guard."

Tom interrupted. "No guard? What are you talking about?"

"Iris told us that Ferguson was needed at the bomb site and wouldn't be coming."

"Oh, no! It's worse than I thought," Tom said.

"It wasn't always easy," Bryan said. "One of us tried to be in the Senate gallery or at least near where she was. I even dressed up as a woman a couple times, and I fooled her friends from Wisconsin. But Mom has this Supreme Court thing coming up, and I can skip just so many classes, so we aren't always there."

"You did this because?"

"We thought she was in danger, and she was close to knowing who killed her friend. Whoever this killer is might even get past your FBI guards."

Tom said, "Bryan, do you know who killed Mr. Tolufson?"

"No. Do you?"

"I think so. I know you're probably dead tired, Ms. Loftis, but this is urgent. Would you call Brenda Samuelson's office and see if they know where she is?"

When he found out that Brenda and Megan had planned to meet Rick Samuelson at La Fontaine, he didn't even say good-bye, but rushed out the door and into the night.


Somewhere in the rosy twilight Megan had seen a workman coming out of the cathedral, a large box in his arms. She edged along the building, looking for a door that wasn't latched.

Looking over her shoulder, she saw a tall man rushing down the sidewalk. *Rick!* She tried one door after another; a small wooden one at the side of the cathedral opened when she pulled the knob, so she darted inside. She was in the cloistered hallway, and she took off her shoes. Like Moses, she thought as she began to run through the building.


Iris flopped onto the sofa as soon as she got in the apartment. She was almost asleep when she heard Megan's voice. Or was it? Yes. Megan's voice, calling, "Help me!" The apartment was empty. But Iris felt certain that somewhere, Megan Likely was in terrible danger.

Iris knelt beside the couch and said aloud, "God, I'm not very good at praying yet. I don't even know the Lord's Prayer by heart.

But please, please help Megan." Then she remembered the little Psalm folder the church pastor had given her that day at noon. She took it out and began to read aloud, "He who dwells in the secret place of the Most High shall abide under the shadow of the Almighty. I will say of the LORD, 'He is my refuge and my fortress; my God, in him I will trust.'"

Megan shrank against a fluted pillar behind the pulpit and waited. She could hear footsteps ringing on the stone floor, but because of the echo, she couldn't tell where they were. Lights behind the altar illuminated the ivory-colored stone wall of carved saints and apostles, but the rest of the cathedral was dark as a cave. How could she escape?

"Megan? Where are you, honey? It's Rick. I've come to help you."

*Help me?* His voice was gentle and ingratiating. She shivered and tried to breathe silently. If only she could see him! And where was Brenda? Was she still in the restaurant, or had she fled when she had the chance?

With her stocking-clad foot she identified the chancel steps, so she knelt and began crawling upward to the choir pews. She heard his footsteps coming closer, so she flattened her body and pulled herself on her stomach to the choir. As soon as she was in the back pew, she suppressed a sigh of relief and waited again.

Suddenly the full moon outside apparently broke free of the clouds: brilliant moonlight shone through the stained glass and threw bright colors across the nave of the church. Chairs and floor stones turned red, violet, and green as the light flooded through *The Last Judgment.* Samuelson was illuminated also, standing below the chancel steps, his face and body a patchwork of bright color. He looked beautiful. Celestial. And she shivered.

She crawled through the pews toward the cathedra, the carved stone bishop's chair on the north side. It was the Glastonbury cathedra, made of stone from that ancient monastery founded by the man who gave Christ his tomb.

She sank onto the chair and clutched the arms. The brilliance from the moon didn't penetrate her corner, but she was worried about the altar lights: would they reveal her hiding place? As she drew up her feet and scrunched herself into the chair, she thought about the note Brenda had handed her. What had it said? *His name is from Sammael.* What was important about the roots of Rick's name?

"Megan!" Rick's voice once more reverberated against the pillars. She could hear his footsteps again, and she peered through the sculpted wood choir lattice to watch him, still brightly lighted by the moon, climb the chancel steps.

"Megan? Why are you hiding from me?"

Why? Because he'd killed Ben and Linderman. Because she'd seen him in the Christmas Eve video and in the news clipping. Because of the memo paper he wrote his pager number on, paper with his name and logo and a raised blue border. Paper matching the address Iris had found in her jacket pocket, the threatening note from Christmas Eve, and the note delivered to the Senate chamber. Because he'd known where the car bomb was placed.

But it wasn't Rick who was in her hotel suite that day before Christmas. It was Brenda. So maybe they were working together.

Nonsense. Brenda had been sending out distress signals, and Megan realized she'd only half heard them until she saw the memo. But would Brenda have married anyone who wanted to hurt people?

Not if she'd known. Megan had seen the tape of the Christmas Eve murder, where Rick Samuelson was standing in the crowd, near the door. Smiling. She was certain the man in the "angel" clipping had also been Rick, holding a camera to look like a reporter. She hadn't known him then; that was the morning after her election, last November, but when Brenda introduced him, he'd looked familiar. He had to have been stalking her then, watching her, learning her habits in case he had to—had to what?

She pushed her hands down on the seat of the Glastonbury

chair so she could change position. As her hands touched the carved limestone, the picture of Joseph of Arimathea and his part in Christ's burial flashed into her mind like a movie scene: Joseph, helping the women take Jesus from the cross, negotiating with Pontius Pilate, buying spices, placing Christ's dead body in his own new tomb. And laughing when he heard the news that his tomb was empty again.

Was the gospel—not Rick's version, but the one she'd learned from her parents and her grandmother—was it true?

Moonlight now poured through the rose window at the south of the church, the window that depicted *The Church Triumphant*. The multicolored light rested on Rick's pale yellow hair, and again, he looked like an angel.... She drew in her breath. An angel...an angel of light, maybe? Someone her grandmother had warned her about?

One bright beam fell on his hands, turning them red and blue, then white, shining on the pistol he held. A 9-mm automatic like the one that had killed Ben Tolufson. Not *like* the one that had murdered Ben. It had to be *the* one, and now Rick was trying to kill her with it!

*Something made me recognize Rick's paper. Something made me ask him about the car seat. Something made me remember that Rick was out of town every time there was a murder. Something sent Brenda to stay at my apartment so Rick would give me the memo sheet. Something told me to hide up here in the Glastonbury chair.*

Or maybe not something. Maybe *Someone*. She turned to look at the carved figure of Christ in Majesty, carved into the reredos behind the altar. Here he was, the Person she had rejected, with his hand raised in blessing. And a million sunbeams danced over the altar like a rain of bright diamonds. What had Ruthie Tolufson said? "Every sunbeam is an angel in disguise." *Then I must be surrounded by angels. I have been, ever since I was elected. And if there are angels, then there's God. God has been protecting me, leading me, pointing to the truth.*

Knowing that God existed wasn't enough. She had to do

something, had to surrender her life, had to acknowledge the Son of God.

*Jesus,* she prayed, *Jesus, you are real, and I love you. Please, help me....*

"Come on, Meggie," Rick coaxed. "It's safe now. I'm here." As he stood in the colored light, she saw his face contort and twist. It was no longer angelic: Now his smile was diabolical, and hatred poured through his eyes.

"Rick! Rick, no!" Brenda's voice cried, and footsteps raced in from the north hallway. Shots, three of them, echoed through the cathedral, the sound ringing across the vaulted Gothic ribs of the building.

Megan knew she had to help Brenda. In the dim light she saw Rick kneel for a moment beside Brenda's inert body, then rise and whirl around. In a voice full of fury, he yelled, "All right, Megan. Now you've killed Brenda. Your best friend. If you had come out when you were supposed to..."

Megan began to sob. Rick cocked his head, smiling, then followed the sound of her weeping. When he was about eight feet away, he grasped the pistol in both hands and fired into Megan's dark hiding place in the Glastonbury chair. As the bullet pierced her flesh, she reached behind her for the stone knobs on the chair, to keep from falling....

And then the light through the windows was gone. She clutched her shoulder: Thick liquid was oozing through her jacket. *Jesus,* she whispered, *Jesus, help me. And if you can't save me from Rick, take me to heaven.* She slid to the floor, half conscious, and waited for Rick to come and kill her.

The lights were on when she opened her eyes. Tom Warburton was leaning over her, along with a paramedic who exclaimed, "Holy Toledo! This is that angel senator. The one from Wisconsin."

"Did you get him?" Megan murmured.

"Don't move," Tom said. "Not until the paramedics can—"

"Brenda…He killed her out there in the crossing."

"She isn't dead, Megan. We've got an ambulance on its way."

A uniformed police officer came into view, asking, "Who did she say did this?"

Megan smiled up at Tom. "How did you find me?"

"I was coming across the grounds just as the police arrived. You were right about an FBI agent named Dobbins. It's Samuelson, all right. When I figured that out, I started trying to find you. The waiter at La Fontaine said a small woman with brown hair had run out of the restaurant, with a tall guy chasing her."

"But how did these others get in here so quickly?"

"Somebody pushed the code pad on the wall over there." He waved toward the wall, where a security panel was installed discreetly next to the Glastonbury cathedra. "Was it you?"

The police officer poked a lock of hair into her ponytail. "Ma'am, can you tell us who fired these shots?"

Megan smiled. She must have punched the keypad. She'd flung her arm out. And prayed.

"Rick," she said. "Rick Samuelson. The congresswoman is his wife. Is she going to be all right?" She began struggling to her feet so she could go see Brenda.

The paramedic looked panicky. "Oh, Senator, don't ma'am, please!"

Megan stumbled down to the area between the chairs and the choir. Brenda lay in blood that pooled onto the colorful mosaic of the floor.

"Brenda, oh, Brenda, don't die," Megan said, kneeling, as Rick had, beside her friend. "I don't know what happened to Rick, but—"

"Rick," Brenda whispered. Her face was the same pale gray as the cathedral's outer walls, and her voice was barely audible. "His…name. From Son of Sammael. It means…"

A small herd of paramedics in blue work shirts whisked up

the grand aisle, and Megan wobbled to her feet to get out of their way. Two of the medics moved her toward a chair; while the others worked over Brenda, they began cutting the fabric of Megan's new red jacket.

"My jacket!" she cried.

"Your shoulder," the paramedic said, patiently pulling the fabric away from her flesh. "You may have a bullet still in it."

"No," she murmured. "I think it just grazed me. The bullets are probably up there in the Glastonbury stone."

They were loading Brenda onto the stretcher, and as they rolled past Megan, Brenda gasped, "Son of Sammael. It's...ancient... means Son of Satan. He made up the name."

# TWENTY-NINE

T he vice president pounded his gavel on the podium. "The chair recognizes the junior senator from Wisconsin." A ripple of applause started, and then in a great surge everyone in the Senate chamber and the gallery rose.

Today, the Senate, having invoked the War Powers Act to prevent the president from sending in more troops or declaring war, at least until further diplomatic solutions were tried, would settle down to vote on the poverty alleviation amendments. But right now they were applauding the small woman whose famous "angel" picture had been under Friday's headline: "Senate 'Angel' Escapes Death; Rep. Penning in Critical Condition."

Iris said Oprah Winfrey's staff had called twice to invite Megan to the show, Ted Koppel used a whole *Nightline* segment to tell the story of the Cathedral shooting and the other murders, and the newly revived *Unsolved Mysteries* was planning to run a program about Rick's double life, his international connections, and his eerie disappearance. For three days, the newspapers had featured stories about Megan and Brenda and displayed photos of Rick with the caption, "Have you seen this man?"

So far, nobody but the majority leader had talked to the police about the simultaneous disappearance of Amelia Hutchins.

Brenda was off the ventilator, and according to her nurse, she had sipped a little water and had remained awake for nearly a half hour. Stopping on her way to the Capitol that morning, Megan peeked into Intensive Care. Brenda rewarded her with a weak smile.

As she left, Megan nodded to the police officer outside Brenda's cubicle. Nobody could enter Intensive Care without showing him a pass. This had been instituted partly to keep visitors out of the room, but also in case Rick showed up.

His picture was on every front page, in every newscast, and on posters around town. His name was given variously as Rick Samuelson and Richard Sammael and as ex-Special Agent Greg Dobbins, fired as a San Francisco FBI agent eight years earlier after he was discovered to have been selling investigation files not only to the tabloids but to the North Koreans. He'd managed to flee Seattle before the matter could be brought to trial. In his arrogance he apparently thought nobody would ever recognize him, though he hadn't done much to alter his appearance: he'd grown a beard and changed his dress style. And adopted a Virginia accent, along with his "southern preacher" persona.

When Tom was telling Megan the details earlier in the day, before the Senate session, she said, "He knew Ben recognized him and might tip off the authorities."

"Right. After he killed Ben, we would never have known except for you. I just wish I'd found out before you and Brenda got hurt. How in the world did you remember the name Dobbins?"

"My grandmother had a dappled gray horse named Dobbins," she said. "When Ben said 'Greg Dobbins,' I immediately thought of that old horse. I wish Ben had said more about it. Ruthie said on the phone last night that Ben had intended to talk to you about Greg Dobbins after Christmas."

Tom smiled down, his blue eyes twinkling. "Too bad Mark Combs didn't get up here for your swearing-in. He could have prevented some of it if he'd seen Samuelson."

"Mark?"

"Dobbins was married to Mark's sister Gail. We now think he followed her to Lake Superior and killed her. It's one of the reasons he was at your election press conference. He wanted to see if Mark had described him and you recognized him."

Megan's hand went to her throat. She felt as if she were choking. "How many people has he killed?"

"Well, fortunately, he didn't hit Agent Ferguson hard enough to kill him. The police found him in a warehouse, tied up, with a bad concussion. Now we're reopening the case on Arlow's first campaign manager," Tom said. "We never were convinced it was suicide."

"I'm still not completely clear on why Rick—or Dobbins or whoever he is—why he was so intent on war in Egypt."

"He started losing big bucks when Libya annexed the corridor between Sudan and Egypt. He owned oil wells in the corridor. If the United States intervened, Egypt would regain the wells, and he could recoup his investment. But there's a worse reason, one we're keeping out of the papers for a while. President Jackson knows now he met with Samuelson the night of the car bombing, when Brenda thought he was in New York."

"Really? How did Rick get the New York hotel to lie for him?"

"He didn't. The number he called in to Brenda was traced to a tiny little office in New York, where apparently someone who has now escaped pretended to be the hotel manager. Apparently Samuelson went to Chicago, killed Arlow, then flew back in and hid out, right in town. Practically in plain sight."

"And you say he met with the president?"

"Late the other night. About the same time the bomb he put in his wife's car blew. He undoubtedly knew she'd been investigating his past. He hit the president with a lot of baloney about atrocities by the Libyans, thousands dying on the streets of Cairo, people in the corridor being slaughtered. A lot of the news reports on the wire services were generated by Rick's cartel."

"Cartel?" Megan searched Tom's face for a clue to what he was talking about.

"As I said, the president knows this, his national security advisor knows, and several senators do. So what I'm telling you is legal to say, but hush-hush. Consider this a security briefing."

He explained that Rick was not only a murderer, he was a traitor, a member of a shadow cartel that had tried to gain control of the oil, nickel, uranium, and other mineral production all over the world, thus undermining the interests of the United States. The problem was that the cartel was so shadowy; it was composed of men whose names were invented, like Rick's, and whose faces were largely unknown. An underground government that wanted the power that would come with owning most of the important raw minerals and metals in the world.

"All that end-of-the-world stuff was about oil?" Megan shook her head.

"Oil, tungsten, copper, every important element. Not the first person to be swallowed up by greed, I guess.... I just wish he and his henchmen weren't still out there somewhere. They're sure to pop up again."

"And now, the police are saying Rick may be with Amelia Hutchins. Unless he's killed her, too." Megan looked thoughtful. "But why did he want to kill Brenda?"

"From what little she's been able to tell us, I surmise that she'd been suspicious. Bryan said she'd been over to Vital Statistics to look up his alleged family connections. Finally she figured out the truth, but she was terrified of him."

"I wish I'd been able to hear what Donnie Thurmond was trying to tell me."

"I hear she's going to make it. If she hadn't gone on assignment to Alaska, Rick probably would have killed her before this, just to shut her up. It was obvious she knew too much about the oil and the Hala'ib corridor. Anyone tracking his interests down in the corridor would have eventually stumbled across the cartel and their power play."

"I'm surprised he didn't follow Donnie to Alaska."

"She'd gone to a dogsled race to Nome, and he couldn't find her until she got home. He apparently called her on pretext of a news story, then loaded her tea with barbiturates."

"Did Arlow know Rick was Greg Dobbins?"

"I don't think so, but Linderman did. He made the mistake of trying to extort money from Rick, just as he tried to blackmail your friend Combs. Then Rick apparently became convinced that Arlow knew, too."

"So he walked into the hospital and killed him." Megan hadn't liked Henry Arlow, but he had once been a fairly good senator before he got bought up by the party bosses. Arlow had deserved a chance to live, to break out of politics and get reacquainted with his family. And he'd been right when he was raving about an "underground government" after all.

Megan let her head rest for a moment against Tom's shoulder; then she said, "I've got to get into the Senate chamber."


As she adjusted the microphone, the applause finally spattered away. Her left arm was in a sling over her black suit jacket; she had pinned the bandage with her mother's topaz sunflower.

"We're glad to see you alive and well, Senator Likely," the vice president said. "For what purpose does the gentlewoman rise?"

"I rise to speak in favor of SB615, the amended poverty alleviation bill."

A collective gasp of surprise swept over both sides of the aisle and up into the gallery. Senator Callon raised his eyebrows in hopeful inquiry. Vice President Barnes pounded his gavel until ninety-nine senators settled back in their antique desks to hear the junior senator from Wisconsin explain why she was defecting from her party's position. Luke Callon's amendment to the bill had squeaked by the day before, but the bill itself was still in danger.

Megan had done her homework. For the three days since Rick's bullet grazed her shoulder, she had haunted the Library of Congress and ploughed purposefully through the World Wide Web, searching and downloading. Iris had sat beside her, printing and making notes.

"You're working way too hard, Iris," Megan told her.

"Megan, I'd do anything for you. Just hush up and work," Iris murmured with tears in her eyes. And now Megan was ready to make her first Senate speech, not on the price of cheese, but on mercy.

"My decision comes after much thought and prayer," she said, touching the topaz pin for reassurance, just as she had reached to touch the Glastonbury stone. "I suggest to my brother and sister senators, especially those who espouse a religious point of view, that mercy is at the center of every major faith or philosophy. And it's time to show mercy to the poor. I can't walk a block in this city without seeing someone poor or homeless. And I know it's the same everywhere. Only a few days ago I gave a man money and watched him rush to buy food with it."

The press had been forbidden to take pictures or videos from the gallery; only C-Span would record her words, and the second murmur of surprise.

"Mercy is first of all Jewish," Megan said. "The prophet Micah knew Judah went into exile as much for her neglect of the poor as for idolatry, and Micah admonished the faithful to love mercy, seek justice, and walk humbly before God."

It was Rick's favorite text, but he'd always stressed the "seek justice" aspect, implying that justice meant punishment and retribution for criminals and freeloaders.

Megan had also known the verse all her life, thanks to Ceelie and Sunday school, but she'd phoned a rabbi for help on the paragraph. She raised her eyes for a moment, wondering what Rick, wherever he was, would think when he heard she had used his favorite text to fight one of his favorite causes, the elimination of all welfare and poverty assistance. His only interest in the poor was to punish or exploit them. And everyone else.

"And to my one Muslim brother in this chamber," she continued, looking over at Abu Karim, the freshman senator from California, "I want to say that mercy is at the heart of Islam. The third pillar of your faith, which you call *sadaqah* and which means almsgiving to the poor out of love and piety, is not only recommended but required." She'd searched the Islamic pages on the Internet for two hours to find that fact.

"And mercy is certainly Christian." She smiled as she added, "Jesus said, 'Be merciful, just as your Father also is merciful.'" How many times had she recited that verse in Sunday school? God had been planning this moment long before today!

"Finally, to those senators who believe in morals but not any religion, remember that Plato said a moral person must injure no one at all. And that has to include injury by neglect or omission."

By now the room was absolutely silent. Megan had left nobody out of her speech: Baptists and Catholics now had to consider mercy in the same moment as did the Jews, Muslim, and the agnostics. There would be other Christians who criticized her for using the scriptures of Judaism and Islam and for appealing to agnostics; but she'd known she had to speak to the whole Senate.

She took a deep breath. "I ask that we all consider the teachings of God and the world's great thinkers and that we dispense mercy to the miserable poor among us: the homeless, families in trouble, all of the downtrodden. I believe God cares what we decide here, because our attitude toward mercy makes us what we are."

She didn't wait for a response, didn't even hear the applause that thundered through the chamber. She glimpsed Senator Callon rising, along with five or six other senators who were rushing to microphones to speak in favor of the bill. She went to the women's room, rinsed her face, swallowed the mild pain pill she'd waited until now to take, and stepped out to the hall. A group of reporters fluttered on the Capitol steps.

"Senator Likely, why did you change your mind?"

"Hey, Angel, are you leaving the party?"

Finally, a brunette woman from CNN thrust out her microphone. "Senator Likely, how did you elude the killer the other night? And did that influence what you said on the floor a few minutes ago?"

"The light of the moon," Megan said. "Moonlight was shining through the stained glass, and I could see where Mr. Samuelson was. And yes, it was during that experience that I realized God is real. A God who demands justice for the poor."

The reporter looked puzzled. "Moonlight?"

"It was gleaming through the stained glass so I could see him clearly," she reiterated patiently. "I was able to hide until he shot his wife. Then I started to cry, and he located me by the sound."

"But Senator, there was no moon that night. Not only was it cloudy, but the moon was dark."

"But I saw——" she began, and then put her fingertips to her lips, realizing that the light she had seen was not from the moon. "I guess the angels were with me again," she said after a moment, and the reporters rushed away to file the words with their wire services.

"Megan?"

She turned to see Tan Luyin, the First Lady, coming from the gallery, surrounded by Secret Service. She said, "It was wonderful, Megan. You've been in my prayers, and now I know why. And I'm not the only one who thinks your speech was wonderful." She gestured toward the stairs, and Megan glanced up to see Iris and and Mark Combs.

"Mark! How did you——"

He threw his arms around her. "Your friend Warburton got me here," Mark said. "Megan, can you forgive me for being a foolish, arrogant idiot?"

"Tom told you to come?"

"He called me yesterday and said if I didn't get down here, he was going to ask you to marry him."

Imagine. A thirty-year-old senator, blushing in the Capitol rotunda! She looked into Mark's dark eyes, bequeathed him by his Ojibwa grandmother, but she couldn't keep Tom's blue ones out of her consciousness.

Which man would she marry, if she ever married anybody? She wasn't sure. But she knew what she wanted to do right now.

"Come on, Iris," she said. "I've got to call Ceelie before we go to the noon church service." A flickering pattern of sunbeams danced over her head as she started walking.

Dear Reader:

Writing a book is always a journey. As I write, I change the story or the characters—and they change me. We journeyed together, the characters and I, and you took the trip with us, even before you read the book, because I was constantly thinking of you.

I also took a literal journey to write *Angel in the Senate;* with my grandson, who had his thirteenth birthday while we were traveling. We flew on a 747 to Washington, D.C. We landed at Dulles in a heavy snowstorm that had already shut down Washington National.

We stayed at Embassy Suites so that the story would be authentic. We trudged through snow to visit the Capitol, Mount Vernon, the entire Smithsonian, and to sit in the Senate gallery; ate at all the places named in *Angel in the Senate;* and walked the length of the Mall so I could write about Megan's doing that. We encountered the homeless in Lafayette Park, across from the White House. We saw the Pentagon and tall, narrow houses in Georgetown. And we went to a service in Washington National Cathedral that still haunts my dreams with its beauty and holiness.

At the center of Megan's story are the angels who guard and guide her, and her coming to Christ, who had always been at her side. I wanted to show that angels are *God's* servants, not ours. And I would like to leave you with the little prayer my mother taught me about my guardian angel:

Angel of God, my guardian dear, commissioned by God to watch out for me here:
Ever this day, be at my side, to teach, to lead, to guard and to guide. Amen.

Yours in Christ,

Write to Kristen Johnson Ingram
c/o Palisades
P.O. Box 1720
Sisters, Oregon 97759